Postcolonial Hauntings

DISSIDENT FEMINISMS

Elora Halim Chowdhury, Editor

For a list of books in the series, please see our website at www.press.uillinois.edu.

Postcolonial Hauntings

Play and Transnational Feminism

SUSHMITA CHATTERJEE

UNIVERSITY OF
ILLINOIS PRESS
Urbana, Chicago, and Springfield

© 2024 by the Board of Trustees
of the University of Illinois
All rights reserved
1 2 3 4 5 C P 5 4 3 2 1
∞ This book is printed on acid-free paper.

Library of Congress Cataloging-in-Publication Data
Names: Chatterjee, Sushmita, 1976– author.
Title: Postcolonial hauntings : play and transnational feminism
  / Sushmita Chatterjee.
Description: Urbana : University of Illinois Press, [2024]
  | Series: Dissident feminisms | Includes bibliographical
  references and index.
Identifiers: LCCN 2024003672 (print) | LCCN 2024003673
  (ebook) | ISBN 9780252045981 (cloth) | ISBN
  9780252088087 (paperback) | ISBN 9780252047169
  (ebook)
Subjects: LCSH: Feminism. | Feminism—Social aspects. |
  Feminism—Political aspects.
Classification: LCC HQ1155 .C537 2024 (print) | LCC
  HQ1155 (ebook) | DDC 305.42—dc23/eng/20240206
LC record available at https://lccn.loc.gov/2024003672
LC ebook record available at https://lccn.loc.gov/2024003673

Contents

Acknowledgments   vii

Introduction   1

1   Becoming Animal, Becoming Transnational   27

2   Translations and Overlapping Belongings: Mapping Queer Transnationalism   55

3   Un-Mithu's Politics: Lingual Anarchy and Playful Undoings   79

4   Feminist Transnationalism and the Political Dimension of Friendships: Thinking through Mithu Sen's *It's Good to Be Queen*   97

5   Spectral Politics   121

Notes   143

Bibliography   159

Index   171

Acknowledgments

This book has been long in the making. Academic writing with its high teaching and service loads is discombobulating—a page here, a paragraph there, disheveled drafts picked up and reworked yet again. Ironically, I was able to finish the book only once I became an administrator. The process of navigating academic life has taught me to appreciate the parts of our material, intellectual life that sustain us even as we struggle with the profound imbalances of teaching, service, and research. One indispensable source of intellectual inspiration throughout my career has been my students. I have always loved my job, mainly because of my students. Day in and day out, in synergetic conversation with them, they have enlivened my thinking and posed new questions.

Friends, colleagues, family, and writing groups have all played a magical role in the development of this book. Among these, Banu Subramaniam and Diane Mines are both friends, colleagues, and mentors, who have, to put it simply, helped me finish this book. I met Diane at Appalachian State University, and we were quick to become friends through our writing-group meetings on Saturdays in Belk Library. We maintained our writing group for years, and it helped me center my work, even if for just one day every week. Diane has been an invaluable listener, brilliant interlocutor, and reliable writing partner. Banu is a dream coauthor. We think and coauthor regularly, working dialectically, with very different strengths. I am forever impressed by how Banu moves ideas and conversations forward through her excellent questions, empathetic style, and amazing mind. Banu kept saying to me, "Get that book done so that you can work on your next!" Thank you, Banu and Diane, for providing wonderful motivational support and friendship.

Many thanks to my wonderful colleagues and friends at Appalachian State University, including Patricia Ortiz, Kim Q. Hall, Jill Ehnenn, Heather Ondercin, Michael Eng, Heather Waldroup, Dana Powell, Anastacia Schuloff, Gayle Turner, Dylan Blackston, Joseph Bathanti, and Jessica Martell. I appreciate, too, my colleagues in Sustainable Development, one floor above my office. Anataoli Ignatova, Jacqueline Ignatova, Brian Burke, Rebecca Witter, and Dinesh Paudel were a constant source of support, assistance and, just as important, merriment. They are fondly missed. My colleagues and friends at Appalachian State University have provided me with beautiful memories of walks in the Blue Ridge Mountains, inspiring conversations, shared meals, and a vast reservoir of love and kindness.

Colleagues and friends in the gender studies world have generously read and provided valuable feedback on chapters of my book, even as they also serve as models for creativity in scholarship. Irina Aristarkhova first drew my attention to Mithu Sen's works and changed the way I perceived art and politics. I benefited greatly from Irina's unwavering support at different stages of my career, and her brilliant mind is always a source of inspiration. Deboleena Roy is a friend and mentor who gave me the courage to step into administration. Her positive spirit and affirming generosity are invaluable. Keya Maitra is also a friend and mentor whom I can call with even the silliest questions and count on her wisdom as a steady and calm force through writing, thinking, and moving. I am always amazed at how Mel Y. Chen thinks through ideas and issues. The path-breaking proclivity in their scholarship opens new vistas for thought and imagination. Kiran Asher's critical mind and engagement with complex questions have provided important directions for my own work. She is a wonderful cothinker. Many thanks to Kimberly K. Lamm for valuable conversations about image and text, for reading my work, and for great meals together that provided food for the mind as we worked on our research projects.

Many thanks to great conversations and feedback from talks at conferences of the National Women's Studies Association (NWSA) and the Women's, Gender, and Sexuality Studies South (WGS South, formerly the Southeastern Women's Studies Association, or SEWSA). Jennifer Purvis and Hil Malatino are my WGS South friends, who have asked great questions and also added merriment to the labor of research. Talks at Augustana College, the University of Massachusetts Amherst, Wesleyan University, the University of North Carolina Asheville, Appalachian State University, and Colorado State University have all been invaluable through excellent feedback, helping me think deeper, and pushing me toward new directions.

I am lucky to have been taught by teachers who inspire students to think creatively and who have never dissuaded me from seeking questions that seem ostensibly trivial like laughter and humor, or ghosts and haunting. Two teachers from very different parts of the world, Prasanta Ray (PR) and Nancy Love, have given me the spirit to probe at politics otherwise, from theorizing deeply about topics ostensibly trivial, such as laughter or ghosts. PR encouraged me to continue my education abroad and instilled an understanding of travel as knowledge. To Nancy, I owe my love for theory and for thinking with concepts and ideas to (un)weave their connections as they structure the material world around us. My teachers have also taught me how to revel in those magical moments in the classroom, where we are changing more lives than we can imagine.

Many people have shaped my questions, prisms, and ways of looking at the world. One stands out. Elora Halim Chowdhury's rich transnational feminist scholarship comes to life as she also actualizes its ethics through her mentoring and support. I continually teach and learn from her scholarship. Elora's thoughtful scholarship that can articulate the many layers of power politics is forever illuminating. She is the kind of scholar that I would like to be.

I really do not know quite how to convey my gratitude to Mithu Sen. I write about her work, learn from her practice. We laugh together, and we agonize together about representations. Our never-long-enough transatlantic chat sessions keep reminding me about the joy in work-play, a hyphenated unity best never separated. Her art frames this book, and no other cover image could have so perfectly framed the politics of this book. Much gratitude to Mithu for her energizing friendship, support, love, and laughter and for keeping me on my toes through her splendidly profuse works that continually inspire me to write.

Friendships nurture and sustain me. Heartfelt gratitude to Azin Neishaboori and Nandini Sen for being dear friends, for your support through many moments in life, and for all the love and laughter. My dear friend Alexa Schriempf has helped me through the hard work of moving boxes and homes across states, listened and supported me through major life events, provided mirth through all idiosyncrasies of life, and been a true friend. Another close friend, stef shuster, provides me with strength daily. stef has been a constant companion providing reason, laughter, and good cheer. Their pragmatism helps calm my mind through too-frequent dental emergencies and many other tribulations and joys.

Many people have helped this book actualize. Many thanks to Anitra Grisales and Diane Mines for their excellent help in developmental editing and copyediting. They absolutely understood the spirit of the book and were willing to converse with it. Much gratitude to my editor at the University of Illinois Press, Dominique Moore, for her help and support through the way. The two anonymous reviewers provided truly excellent suggestions and generative comments, and the book was much strengthened with their feedback. Mary Lou Kowaleski and Jennie Fisher have provided valuable help in the book's production process and cover design.

I still remember the day that I ventured forth to Penn State to do graduate studies. Following my uncle Kalyan Chatterjee through the major airports, I was absolutely clueless about the major step that I had just taken. My aunt and uncle, KumKum Chatterjee and Kalyan Chatterjee, helped me settle into my new life and provided a family away from home. I fondly remember KumKum pishi (her death still feels unreal), her fabulous cooking that was the envy of all my roommates, and her words of advice that ring true every day.

My two sisters, Relina Barman-Roy and Sahana Chatterjee, enrich my life and its experiences on a continuous basis. My father, Arindom Chatterjee, had a famous sense of humor. My thinking has been influenced in countless ways by his laughter and his joyous way of being in the world and how he delighted in every meal and conversation. It cannot be an accident that I write on play, laughter, and the buoyancy of life. My mother, Surjit Chatterjee, is with me everywhere, in my work, life, and how I see-act. She constantly inspires me to understand the bigger picture and enjoy every journey. This book is possible because of her.

Postcolonial Hauntings

Introduction

> The past is neither inert nor given. The stories we tell about *what happened then*, the correspondence we discern between today and times past, and the ethical and political stakes of these stories redound in the present.... If the ghost of slavery still haunts our present, it is because we are still looking for an exit from the prison.
> —Saidiya Hartman, *Lose Your Mother*

> So the borders here are not really fixed. Our minds must be as ready to move as capital is, to trace its paths and to imagine alternative destinations.
> —Chandra Talpade Mohanty, *Feminism without Borders*

I believe in ghosts. Apparently, I am not the only one. Ghosts seem to haunt our most sacrosanct edifices and categories. They disrupt analytic distinctions between living and dead, here and there, past and present. They bother every anthropocentric structure through which people try to control the world, so much so that present day political and social theorists proclaim persistently that they are "haunted" by some conundrum, issue, context, or situation. Being haunted situates a continually insatiable moment in thinking and activism where it is used to grapple with unrecognized violence in the present, whether in the context of crises like climate change and COVID-19 or persisting structures such as sexism and racism. The stubborn proclivity and agonistic pronunciation of being haunted demand attention for its prolific use and repeated occurrences. Inspired and agonized by the politics of haunting, I ask in this book: What is the work of haunting?

The critical value of the concept and sense of "haunting" in the humanities and social sciences is inspired in large part by Jacques Derrida's "hauntology" where he questions our ontological certitude.[1] This book argues further that to fully engage with the ghosts that upend our ontological certitude, we need to understand them not only as unrelenting vestiges of past tragedies nor simply as farce but, rather, more complexly as play.[2]

Like hauntings, play has received much analytical attention, especially in feminist and queer theory, critical theory, cultural studies, cultural anthropology, game studies, and radical geographies.[3] Play and hauntings have been each separately analyzed as critical concepts in an epistemology of resistance. I argue through *Postcolonial Hauntings: Play and Transnational Feminism* that the separation between play and hauntings fails to discern how hauntings and play *together* frame postcolonial predicaments. They are necessary and significant accomplices. *Postcolonial Hauntings* thus intervenes in the literature on both play and hauntings by showcasing their braided workings in social and political fabrics rather than situating them in isolation. Working with play and hauntings as entangled events enables us to reckon with the persistent nature of a ghost's entry and exit and its playful stubbornness. Akin and distinct from a ghost's repetitive presence-absence, play also flits through social fabrics, unsuspectingly and stealthily. This theoretical emphasis reckons with histories, processes, traces, and patterns that contextualize events, words, and structures.

To understand how hauntings and play are necessary coconspirators, think with me through Indian filmmaker Satyajit Ray's 1969 film *Goopy Gyne Bagha Byne*. This panoramic visual feast and musical splendor effectively elucidate the politics of haunting and play.[4] Distinct from Ray's films that were melancholically realistic and emotionally intense, *Goopy Gyne Bagha Byne* is a ghostly comedy that has endeared itself to every generation of Indians, especially ones speaking Bengali. Framed around boons from a ghost king, the film uses play and hauntings to deliver a biting social and political critique about the plight of common people in ostensibly rich kingdoms. Goopy and Bagha are musicians in their village, but the villagers drive them out because, despite their best aspirations, Goopy cannot sing, and Bagha cannot play drums. Scorned for their music and living in abject poverty, the two find themselves in a jungle surrounded by animals and ghosts. Goopy's voice and Bagha's drumbeats that the villagers consider terrible are loved by the ghosts. The ghost king emerges to grant them three boons. The boons they choose are to be always well fed and clothed, to be free to travel wherever they want, and to let their music leave people spellbound. What follows is a grand adventure movie where Goopy and Bagha help people, prevent war and massacre, and even marry princesses. Depicting the abject poverty of common people alongside the wealth of landlords and kings, the film combines realism with the fantastical. Viewers are treated to a lengthy ghost dance depicting the caste-and-class structure in India and also consisting of British men, missionaries, and the local elite. This eerie dance, combined with eclectic musical genres, holds sway for almost eight minutes of the film. The ghost dance haunts the narrative that critiques war and the abject hunger of common people who do not benefit from war. This episode frames the entire film, and it is no coincidence that Ray himself voiced the boons from the ghost king in a ghostly sing-song voice. It is only the ghosts who can facilitate social change by providing Goopy and Bagha with other-worldly powers that play with the world around them, for instance, when making it rain sweets from the sky to stop a war. The film portrays how hauntings and play can disentangle oppressive structures and herald utopic energies. This film serves as an important cultural benchmark that frames my own perspectives on play and haunting and continues to mesmerize me with its scathing social critique packaged as a children's movie, alongside its ability to push us toward a less oppressive world through the boons of a ghost king.

Guided by the politics of play and hauntings, *Postcolonial Hauntings* intervenes in central debates and impasses within transnational postcolonial feminisms. Transnational postcolonial feminisms struggle persistently against the closing of borders and ontologies arbitrarily effected in before-and-after pictures of colonialism and independence. Additionally, they struggle against imperial politics coded within images of "third-world" women waiting to be saved and alongside violent histories of animalization, homonationalism, and erasure. Binary thinking that theoretically and practically instills frames of developed versus undeveloped and man versus animal haunts the work of transnational postcolonial feminisms. Play enters the world through these hauntings. It is in the inextricable entanglement of play and hauntings that I situate possibilities for justice. Thus, when the frame of animal haunts postcolonial studies in terms of its counterposition to the truly human that can never be the colonized, I use play to undo frames of animality and animalization. When hegemonic language and meaning codes haunt postcolonial subjects and their modes of belonging to language communities, I situate the importance of playing with language through works of translation.

By centering the work of play and hauntings, this book converses with central conundrums in transnational postcolonial feminisms on the impossible echoes of translations, differential waves in renditions of "queer," becoming animal of (post) colonial subjects, and possibilities of solidarity beyond fraternal friendships that cement nation-states. Through invocations of these debates, *Postcolonial Hauntings* critiques the role of binary categories by showing in successive chapters how postcolonial subjects use animality to play with static positionality, how they tug at language-use to haunt and play with "queer," and how they build modes of relationality that subvert imperial habits of friendships. Play and hauntings are the attempts to undo frames of static positioning, loosen binary thinking, and anchor postfoundationalist ethics as the inspiration for responsibility and responsiveness to histories and traces. The remainder of this introduction elucidates how play and haunting shadow social structures in an irreducible conspiracy and review how transnational feminist scholarship makes use of the concepts of play and hauntings, separately and in tandem. Along the way, I also draw out the theoretical frames for the book, postcolonial and transnational, and their particular investment in play and hauntings.

Hauntings

Hauntings undo the world as we know it. "Haunting" is a fittingly amorphous word that I use to encompass all sorts of ghostly experiences, whether a general phenomenon of dislocation, a tormented state, or the sense of feeling frightened by something unexplainable, whether seeing ghosts, being possessed, or exorcising spirits. Although some would compartmentalize a general sense of haunting from a specific spectral visitation, such a sharp, logical differentiation among "types" of hauntings forgets its boundary-transgressing prowess and uniquely intimate politics. Ghosts are illegitimate social actors; they undo binaries—dead and alive, for instance—that help society make sense of itself. Their persistent hauntings keep the present attentive to the past, as ghosts derail a comfortable linearity that presumes the progress of the past into the present. By being at once past and present, ghosts riddle political temporality and remind us that issues and events cannot be contained within bound discourses or temporalities. While some ghosts can discipline or welcome, others convey terror and horror. Ranging from personal ghost stories to ghosts that trouble violent landscapes, hauntings are characterized by connections, infiltrations, and excesses that tease or make impossible any closure of categories.

Hauntings can magnify specificities, as well as erase them. Indeed, the process of being haunted may wipe away the specific context and connect moments, times, places in a voracious somersault and so constitute a realm of counterworldly politics I call hauntings. The *work of hauntings* is a critical aspect of postcolonial societies, subjects, and experiences.

My attention to ghosts and hauntings has early origins and has traveled with me through different worlds. The only thing that ruffled our old South Calcutta house of enduring cement and brick were stories of ghosts and hauntings. The house owned many kinds of noises, largely from metal pipes that supplied water to the whole structure, that were made more palpable through intense monsoon months of water-logged streets. The ghostly noises swishing through the metal pipes were used to discipline us as children to do our homework and be good. But it is not simply the daily sensorium of living with ghosts that pervades my memories of growing up in India; it is also the fantastical story, retold so often, of a good ghost blessing my mother in my grandparents' ancestral home in rural Bengal. On a visit to that house, which was hundreds of years old, my grandmother alerted my mother to the presence of a hand stamp on her body; the discernible print of five fingers at the back of her neck. She was told that it was the hand of the good ghost that protected our household as a guardian spirit and welcomed new members to it. My Punjabi mother was as thrilled to be accepted into a Bengali community as she was chilled by the ghostly fingers that delivered this uninvited blessing. She entertained us with this story countless times as we lay listening to the heavy rain and swooshing pipes.

While the ghost stories and repeated viewings of Ray's film *Goopy Gyne Bagha Byne* have traveled with me through the years, the nature of hauntings has changed considerably in my life as an academic now in the United States. In rental apartments whose stories I do not know, I remain unfazed by ghosts. As I jokingly relay to my friends, if I don't know the stories, I cannot be haunted. Ghosts and hauntings come about through stories, experiences, and a complicated sensorium wrapped intricately around a place and time. A deep attachment to that place and time precedes the experience of being haunted. One must be attentive, in many ways, to see ghosts. While the experience of being haunted and seeing ghosts is deeply personal, it is also complexly communal and situated within landscapes of belonging or unbelonging and in categories of being in-place or out-of-place. My invocation of ghosts and hauntings through this book treats them as undoing binaries of life and death, here and there, human and animal, and friend and enemy. Permeating places and times and nudging their contours, ghosts and their hauntings are used in the book as a remembering of histories, exclusions, and violence.

My emphasis on the critical role of hauntings in understanding postcolonial contexts is inspired by Marxist literature, especially by Derrida's and

Gayatri Spivak's writings on the work of specters that haunt social fabrics to denote its exclusions and injustices. The first line of the *Communist Manifesto* rings in my ears as a constant reminder of the political potency of hauntings: "A spectre is haunting Europe—the spectre of Communism."[5] Commenting on the future of Marxism in *Specters of Marx*, Derrida reiterates the significance of thinking about contemporary capitalism with specters that denote the critical potency of Marxism. The specters of Karl Marx have not outlived their relevance. Derrida states, "Haunting is historical, to be sure, but it is not *dated*, it is never docilely given a date in the chain of presents, day after day, according to the instituted order of a calendar."[6] While haunting is about the old and the dead, it is also significantly present and disobeys the linearity of a calendar. Between life and death and irreverent to the distinction of life from death, haunting stealthily reminds us about the past in the present and the present as part of the past as we seek to decipher contemporary moments of crisis and capitalism. Tracing the role of the specter in Marx's writings, Derrida situates it as an inextricable element of Marxist radical politics that continually disturbs the status quo.

Spivak notes the value of Derrida's method of deconstruction to read Marx, but she takes exception to the invisibility of women in the narrative. In "Ghostwriting," she draws out how *Specters of Marx* itself creates yet other specters, such as women, who are kept in the shadows.[7] She contends, "Woman is the dubiously felicitous out-of-joint subject of the strictly Marxian vision."[8] Thus, although Derrida notes the out-of-joint appearances of the specter through time, he fails to engage with women who remain doubly out-of-joint. Spivak's engagement with Derrida's text has significantly influenced *Postcolonial Hauntings* as a persistent reminder to continually read for the shadows. While hauntings relay inclusions and exclusions in any particular context, Spivak brings to the forefront how hauntings must be open to their own complicity with regimes of power as some specters are forever unintelligible, even as specters, as some are rendered doubly spectral. Ghosts can create other ghosts. Thus, when moving through the debates in postcolonial transnational societies about animality or being queer, I remain thinking with Spivak about grids of intelligibility and spectral politics. Spivak's approach influences the methodology of hauntings in this book through attentiveness toward noting that we are never purely inclusive, even when working with ghosts, as some issues, contexts, and people are never seen. By centering race, gender, sexuality, and nation in its frames of analyses, *Postcolonial Hauntings* situates the uneven politics of ghosts and their echoes.

Postcolonial Hauntings

The hauntings and ghosts that saturate these pages are residues of memories and histories. They emerge out of the violence that characterizes vastly stratified societies, out of the enormous power differentials within and between nations and out of continuing histories of exploitation and expropriation. Saidiya Hartman describes it best when she refers to the present as the "afterlife of slavery" or "living in the future created by it": "The perilous conditions of the present establish the link between our age and a previous one in which freedom too was yet to be realized."[9] The hauntings that proliferate through these pages emphasize that colonialism is far from dead.

Arundhati Roy's 2020 Clark Lecture "The Graveyard Talks Back" further situates the significance of haunting to a postcolonial world. In this lecture, Roy talks about her 2017 novel, *The Ministry of Utmost Happiness*, about Muslim graveyards in India and about the status of Kashmir. Kashmir has been the site of a protracted and complex territorial dispute implicating Pakistan, India, Kashmiri nationalists, and China, resulting in the deaths of many citizens and soldiers. Roy explains how Kashmir has now become one large graveyard strewn with myriad smaller graveyards.[10] Roy's novel converses not only with this graveyard that is Kashmir but also a second graveyard as well, in Delhi. Anjum, a protagonist in the novel, builds a guesthouse on top of the graveyard in Delhi. This house provides shelter to many and is named the Jannat Guest House, translated as the "Paradise Guest House."[11] Weaving her way through fact and fiction and through a conversation between two graveyards, Roy writes about postcolonial Kashmir as a land of "talking graves": "In our Kashmir the dead will live forever; and the living are only dead people, pretending."[12] Graveyards in India usually signify Muslim graveyards, and with the rise of communal violence toward Muslims, "talking graveyards" articulate resistance and dissent against Hindu nationalist rule. Kashmiris today live under military rule with every civil and political right disenfranchised. This land looks like paradise with its heavenly mountains and scenic valleys, yet it has become nothing more than a graveyard through years of war and bloodshed. What does it mean for a graveyard to talk back? And how do the talking graveyards that lie between the ever-living dead and the barely living disturb the "post"-colonial rhetoric of liberation and nationalism? Talking graveyards, the ever-living dead, and the living who are ever-dead poignantly situate the uncontrollable proliferation of hauntings in postcolonial societies.

Questions about who counts as living and whose death gets recognized have framed much conversation in critical race, feminist, and queer theory, alongside analyses of colonialism's restive presence.[13] As Sharon Holland lucidly emphasizes, the binary between living and dead forms the binary for straight and queer, White and Black.[14] Working with frames of recognition such as human and animal, straight and queer, I converse with ghosts and hauntings that break through our tightly contained formulations. Continuing with the emphasis on "necropolitics" that draws attention to "who is able to live and who must die," "postcolonial hauntings" questions the framings of life and death by drawing attention to areas in-between and in excess: those who can never live and those who never die.[15]

The afterlives of colonialism proliferate not only in settler colonialism and neocolonialism but also in the imposition of hegemonic meaning patterns in even the most-everyday contexts of representation and relationship building. The ordinary frames we use to designate self, other, human, animal, friend, and terrorist continue the violent politics of civilizing the "other." So, while "animals" are an unchanging kernel, "humans" are sentient and civilized; while a "friend" looks like oneself, a "terrorist" is a monstrous virus that is best annihilated from the body politic. Looking at frames of representation, such as animal versus human, and means of relationship building, such as translations and friendships, this book traces postcolonial hauntings that pervade these specific moments of politics. Working with frames of recognition such as human and animal, straight and queer, friend and other, I converse with ghosts. Through historical residues and present conditions, the ghosts that flit in and out of these pages emanate from barricaded ideas about who counts as human, animal, friend, or enemy. *Postcolonial Hauntings* endeavors to converse with the many afterlives that haunt questions of animality, friendships, and translations.

What then of the "post" in postcolonialism? Does it point to such "afterlives" as those Hartman writes about? In fact, there has been an upsurge of interest in postcolonial feminisms, often productive, but at other times ironic and bafflingly literal in its understanding of the "post" in postcolonial. Of course, many would attest to postcolonial theories' upsurges and proclamations of demise for many years.[16] One could even discern cycles of upsurges and downsurges, for example, in conversations comparing postcolonialism to postmodernism and most recently comparisons between decolonial and postcolonial feminisms.[17] With differing emphases, scholars often distinguish the postcolonial from decolonial approaches, while others coalesce the postcolonial and decolonial as anticolonial, or some declare the demise of the postcolonial with the rise of "decolonial" as an activist praxis positioned against "postcolonial" as elite theory. Notwithstanding the differing ways in which the postcolonial and decolonial are used in recent feminist conversations, we can safely generalize that these two terms have dominated many feminist forums seeking to grapple with Western modernity, the production of knowledge, and exclusions inevitably produced in the wake of dominant discourses about human, truth, science, culture, and nature. Kiran Asher lucidly writes about points of contact and dissonance between decolonial and postcolonial feminisms and warns against "simplistic claims about decolonial ontologies and postcolonial futures."[18]

Centralizing the politics of play and hauntings shifts how we attend to the postcolonial and transnational. My engagement and interest in postcolonial studies and the naming of "postcolonial" derive from the stark realization that "postcolonial" cannot denote something that *is*. So, as such, the postcolonial cannot be an "identity" and might even best be seen as an "anti-identity." It is in this sense a ghostly category, particularly hospitable to the work of play and hauntings. Let me explain. First, let us ponder the fact that most of the names popularly associated with postcolonial studies have vehemently disapproved of the frame per se; in other words, they have never called themselves "postcolonial."[19] Rather than a form of identity, as we would call being a "feminist," postcolonial scholars are ironically associated with postcolonial studies because of their assessment of the problems inherent in the naming of "postcolonial" in the first place, not to mention the politics about who gets to count as the postcolonial subject. For example, in *A Critique of Postcolonial Reason*, Spivak provides her first full book on the role of the postcolonial critic and the "implicit collaboration of the postcolonial in the service of *neo*-colonialism."[20] She says in the preface to *A Critique of Postcolonial Reason* published in 1999: "After 1989, I began to sense that a certain postcolonial subject had, in turn, been recoding the colonial subject and appropriating the Native Informant's position."[21] She also charts her transition "from colonial discourse studies to transnational cultural studies" as she studies philosophy, literature, history, culture, and the role of the "native informant."[22] Spivak's critique explicitly calls out the posturing of postcolonial subjects for continuing a colonial project of representing authentic local information.

In her book *Strange Encounters: Embodied Others in Post-Coloniality*, published a year after Spivak's *Critique of Postcolonial Reason*, Sara Ahmed continues to grapple with the tensions and conundrums saturating the terrain of postcolonialism: "It is hence about the complexity of the relationship between the past and the present, between the histories of European colonization and contemporary forms of globalization."[23] Her analysis situates the problem in considering colonialism as a sole determinant or totality of social relations. For her, postcolonialism is "*failed historicity*; a historicity that admits of its own failure in grasping that which has been, as the impossibility of grasping the present."[24]

Introduction 9

I persistently emphasize that an important aspect of postcolonial theory lies precisely in the tensions and agonistic politics that prevent it from being situated. In many ways, "disidentification" would best frame a relation to the postcolonial. José Esteban Muñoz describes "disidentification" as "a strategy that works on and against dominant ideology. Instead of buckling under the pressures of dominant ideology (identification, assimilation) or attempting to break free of its inescapable sphere (counteridentification, utopianism), this 'working on and against' is a strategy that tries to transform a cultural logic from within."[25] Disidentification presents myriad ways of working on and against a system, with full responsibility of complicity. Writing within Western academia, acknowledging the politics in the production of knowledge and the role of the native informant, it is our responsibility to move with a "productive acknowledgment of complicity," as Spivak reminds us.[26] Thus, in this book I resist an anchoring of the term or theories of the "postcolonial," recognizing its ethics in critiques and disidentifications. Being constantly attentive to exclusions produced by our terminology and theory enables us to broaden and deepen terms of engagement that would be foreclosed if we worked with it as an identity for something that *is*—spatially or in temporality.

Working with the many guises of colonialisms, where colonialism is far from dead and resurges in every landscape, it is useful to think with the many lives of colonialism and its temporal anarchy. Moreover, recognizing that not everyone engages with time in the same way, embedded as they may be within different socioeconomic structures. Achille Mbembe in *On the Postcolony* puts it perfectly about the combinations of temporalities: "In the case of the postcolony, to postulate the existence of a 'before' and an 'after' of colonization could not exhaust the problem of the relationship between temporality and subjectivity, nor was it sufficient to raise questions about the passage from one stage (before) to the other (after), and the question of *transit* that each passage raises, or again to recognize that every age has contradictory significations to different actors."[27] In its temporal discontinuities, there lies a spatial disorientation. Although colonialism draws many maps and obliterates others in its hunger for optimum resource extraction, spatially we are continuously within dislocations, drawings, and redrawings. The borders of nations and of communities of belonging spiral outwards or inwards, and we are constantly negotiating shifting terrains of nationalisms and transnationalism. Market flows, diasporas, refugees, immigration, and activisms are continuous trajectories in globalization and our contemporary structure of world politics and economics.

Postcolonial studies have contributed significantly to critiques of temporality, as seen in conversations about queer temporality.[28] As Mbembe marks the occurrence of multiple and contradictory temporalities in the passage above, queer theorists have also critiqued a linear temporality and "reproductive futurism."²⁹ *Postcolonial Hauntings* contributes to this conversation by situating the use of asynchronous temporality in politics of various kinds, left and right, whereby power configurations are destabilized or further stabilized. Rather than simply situating the radical potential of play and hauntings, this book notes their heterogeneous and layered nature through meaning-plays in queer transnationalism, for example. Queer subjects in India play with the term "queer" and are haunted by it within a global political economy of needing to look queer, as measured through a Western prototype, to be considered really queer. By addressing the roguish nature of play and hauntings, this book frames temporality as political, shifting, and multiple and forever manipulated. Noting the mischievous nature of politics, our terms for theory making work at all times through hauntings.

My emphasis on the postcolonial and the transnational throughout this book situates them as hauntings. We have never been *post*colonial, nor has the transnational ever really moved beyond the state, unless we choose to ignore citizenship privileges and global hierarchies that govern movement between borders. While postcolonial and transnational feminists work tirelessly against capitalism and globalization and work to build feminist solidarity, I argue that only in positioning the postcolonial and transnational as persistent hauntings can we hope to achieve a feminist ethos of justice. The work of hauntings and play rises from the asynchronous temporality and spatial mappings that postcolonial studies highlight, albeit through a critique of the term "postcolonial." Antithetical to a settling in with a politics or ideology, postcolonial studies works through a distancing, or in other words, a proclivity to read through the lines that demarcate transitions from colonialism to liberation, oppression to freedom. As certain subjects, even in ostensibly liberated societies, continue to be excluded from political gains and victories, emphasizing the "postcolonial" remains an ironic haunting per se.

Because discussions about the postcolonial and/or the decolonial riddle many feminist conversations in our contemporary moment, I reemphasize briefly some oft-noted critiques of the postcolonial, for example in the works on Leela Gandhi, Ania Loomba, and Anne McClintock. My attention to these critiques is inspired by the need to engage with the "postcolonial" while attending carefully to its exclusions, which emerge as an inevitable part of the epistemology that it unfolds. Gandhi, for instance, writes about "postcolonialism" as a "diffuse and nebulous term" that simply projects the needs of the Western academy and helps to situate the works of non-Western subjects who are now part of the West.[30] Loomba notes the many practical problems that saturate conversations on the "postcolonial," for example, when a country can be simultaneously postcolonial (after a national liberation struggle) and neocolonial (dependent on colonial economic processes).[31] Moreover, Loomba notes that there is nothing "post" about those who remain oppressed under new regime forms, as their colonization is far from over.[32] McClintock's study of the postcolonial similarly interrogates the "post" in "postcolonial" and emphasizes that "the historical rupture suggested by the preposition 'post-' belies both the continuities and discontinuities of power that have shaped the legacies of the formal European and British colonial empires (not to mention the Islamic, Japanese, Chinese, and other imperial powers)."[33]

These critiques of postcolonial studies remind us that changes in political structures are not necessarily indicative of economic redistribution in favor of those lower in economic status and that the cultural valance of virtues, morals, and language—among other systems—persists through time with complex permutations and combinations that are not captured when we think about institutions as contained within only one temporal specificity, that is, postcolonial. Working with attention to hybrid and multiple temporalities, and dissonances, *Postcolonial Hauntings* situates an incessant conversing with specters as its core yearning. Thus, haunted through its own nomenclature and always living with ghosts, *Postcolonial Hauntings*' epistemology of play enables an emphasis on reality as it is—haunted and play inspiring—and heralds a politics of hope through exaggerations and border crossings.

The Politics of Play

Inspired by the mood Ray strikes in the eerie, topsy-turvy ghost dance, I work in this book with spirited buoyancy, with play and mischief, noting their incredible prowess in helping us both discern and undo modes of violence, including the violence of hegemonic categories, often inherited from colonial practice. I have always taken play seriously. Not simply in its more mirthful incarnations, like when we laugh. When laughter shakes the body and mind, fixed categories, solid conditions, and stubborn ideologies are nudged and prodded with an effervescence that deems hilarious the proclivity to consider something stable, true, or even real. Play comprises laughter, humor, satire, and/or irony, all of which have a complex history in feminist and queer politics, and it can also nudge at categories deemed sacrosanct, subvert stereotypes, and make mischievous exaggerations. While play may take many forms, subversive or exploitative, in this book I draw attention to manifestations of play in the context of postcolonial and transnational feminism, a politics of creative resistance that can help us survive systems and structures of violence.

When I was growing up in Kolkata, India, my first inkling that play was serious business came from the fish markets. I often accompanied my mother to our local fish market in South Kolkata, and it is this imagery that helps me best situate the politics that I have in mind. The fishmongers were typically seated in rows on a slightly raised platform with shiny knives and gleaming fishes. The fish scales sparkled in the reflection from the lightbulbs hanging precariously from black cords. There were fishes of all shapes and sizes, many still alive and splashing water all over with the force of their tails. We would walk through the muddy alleys of the fish market, first simply observing and taking stock of what was available. As a child, I was intrigued by the large fish and the way this part of the market had a covered roof and was separated from the rest of the market. After my mother saw the fish she wanted to purchase, a spirited back-and-forth ensued between her and the seller to fix the price. No fish-buying expedition was complete without it. While the seller spoke at length about how fresh the fish was and how unjustified my mother was in asking for a lower price, my mother made her own performative remarks and gestures. Although our Bengali Brahmin relatives congratulated my Punjabi Sikh mother on the low price of the fish that she managed to procure, they preferred not to get into this mode of bargaining.[34] Years later while thinking back on these ostensibly innocent childhood memories, I am struck by the many layers of meaning in this daily walk through the fish market.

A deft play between buyer and seller framed my mother's interaction. Without romanticizing these instances as more than economic relationality, I am unconvinced that those moments were only of economic consequence or simply about the price of a commodity. Now, I remain delightfully haunted by the mischief, stories, and spirited back-and-forth that infused these bargaining events. While the seller spun tales about the freshness of the fish and its great value, my mother answered with her own version about how the fish did not look so fresh. What all this back-and-forth brought forth was a creative relationality that did not ignore the power relations between a buyer and seller but that still managed to express humanness made of stories, imaginations, and revelry. Other politics—of gender, of community—and many histories also jostle forth from this memory, but here I simply want to draw attention to a gleeful exchange of relation building within the confines of societal norms that also imbue actors with many forms of agency. Maybe it was through this performative act of buying fish that my Punjabi mother, coming from a family of vegetarians, was able to become Bengali, part of a community of avid fish-eaters, at least for a little bit? While histories between communities, classes, and genders permeate this playful interaction, its immediate nudge at everyday social relations persistently resonates. Thus, while I draw the politics of play in broad strokes, as narrowing it would inhibit its border defiance, its specific occurrences as they strike out as mirthful, mischievous, and/or nonsensical and provide levity and force to circumstantial constructions.

This example of my mother at the fish market evokes the central themes of the book: animals, translations, community, nation, and the border crossings that are inescapable for postcolonial subjects. To begin with, "India" signifies attempts to project a homogenous national unity, even while the realities of belonging to specific communities, that is, Bengali versus Punjabi, continually fracture the picture. And while Bengali fish markets in Kolkata include fisherwomen and fishermen, the early morning visits to the fish market are mostly the prerogative of Bengali men. But here is my mother, participating in the same protracted negotiations exercised by Bengali men but, through that participation, still always excluded because of gender and her designation as non-Bengali. What about language? Translations and the transnational are necessary cotravelers that always unsuccessfully attempt to catch up with each other. My mother's fluency in Bengali, learned from growing up in Bengal and intensified by her rapture with the songs of Bengali poet Rabindranath Tagore, serves her well in terms of her ability to converse with the fish sellers, but again it also marks her as separate from them. Her community markers as a Punjabi Sikh woman wrestle silently with her ostensible fluency in the Bengali language. Transnationalism's attempts at translations are forever tensed and persistently spirited.

The final important theme my mother's story draws out is, of course, the ubiquitous animal, here the fish, that serves as the slippery negotiator between gender and community. The fish shimmers as the object of desire and sale, and as such it brings buyers and sellers together along with matters of nation, community, gender, and translation, all the while remaining also separate from these matters. While Bengalis are avid fish eaters, Punjabis are mostly vegetarian. The immigrant Punjabi community in Bengal has long picked up the love for eating fish, and the battered and deep-fried fish is a common presence in Punjabi social gatherings. The act of buying fish, in a Bengali fish market, by a Punjabi woman who speaks fluent Bengali marks reverberating acts of translations and transnationalism and the work of play and haunting. The playful negotiations on the right price for the fish are frames that are continually haunted by gender norms and community. Thus *Postcolonial Hauntings* demonstrates the continuous transactions that are part and parcel of postcolonial lives and its effervescent swerve, push, and pull against determined outcomes and meanings, alongside the seething reminders of community and gender that haunt the "world-travelling."

My understanding of play has evolved in response to Maria Lugones's emphasis on play as "'world'-travelling" in her essay "Playfulness, 'World'-Travelling, and Loving Perception" and to Sudipta Kaviraj's emphasis on how play can wreak havoc on colonial modernity in his book *The Unhappy Consciousness: Bankimchandra Chattopadhyay and the Formation of Nationalist Discourse in India*. Lugones, speaking of her experience of White/Anglo structure in the United States as a woman of color, writes about "travelling" as learning to love another by being able to enter into the other's "world." Her use of the word "world" looks upon it as a constructed sense of self and others. By being able to travel to each other's worlds through the translation of experiences, playful traveling, we are able to love each other. Playfulness in "world"-travelling, as Lugones emphasizes, means nourishing a creative sense of self, being open to wonder, open to being proved wrong, and open to even being a fool. Play, very different from a game or sport as seen in the work of Johan Huizinga, for instance, is not about the conquering or winning that can be seen as supporting an imperial spirit. Rather, play extols not being trapped in a "world": "We *are there creatively*."[35] A creative buoyancy with no permanent rules weaves its way through Lugones's work with play.

Kaviraj's *Unhappy Consciousness* describes the work of Bankimchandra Chattopadhyay, a nationalist in colonial India who critiqued colonial modernity through play and humor. For example, in his work, Chattopadhyay uses the character of Kamalakanta described as a homeless, jobless drug addict, and "a sayer of the unsayable" as a foil against colonial modernity to play with the "grammar of reality." Playing with colonial structures of education, rationality, and economic productivity is Kamalakanta's forte. And, in this play, Kaviraj discerns a critical subversiveness that is full of hope: "It is hopeful precisely because in ridiculing the reality of social relations it asserts the important fact that the world that exists is always short of, is a travesty in a sense, of the world that ought to be."[36] Kaviraj uses play and humor to delineate a utopian energy for moving beyond reality as we know it, and the incidence of playing with social relations indicates the hope for a better world that stands as a foil to the present world.

There are significant differences between Lugones's and Kaviraj's use of play, mostly arising from their use in different and very specific time periods and places. But the way they make use of the work of play to create social change and puncture the colonial "grammar of reality" informs this book throughout. Their influence is most apparent in my concept of *meaning-plays*, by which I mean the creative acts where postcolonial subjects play with language, identity, or a context to overturn its original intentions: a playful, affirmative sabotage. Embroiled with colonialism and its histories and attentive to the hauntings that are generated by colonialism, meaning-plays signal toward eclectic negotiations through multiple worlds by postcolonial subjects. In these playful movements, in language and beyond, we discern the kernel for creative reactions in postcolonial societies. This politics of play that cuts across multiple locales has much to tell us about structures of power and methods of negotiating with them. Often we sequester issues, subjects, and places as if distinct, isolable phenomena, failing to attend to the mischievous ways in which they intermesh. In addition, we bracket some subjects as helpless, forever maneuvered. Think about a woman selling vegetables in a busy Indian market who reserves the discretion to give a customer a clean or a dirty note, depending on the tone of the customer's voice when they talk to her. Think also about the tourist who walks through the streets of a third-world locale taking pictures of downtrodden women and children and who ends up paying eight times the price of a trinket from the street vendors and the gleeful smirk on the faces of the local inhabitants as he walks on unaware. These moments of creative effervescence are what I consider "play" that bother structures of power that are unmoving and exclusionary. These are frequent, not special, events. However, they persist resiliently through structures of power and continue to demand attention for their sleight of hand with power configurations.

These instances of the woman selling vegetables in an Indian market or the tourist meandering through third-world streets incorporate many different meaning-plays. The specificities of the situations of woman selling vegetables or tourist walking must be read in tandem with mappings such as Indian market and third-world locale. Mappings and their meaning structures overlap when we think about how most Indian markets have their own cartography dictated by cultures and customs with clearly demarcated areas and how "third world" operates as a misnomer in a binary model of mapping. In reality, the third world exists within the first world and vice versa. Vast histories of class position precede the woman's situation in the market selling vegetables, alongside the consideration of the history of tourism in less privileged locales. Thus, understanding these two frames of play requires translating mappings, binaries, and structures of relation building and being haunted by the histories they entail. The woman plays with her customer through the dirty note, and local inhabitants play with the tourist. They draw attention to what Hartman calls "infrapolitics of the dominated." Hartman's "infrapolitics of the dominated" includes "stealing away, the breakdown, moving about, pilfering, and other everyday practices that occur below the threshold of formal equality."[37] Through showcasing play with binaries, mappings, translations, and relation building, this book emphasizes meaning-play's multilayered politics that strike through formal structures.

In recognizing the importance of play in creative forms of relationality, different from a major social event or paradigm shift, throughout this book I follow many guises of play as it dances forth within social and political structures. Going back to the scene from the fish market, the fishmongers and my mother were actively engaged in puncturing the grammar of reality through their playful exchange. The "world"-travelling happens through engaging myriad mappings that situate self and the other. In noticing the everyday occurrences of play, as Lugones and Kaviraj articulate, we see social structures and attempts to unbalance them. Exaggerations, border crossings, shape shifting, performing, drawing, and simply talking can be playful manifestations when they engage with a set system, such as language. Meaning-plays illuminate the use of language as haunting, confuse reality as it is, and inspire different becomings. Central to shifts of meaning in language use, meaning-plays, as I study through the book, move with transnational politics. Play travels between and through borders, displaying their constructed nature in play's irreverence for static structures. Haunting social forms with its fleeting movements and persistent questioning, play illuminates social investments in rules and regulations, and it nudges at them mischievously.

With an emphasis on play's multihued politics, *Postcolonial Hauntings* traces how meaning-plays travel through a postcolonial and transnational world. The meaning-plays I highlight in this book refer to practices of translation that move with the use of words, identities, and events as people negotiate their position within multiple mappings of identification and disavowal. My attention to translations in situating subject positions—queer, for example—underlines how people resist hegemonic structures through their own meaning-plays with categories and identities. In noting the excesses, errors, and slippages that move with translations understood as linguistic and political, I highlight how meaning-plays can help us understand subject formation and resistance to naturalized forms of being and doing.

Postcolonial Hauntings connects meaning-plays to the politics of play and hauntings and in so doing significantly intervenes in feminist and queer conversations about relating through differences and working with inlaid practices of power and resistance. It showcases how subjects traverse overlapping spatial and temporal locations in a transnational postcolonial world by playing with a supposedly achromatic issue or event and saturating it with colors and meanings that speak to histories and hauntings. Meaning-plays are a manifestation of hauntings and play as they are shadowed by histories and play with a supposedly sacrosanct connotation. The emphasis on play and hauntings is concomitantly timely and untimely with play's attention to contemporary conversations in queer and feminist theory, alongside its continual undoing of the place and time of an event.

Reckoning with play's multihued configurations, I thus beckon us toward a specific kind of politics: a politics of playful irreverence, of moving back and forth, not necessarily of winning or losing or stating unchanging propositions. Working with play enables us to move through layers of place and time-braided positions—without presuming linearity or progress; it also inspires imaginative formulations that enable survival or persistence in new and unexpected ways. Disobeying prototypes of the abject third-world woman, the animal that does not talk, and the Westernized, queer, third-world subject, this book showcases a play with categories and the language used to describe the "other." We can find these playful negotiations with structures of power all around us as we look at our social and political world and attempt to make sense of it. Working in different garbs and through multiple avenues, play subtly dislocates hegemonic tropes and provides our imagination with inspiration to run in different directions.

By riddling social structures, play becomes an epistemology of grappling with the world as it is, haunting it to illuminate and shuffle the status quo. This book emphasizes play as politics, a yearning that negotiates with power hierarchies to help us discern the many layers of life and nonlife, place and its shifting terrains, along with the responsibility to engage with the past as future. A transnational postcolonial sensibility echoes through these pages, urging a consideration of our places and scales of analysis. However, the transnational and postcolonial prism that I deploy for this project cannot be terms of identity. Owning these labels, transnational and postcolonial, is ironic on multiple levels. How responsible would it be for academics to pronounce themselves transnational and postcolonial without acknowledging the power profiles and passport privileges that enable them to engage with borders or to fail to recognize that our language and terms of discourse have violent genealogies within which we remain embedded? Thus, throughout these pages, I urge us to reframe our political imagination through a holistic engagement with the transnational and postcolonial, understood as multilayered positionalities and useful for a feminist project only through persistent critiques and attunement to hauntings.

Transnational Feminisms and Shifting Terrains

Attentive to multilocal and multipronged activisms, transnational feminism, as Elora Halim Chowdhury emphasizes, "adheres to a lens and set of practices that pay attention to various overlapping systems of power such as capitalist development, globalization, imperialism, and patriarchy."[38] Its concern with histories and systems of power attempts to discern "scattered hegemonies," such as flows of economic processes, nationalisms, local and international policies, and frames of oppression.[39] Different from a global feminism that works with a universal frame for women's emancipation hinged on ideals of Western modernity—and keeps intact the center/periphery, developed/undeveloped, first-world/third-world binaries to "help" women in other spaces—transnational feminism strives to stay attuned to the workings of power that create frames of self/other. Transnational feminism continually engages with different kinds of borders, and as Chandra Talpade Mohanty writes, "I choose to stress that our most expansive and inclusive visions of feminism need to be attentive to borders while learning to transcend them."[40]

As Chowdhury reminds us, it remains crucial to situate the politics of transnational feminism and postcolonial studies in diverse discussions about nationalism, patriarchy, and imperialism, whereby the congruence between transnational feminism and postcolonial work remains tensed and agonistic.[41] A certain central point of contention is the figure of the third-world woman. As Gandhi, Mohanty, and Trinh T. Minh-ha, along with others, have showcased, we are kept oscillating in an eternal balance between an imperial feminist project and its concomitant projects of global sisterhood, with the third-world woman as a static victim of culture waiting to be saved. In addition, on the other hand, a nationalist project of safeguarding tradition and "their" women animates our postcolonial brothers. As a transnational postcolonial project traverses its multilocal parameters, the conversation must be attuned to overlapping structures of oppression that envelop local to global spaces.

How do we build transnational alliances through borders knowing all the while that forces of globalization move steadfast through the same channels and often at the same time? M. Jacqui Alexander alerts us to this question when she comments that the "category of the transnational—which has itself been put to multiple uses—continues to be haunted by relativist claims that effectively reinscribe dysfunctional hierarchies and obscure the ways in which national and transnational processes are mutually, although unequally, imbricated."[42] In other words, transnational feminism ironically reproduces the very conditions that it intends to counter. The ability to move across borders flows along the same power hierarchies that enable the movement of capital and privilege; those in global economic centers move relatively easily across borders, while those moving from the periphery to the centers are hindered by migration checkpoints and attitudes that castigate migrants as interruptions in need of aid. These differential power hierarchies haunt transnational postcolonial feminism as it negotiates theories and activisms on national and transnational scales.

Attuned to the politics of this double bind, Spivak suggests that we "learn to use the European Enlightenment from below." She elaborates that we want some of the useful changes that emerged from the Enlightenment, for example when thinking of the public sphere or questions of privacy. Yet, we must resist the colonialism and "free trade" that it also heralds. Spivak notes that we are indebted to Gregory Bateson and his *Steps to an Ecology of Mind* (1972) for the phrase "double bind," which he uses to understand childhood schizophrenia. A double bind is a no-win situation, in which whatever course of action one chooses results in punishment or re-creates the problem one is hoping to solve. Transnational feminism finds itself in such a bind when it reproduces the very conditions it criticizes, without seeing any other alternative. For Bateson, the only way out of the double bind is to call out its form, to see how it operates. In his theory, this necessitates a therapist who can break the frame, so to speak. In his essay "A Theory of Play and Fantasy," he elaborates about how a therapist negotiates the double bind by maneuvering between the abstract and the concrete; Spivak calls it "play training." In Spivak's theory, escaping the double bind requires what she calls an "aesthetic education," an epistemological grounding to get at "the double bind at the heart of democracy. . . . Contradictory instructions come to us at all times. We learn to listen to them and remain in the game."[43]

This is to say that both transnational and postcolonial theory necessarily work with an insidious aporia and double bind, one that cannot be reduced to a simple contradiction. This is what Spivak is suggesting in *An Aesthetic Education in the Era of Globalization*: "When one decides to speak of double binds and aporias, one is haunted by the ghost of the undecidable in every decision."[44] Hauntings riddle, push, and pull at the contours of the postcolonial and transnational, revealing their workings and imbuing them with a politics of responsibility to history and to the contemporary moment, where colonial and neocolonial processes continue to operate through frames of the national and transnational.

An attunement to the double bind when working with postcolonial transnational feminisms animates this study. This book ponders the possibilities and ethics of play, what it means to be played with by unequal power structures and what it means to suggest that play may become a route out of the double bind or even offer a solution.[45] By centering play and hauntings as epistemological partners and meaning-plays as a way to reframe the double bind and so expose it, *Postcolonial Hauntings* works with theory that is restless and buoyant and persistently endeavors to undo frames of meaning-making that reiterate cycles of violence. As we are haunted with the exclusions in our feminist and queer politics that reflect the status quo of the present, even when trying to unsettle it, how do we work toward a more responsible politics? If certain people are always less than human—animals—can we play with this categorization to create a space for all to flourish? How do we broaden our terms—such as queer, animal, and friend—and theories of meaning-making to include affirming possibilities?

India

My use of multiple genres and media in this book is inspired by the politics of play, to continually endeavor to see hidden meaning-plays in frames that we suppose are sacrosanct. I study graphic narratives, children's books, ghosts, multimedia art performances, and forms of prose to situate their politics. When reading Suniti Namjoshi's animal becomings or following maps with Alison Bechdel and Amruta Patil in their graphic narratives, I draw attention to our frames of understanding through an analysis of what they include and exclude. India dominates these narratives as I question its framing within transnational trajectories through an attention to overlapping maps and shifting borders. "India" offers a particular vantage position through which overlapping maps are discernible because of its growing diaspora and subnationalisms as seen, for instance, in being Bengali versus Punjabi. The sustained elaboration on the art of Mithu Sen, who is Bengali and a prominent Indian artist with global presence, points to maps that pull in different directions. Through the book, I analyze many Indian artifacts, for example, in Sen's art and images of a talking cow, and by situating them within transnational circuits and meaning-plays, I complicate their geopolitical positioning and our frames of perception. The cow takes on many personas through its transnational travels, and so does Sen's art. By constantly complicating assumptions of static positionality, whether that of animal, woman, artist, or India, I draw attention to nationalism's maps and the meaning-plays that subvert them, both at home and abroad.

Deepti Misri turns our attention to "India" as a "floating signifier" with differential meaning-plays, seen, for example, in India as a postcolonial nation, rapidly developing economy, and dominating regional presence, alongside other metrics of accomplishment and disreputation.[46] She describes how "the meaning of this floating signifier, 'India,' is secured and unsecured time and again through violence."[47] My choice of texts in the current book showcases meaning-plays around "India" and subversions, exaggerations, and translations of its multipronged signifiers. While not making a case for uniqueness in India and being alert to the exceptions that pave claims for being special, my focus on texts around India are inspired by an attempt to showcase *Postcolonial Hauntings* or how a postcolonial nation-state entrenches and is entrenched within cycles of violence that could be spiritedly maneuvered, an attempt to emphasize the politics of framing and its undoing. While casteism, communalism, sexism, and manifold violences engulf the postcolonial nation and define it, the meaning-plays are demonstrated by differential life and death possibilities for its people.

Postcolonial Hauntings frames India to questions its borders, that is, how it differentiates between holy and queer and how its borders overflow through transnational travels. Our frames for understanding and categorizing the world create specific ontologies for life, death, and animals, legitimate and real, colonial and postcolonial. Judith Butler writes in *Frames of War: When Is Life Grievable?* "To learn to see the frame that blinds us to what we see is no easy matter. And if there is a critical role for visual culture during times of war it is precisely to thematize the forcible frame, the one that conducts the dehumanizing norm, that restricts what is perceivable and, indeed, what can be."[48] Thus I continually ask through the book what frames are doing and displaying and how playing with them illuminates their work.

While India is shown as traveling with meaning-plays through the book as in renditions of animals or queer, my own experiences and travels are also entwined in these narratives. The everydayness of play and hauntings seeps through the personal and political adding layers to their working. My visits to the fish market in India with my mother and grappling with colonial and postcolonial texts as an academic in the United States are all experiences that knit *Postcolonial Hauntings*. I would not have understood the play of hauntings without the experience of constantly moving between positions and places. I am struck by the surreal and always ghostly feeling that overtakes me as I emerge from a transatlantic flight to India or the United States. Suddenly, everyday exchanges are colored by instances of play and hauntings that would have been impossible to discern without the constant comings and goings, entries and exits, without the movement between places that shapes my personal and political experiences. The materiality of being a tenured faculty member in American academia, on a visa, where tenure has no bearing on the status of material entry or exit into a country has enabled me to keep the ironies of living in a transnational world close to my heart and head. I hope that the biographical traces marking this text are taken as overtures of friendship with the reader and as invitations to think together about what we call nation, queer, animal, or friendship.

Themes, Trajectories, Contributions

Postcolonial Hauntings argues for a politics of play that reckons with ghosts to open ethical alternatives for living in a transnational world. In hauntings that play with a postcolonial transnational world, I find a politics of hope amidst myriad forms of power imbalances among the continuities of colonialism. Each of the first four chapters builds on a theme or topic that showcases play and hauntings. First, I show how the binary framings of "human" and "animal" can be haunted through mischievous exaggerations and artful counterframings. Second, graphic narratives are considered that perform meaning-plays with political maps, undoing their Cartesian imperialism with overlapping storied cartographies. Third, an artist in spirited subversive performance startles us to consider new ways of relating across differences by playing with hospitality and friendships. The final chapter concludes by conjuring many kinds of ghosts to argue how persistent hauntings serve to make possible a new way of thinking about an ethics of justice in postcolonial transnational feminisms. As I argue, in the entanglement of haunting and play we can find a unique and creative way to reconceptualize cartographies of struggle.

Chapter 1, "Becoming Animal, Becoming Transnational," presents playful subversions of the binary human versus animal. I emphasize the hauntings of "human" and "animal" as frames and showcase playful subversions of categorical assertions that situate them in a binary status quo. Working with the grandiose ambition of expanding the frames of what constitutes human and animal, while also challenging the binarism implied, the chapter situates zoomorphic and mischievous counterpolitics of the category "animal." Lesbian feminist writer Namjoshi's novel *Conversations of Cow* anchors this chapter. I juxtapose Gilles Deleuze and Felix Guattari's "becoming animal" with Namjoshi's animal politics to theorize meaning-plays, disrupt framings of the animal, and visualize playful counterpossibilities. While Deleuze and Guattari's antiteleological politics counters the man/animal binary, it fails to travel to landscapes that simultaneously include and exclude the animal and worships and neglects them, as the status of the Indian cow demonstrates.

Continuing with the emphasis on transnational studies and meaning-plays, chapter 2, "Translations and Overlapping Belongings: Mapping Queer Transnationalism," analyzes how the translation of words across language systems and cultural structures creates excesses, errors, uses, and misuses and in this way constitutes a postcolonial haunting. Two graphic narratives, Alison Bechdel's *Fun Home: A Family Tragicomic* and Amruta Patil's *Kari*, draw out the way translations become meaning-plays with consequences for postcolonial transnational feminism. These graphic narratives offer an invaluable prism to study lines and frames and the spaces in-between both as stylistic devices and identity work. *Kari* and *Fun Home* emphasize multiple mappings and the politics of translation as the protagonists negotiate their identities and their places in the world. I argue that understanding overlapping maps and meaning-plays moves us beyond singular stories of sexual identity and homogenous identity that haunt a postcolonial world. "Queer" moves through grids of power with a politics that always exceeds its translation, and sexual subjectivities move with multilayered attunement to experiences of life, death, loss, and belonging.

Chapter 3, "Un-Mithu's Politics: Lingual Anarchy and Playful Undoings," traverses selected art exhibits and performances by Mithu Sen. A transnational artist who has exhibited in localities around the world, Sen in her aesthetic politics mischievously tugs at the borders of what it means to be an Indian woman, an Indian artist, and an exotic subject on international art platforms that read her skin color, long black hair, and persona with their own gaze. This chapter emphasizes how Sen works to undo linguistic meanings and rules through what she calls "lingual anarchy." A play on societal expectations inspires this approach and provides it with a buoyant energy to showcase their inherent exclusions and injuries and our normalized frames of behavior encoded through language. Whether speaking gibberish, appearing possessed, or giving away fragments of the Taj Mahal, Sen's works provoke and inspire; hers is a macabre and festive counterpolitics.

While chapter 3 tours Sen's art to draw out the politics of play, chapter 4, "Feminist Transnationalism and the Political Dimension of Friendships: Thinking through Mithu Sen's *It's Good to Be Queen*," concentrates on one exhibit, *It's Good to Be Queen*, to reframe relation building. Practices of imperial inhospitality haunt transnational relations and friendships, for it is not possible to shed the frame that posits friendship to manifest fraternal bonding among likeminded persons. Situating friendships as a postcolonial haunting, chapter 4 interrogates the impossibilities of friendship amidst unequal power divisions. Sen's art exhibit *It's Good to Be Queen* uses hair, notes of absence, and varied forms of art to illuminate the frames that dictate protocols of being a friend and host. Sen's play with hospitality and her urge to create new forms of friendships offer a valuable place to think anew about transnational friendships. What does it mean to host and be a friend? How can one be a democratic friend in the context of power stratifications and histories of violence?

Chapter 5, "Spectral Politics," emphasizes the importance of conversing with ghosts as an ethical imperative. I enter into dialogue with a range of ghosts who appear in the works of Art Spiegelman, Marx, Derrida, Muñoz, Spivak, Gloria Anzaldúa, and Toni Morrison. These ghosts play with frames of "the normal" and effect a countervision. Oftentimes these ghosts are haunted by other ghosts. We read how communist ghosts don't include ghost women, while queer ghosts riddle heterosexual visions. Ghosts enter and exit life and consciousness as a seething presence that signals continuities between the past and present. Ghosts exist as exclusions that tug at the borders of our political imagination. Spectral politics serve as a continuous reminder of responsibility that speaks to the past and future and aims to move toward ethical futures that do not keep reenacting violence. Hauntings and play undo the hubris of a "now" and "then." Looking at play or haunting as singular occurrences contained to just one situation largely misses histories and traces, a weaving in and out, and a continuous exit and entrance that marks the work of play and haunting through place and time.

CHAPTER 1

Becoming Animal, Becoming Transnational

> What goes for the animal goes for the native.... [T]he colonized has no freedom, no history, no individuality in any real sense. Like the animal, he/she simply "represents" a sort of eternal essence.
> —Achille Mbembe, *On the Postcolony*

> It is as if everywhere we go, we become Someone's private zoo.
> —Trinh T. Minh-ha, *Woman, Native, Other*

A very wise woman, wrinkled with age and years of hard labor, worked in our family home in Kolkata. She helped my mother in the kitchen, cleaning produce and cutting fish, all the while saturating the kitchen with stories and gossip of all kinds. I hung around in the kitchen a lot, hoping for the first taste of the sweet chutney right off the fire or the piping hot bowl of lentils hot off the stove. The woman, Maashi, as we called her, was often absent, much to my mother's dismay. She was never gone for very many days, just one or two after a span of intense work in the kitchen for a festival or a family function. Following her return from one of these inconvenient absences, she explained her nonappearance to my mother. I remember the day very well. I entered the kitchen hoping for a quick snack and saw Maashi tell my mother, with a very straight face, that the reason she was absent was that her daughter-in-law had given birth to a cow. I was struck by the improbability of the story. I was also struck by the fact that my mother chose not to engage in it and instead simply asked her to start her work for the day.

Maashi's quick rejoinder to my mother was saturated with an irreverence to the status of cow as holy mother in India and an irreverent play with categories. It is hard to say exactly why she thought to excuse her absence with such an absurd explanation. Maybe she was not particularly fond of her daughter-in-law or the reverse: maybe she was particularly appreciative of her and saw her as giving birth to a divine entity. Or perhaps Maashi was attempting to completely veer the frame of reference in that kitchen toward the improbable, one that would avoid further inspection. Myriad explanations muddy the waters of this interaction. Its mirthful play with the given situation and, with classifications such as human and animal, guards against an undue intellectualism. Class and caste norms disturb the borders of this story, whose play with categories is significant through the histories that it subverts. "*Maashi*" translated from Bengali means "mother's sister," and thus the presumed commonalities of sisterhood also haunt this instance of subversion, which conjures meaning-plays of animal and cow that, in turn, destabilize an unequivocal understanding of human.

I have carried this episode in my mind, through years of animal-studies reading groups and conversations, as a biting rejoinder that alerts us to the fact that there may be many and varied frames for what constitutes an "animal" in postcolonial worlds and that messy cohabitations—punctuated with gender, race, class, caste, and religion—lace categorical assertions of "human" and "animal." Moreover, this example illustrates that playing with frames and their contingent categorizations enables us to imagine social life in different forms. Maashi's cow grandchild seems to playfully invoke what, in *The Wretched of the Earth*, Frantz Fanon refers to the "bestiary" central to the colonial imagination where the colonized subject inhabits the place of the animal: "The colonized know all that and roar with laughter every time they hear themselves called an animal by the other."[1] The cow in the room mischievously maneuvers to defy frames of intelligibility and uses categories of human and animal to subvert them. This chapter, with the help of Suniti Namjoshi's *Conversations of Cow*, analyzes a particular "roar" that emerges in "becoming animal," where play forms a particularly resonant and haunting strategy to undo the violence of categories.

Animal Politics

How do we enlarge the contours of our theories and definitions for what counts as human or animal? To answer this, we must understand how discourses of patriarchy, homophobia, and colonialism both construct and haunt our conceptualization of human and animal. The varied formulations of human and nonhuman animals, alongside projections of animality and animalization, at play in this chapter gnaw like rats at the contours of each other's neatly demarcated definitions and communities of belonging.

The status of the cow in India is a good place to think through how animals, animality, and animalization constitute a central place in politics. The cow occupies a unique role in India's political imagination, and India, as a state with a majority Hindu population, has historically traversed a complicated relation with the cow. As many report, today the "cow is India's most polarizing animal," sharply dividing the country along communal lines: those who eat the cow and those who want to save the cow.[2] While the figure of the cow has mythic status in Hindu nationalism, it is not as if all cows are universally worshipped in India.[3] Being sacred is a political matter. It comes with changing criteria, regional disparities in the treatment of cows, and distinctions among kinds of cows. The sacredness of the cow and its place in Hindu nationalism today was in part wrought during the colonial period as an Indian nationalist, anticolonial stance that allowed the British to be "excluded" and cast out as beefeaters. Since the Bharatiya Janata Party (BJP) won national elections in 2014, the issue of beef consumption and the status of the cow in Indian society have intensified in national and regional politics. Most of India is currently under beef-ban laws, and slaughtering cows is a punishable offense. Cow-protection armies and citizen groups vigilantly guard the cow's right to live, while they take away the right to live of Muslims, Dalits, and those as accused of eating beef or aiding cow slaughter. Frenzied crowds beating up, killing, or driving Muslim families from neighborhoods and villages is a common occurrence in states where eating beef is illegal.[4] The Hindu cow is a postcolonial haunting as violence against Muslims, Dalits, and lower-class communities has spiraled all in the name of protecting cows.

Now think of a fictitious lesbian Hindu cow. Moreover, one that likes to drink scotch and constantly changes form and identity. What kind of blasphemy does it project? This unabashedly lesbian Hindu cow, at odds with a purposeful Hindu national cow that actively maintains communal borders, is an avid transnational traveler who mischievously plays with categories of human and animal as she moves through varied locales. A context that amplifies the play of the sacrilegious cow is that India only recently, in September 2018, decriminalized homosexuality.

The lesbian cow is certainly a counterfoil to the Hindu cow. But although the Hindu cow clearly shows us how some people are treated like animals and certain animals are positioned as superhuman for human ends, I struggle to find a theoretical frame that can adequately engage the becoming animal of the lesbian cow. The search for such a theoretical frame leads me to Gilles Deleuze and Felix Guattari's oft-cited "becoming animal." The concept of "becoming animal" for Deleuze and Guattari is a minoritarian becoming, like man becoming woman or mineral. With the concept they aim to undo binary thinking and teleological schemas of progression or regression. "Becoming animal" celebrates intensities and profusions of energy that work against hierarchical categorizations like man opposed to and also above animal. While animal studies has certainly reckoned with Deleuze and Guattari's "becoming animal," play and hauntings draw out further the inadequacies of our stubbornly Eurocentric concepts and theories.

This chapter engages with three frames for understanding how animals, animality, and animalization help us think through the formations of political communities. The first frame situates animals as central to national politics using the case of the Indian cow. The Hindu national cow contributes to the creation of an imagined political community instilled through projects of nation building. Such nation building creates communities of insiders and outsiders, alongside the need to firmly define outsiders, for instance, as beefeaters or queer, so that we can bestow legitimacy on the insiders. The second frame draws on Namjoshi's works and especially the novel *The Conversations of Cow* (1985) to situate the cow as a particular postcolonial haunting that also works across transnational circuits. How do animals figure in transnational imaginations?

The third frame considers becoming animal as presented by Deleuze and Guattari. Might there be a counterpolitics to becoming animal that would highlight and subvert the binaries between man and animal and could we go even further and imagine a transnational frame to this politics? By this, I mean that when the imagination of the animal is centrally anchored as "other" to Man's communities of belonging, how might a transnational counterpolitics subvert this binary imagination? I emphasize how these three frames struggle persistently against each other. Further, to add to this interrogation, by working with transnationalism, how might we look anew at animals, animality, and animalization in a way that could sabotage nationalistic and Western framings? *Postcolonial Hauntings* emphasizes the fluid mappings and unmappings of East and West. I remain attentive to theories and people that can move more easily than others across mappings and unmappings and to the fact that the "West" refers to a hegemonic position that is not restricted by geographical mapping. The interrogation of "Western framings" is centrally concerned with how certain theories and concepts, along with resources, become the repository for knowledge and even counterknowledge.

Overall, I am concerned with the potentials of becoming animal for feminist politics, particularly, transnational feminist politics. The significance of this question reckons with a feminist democratic imagination that endeavors to think otherwise. While noting the manifold violence in becoming animal, a creative counterpolitics has manifold uses. For example, although a true human is positioned on the basis and biases of White, male, cis, heteronormative, able-bodied, English-speaking, and first-world citizenship, the criteria for a true animal are never so easy to spell out. Oscillating perennially as the other to Man, the animal is always an inadequate match or an uncontrollable excess. A counterpolitics to the violence of becoming animal could thus posit animals, animality, and animalization as an explicit political strategy for illuminating a world that functions through such markers—in other words, an exaggerated way to ruse the workings of power.

Before proceeding, let me note that Gayatri Spivak's concept of "affirmative sabotage" helps me delineate the politics at play in the counterpolitics to becoming animal. Spivak comments, "Affirmative sabotage is to change the instrument so that it can be used to undermine its felicitous end." For example, a lesbian transnational Hindu cow can be used to undermine the Hindu nationalist cow. As counterpolitics, affirmative sabotage is never outside the politics it critiques. It is only when we recognize "complicity" as Spivak points out that we can call a strategy an example of "affirmative sabotage." That is, through "critical intimacy" and an acknowledgment of complicities, affirmative sabotage can ruse the workings of power.[5] I use the term "counterpolitics" not as an "other to" or "contra." Rather, when seen as a countering or mode of incessant engagement, counterpolitics may not be a naïve political move. For instance, in countering the positioning of animals, animality, and animalization, a counterpolitics working through associative logics and playful exaggerations may use these very categories to subvert their meaning. The playfulness in affirmative sabotage, its counterpolitics, helps to highlight the workings of power, even when haunting them.

The Political Animal

The animal is a political actor and invoked repeatedly in national and transnational conversations. The animal's inclusion in political conversations is marked by estrangement and a mode of presence that is simultaneously absent, much like a spectral presence and absence. As a postcolonial haunting the Indian cow riddles current frames of analyses of the animal in politics. This section is about the Hindu nationalist cow amidst conversations about the framing of political animals. Larger than life, as mother, a life-giver, and protected property, the cow's role in the Indian polity haunts frames of inclusion and exclusion. Trapped within nationalism's family, the Hindu cow has limited traveling potential but moves symbolically through a diasporic Hindu nation. I will first briefly parse the role of the animal in Western national and transnational imaginations to then starkly juxtapose its meaning-plays under an Indian framework. This complication helps to situate Namjoshi's play with animals that straddles Eastern and Western worlds, without reifying the positions. Namjoshi's use of "East" and "West" blasts the categories even while using them.

The National Political Animal

The animal is frequently invoked in Western treatises on the nature of politics, where the political imagination of "animal" frames the formation of states and their borders through selective inclusions and exclusions. The double-edged nuances to Aristotle's founding description of man as a "political animal" instills becoming animal or becoming a political animal as integral to politics and the state, albeit in many ways, which rules out those considered to be like animals or to have their qualities. Varied modes of becoming animal are involved in state-bound politics, whether as conformism or resistance, often couched as radical counterpolitics to binary formulations that define liberal governance. Adding a transnational imagination to narratives of becoming animal, I hope to visualize undoings of state-bound scripts of becoming animal, the crossing of borders, as well as the politics that change the nature of borders through subversion.

How can the animal be an outsider to political communities yet still cement the legitimacy of communions formulated by its estrangement? Working with the possibilities of a democratic imagination, we notice that "animal" is tied to the framing of nation in many ways. While helping to draw the contours of national borders, the animal is firmly included and excluded in frames of political imaginations. It is important to delineate this border politics as we move toward a transnational imagination that could subvert postulations of animals, animality, and animalization. To start with, in Aristotle's designation of man as a "political animal" in the founding treatise for the establishment of the polis, we can discern a broad and clear trajectory in Western political thought about the state-making man. It demarcates the boundaries of the nation-state as a clear dichotomy separating the man of the state from the animal outside. Man is a political animal and at his most pristine when functioning within a state, with logos, language, and when clearly separate from nonpolitical animals. However, thinking only in terms of exclusions ignores the manifold ways through which animals are also *included in* politics.

In *Homo Sacer: Sovereign Power and Bare Life*, Giorgio Agamben works with Michel Foucault's theory of biopower to trace the development of sovereignty and the rights-bearing man.[6] In describing the consolidation of sovereign power, Agamben asks us to interrogate the constitution of politics through the "exclusion of bare life," or life outside of rights. For Agamben, Western politics is founded on the binary of bare life and politics: "In Western politics, bare life has the peculiar privilege of being that whose exclusion founds the city of men." However, the exclusion is formulated through a concomitant inclusion because political life is defined as separate from nature and as "natural." Agamben comments, "Man is the living being who, in language, separates and opposes himself to his own bare life and, at the same time, maintains himself in relation to that bare life in an inclusive exclusion."[7] Understanding politics, the frame of the state, and the constitution of sovereignty through the lens of "inclusive exclusion" enables us to see the mechanisms in place to exclude nature and animals from the proper sphere of politics and state, even while they haunt the borders of Man and his state.

Agamben's stress on "inclusive exclusion" makes significant contributions toward marking the double logic of inclusion and exclusion that never works in isolation; for example, including some always excludes others, and inclusion does not come with holistic respect and thus carries exclusion alongside itself. If one thinks closely, inclusion and exclusion are not binary terms as we often purport. Rather, inclusion is already an act of exclusion and so includes exclusion in its ambit. Playing with Agamben's "inclusive exclusion" a bit, let me offer that an "exclusive inclusion" might better fit the place of the cow in Indian politics. The cow is exaggeratedly present in ceremonial rituals and practices, political slogans, and election manifestos, and it is illegal to kill it for meat in most Indian states. Cows are thus ostensibly included among the national citizenry. At the same time, being worshipped and so included does not mean that cows are cared for; abandoned cattle roam around cities and frequently fall prey to vehicle accidents or toxic poisoning from rummaging through human garbage.[8] Cows are property, god, and mother in India, none of which warrants the inclusion guaranteed to property-bearing Hindu men. The exclusion is no less starkly visible in cow becoming an explicit signifier of reverence: an unrestrainable projection by human politics.

The insidious politics of "inclusive exclusion," while carefully erecting barriers between man/animal, seeks also to control the animal within man. Liberalism's frame of democracy is designed to prevent citizens from becoming animal. Ironically, while distinguishing citizens from animals, governance is also about controlling the beast in man, the animal in the state. In other words, in liberal democracies, "politics is zookeeping," in the words of Benjamin R. Barber. Barber articulates liberal democracy's control of the political sphere in the following words: "In that poor and brutish war, the beasts howl in voices made articulate by reason—for zoos, for cages and trainers, for rules and regulations, for regular feeding times and prudent custodians.... Liberal democracy's sturdiest cages are reserved for the People."[9] A domesticated citizen-subject formulates the basis for liberal democracy and enables obedience to law and the concomitant overture of rights framed by law. Working through the different restrictions, inclusions, and exclusions to becoming animal in liberal democracies, it is important to bear in mind that not all people are subject to the same frames. For instance, critiquing liberalism's body politic based upon the exclusion of women, children, and slaves, Moira Gatens reminds us of the inevitable animalization of woman when she enters the public sphere. Gatens writes about two strategies used to silence women who enter public spaces: "The first is to 'animalize' the speaker, the second, to reduce her to her 'sex.'"[10] For instance, Gatens reminds us that Horace Walpole called Mary Wollstonecraft a "hyena in petticoats" when she fought for women's rights.[11] Not becoming animal thus bears irrevocable relations to becoming a citizen, and framing animality is a persistent device in politics to selectively exclude in order to form an inclusive community of citizen-subjects.

These theoretical prisms that include and exclude the animal are muddied when we add the frame of cow as mother and cow as symbol of Hindu nationalism. Frenzied developments in Indian politics since 2014, with genealogies reaching back along diverse strands of Hindu nationalism, forefront the cow as mother. She is sacred and inviolable, notwithstanding the ironic plight of many human mothers (and cow mothers) in India living without access to basic infrastructure and care.[12] Rajasthan, a state in India, appointed a cow minister in 2015, and the Indian government has articulated its intentions to provide all cows with a safe identification number to prevent them from being illegally transported across borders.[13] The cow in India is almost a supracitizen, guarded by citizen groups, whose body is inviolable. Indeed, the cow serves many functions in Indian society, as Naisargi N. Dave writes: "Cows are symbolically dense animals in India, sites of attachment for all sorts of fantasies about maternal love, communal encroachment, and the stability of a Brahmanical order."[14] Adding all these nuances to our imagination of the "animal" complicates our understanding of animals, animality, and animalization. Muslims and lower-caste Indians are animalized in their projected hunger for the meat of the mother, and the cow suprahumanized becomes the epitome of purity and the authentically national. Here we see how the question of the animal, labels of animality, and processes of animalization are irrevocably bound with identity and framings of nations in different ways across the world. Liberalism's politics as zookeeping meets a startling counterpart in Indian politics where the "right" animal in the zoo bears more rights than many citizens.

The Transnational Political Animal

Thinking of animal lives transnationally is an intriguing provocation. When we divide humans and animals, we tend to group all animals together, the universal Animal with a capital A. In this way we transpose an anthropocentric understanding of political community to the broad spectrum of who and what we posit as Animals. To state the issue simply, we talk as if all zebras and/or elephants know each other and so impose upon them a sort of nationalism or imagined community, as if they have all read Benedict Anderson, too. Anderson's invocation of the nation as an "imagined community" haunts political configurations in our contemporary world, nationally and transnationally.[15] Anderson, recall, understood the nation as an imagined political communion working in perfect synchrony. Such a community requires a firm delineation of borders and the positing of someone or something outside of them. Ironically, imposing an imagined community or nationalism on animals is intrinsic to our definitional mapping of animals. Seeing animals transnationally would involve reckoning with many differences, travels, and other formulations of nations and political economy.

One way of thinking about animals transnationally is to discern the routes—the illegal trade, passage from nation to nation as frozen meat, and in the transmission of bacteria and viruses—that defy political boundaries and even threaten them. Reading the *trans* in transnationalism through the way Aihwa Ong describes, as "moving through space or across lines, as well as changing the nature of something," we could describe transnationalism as movements across borders that change actors, borders, and communities.[16] Donna Haraway writes about how the chicken has traveled the world: "Follow the chicken and find the world."[17] Haraway draws our attention to the global poultry trade, avian flu, and other uncontainable aspects of how chickens have circulated. Rebecca J. H. Woods notes how the transit of frozen meat was intrinsic to the politics of empire in the mid-nineteenth century, and a great deal of engineering technology was invested in transporting meat from Australia to Great Britain.[18] Whether noting the politics behind the transit of frozen meat, livestock, the illegal animal trade, or avian flu, it is undeniable that animals are transnational actors that move through space and change its nature in a way that warrants many more inquiries, as recent scholarship in posthumanism, animal studies, and trans disciplines demonstrates. Elizabeth Povinelli in *Geontologies*, for instance, inspires us to reckon complexly with late liberalism's conception of life and nonlife through the figure of the virus: "The Virus is also Ebola and the waste dump, the drug-resistant bacterial infection stewed within massive salmon and poultry farms, and the nuclear power."[19] Described as the "aggressive rotting undead," the virus is omnipresent, nationally, transnationally, and as an irreverent actor in-between.[20]

The Hindu cow is seen to bear a particular relation to the virus. Political leaders from Hindu organizations have been hosting cow-urine drinking parties as a cure to COVID-19 and extolling the virtues of the Hindu cow to a global community as a spirited opponent to the virus.[21] Seen as larger than life, the Hindu cow travels in unusual ways. Invoking the becoming transnational of animals undermines and subverts the false universalizing implicit in treating animals—Animal with a capital *A*—as if Animal is itself a coherent "imagined community." The cow as a transnational animal faces a specific dilemma. It remains the mother to a transnational Hindu nation, and its travels are scrupulously monitored. The cow's presence as supracitizen muddies modes of transnational travels and situates animal travels in new ways.[22]

To tease out in some depth the political possibilities of a transnational animal and move the question of becoming animal far beyond its Western framings, I now turn to an author who has received little attention in animal studies, queer theory, or postcolonial transnational studies but whose works inspire varied imaginative plays with identity that enable effusive animal travels and transnational becoming animal. Namjoshi demonstrates how the literary imagination can provoke creative counterpolitics to becoming animal, from the national to a transnational imagination. Her works plait the East and the West, deepening and complicating the meaning-plays of cow, animal, queer, and human and adding new dimensions to animal travels in a transnational world.

The Conversations of Cow offers glimpses into becoming animal that critique and engage with gender and sexual identities. Namjoshi is a prolific author, and in an anthology of poems, *The Jackass and the Lady*, she was "the first Indian female author to openly declare herself a lesbian."[23] Caught between disparate worlds—India, the West, lesbian, queer, Indian woman—Namjoshi employs animals in most of her works to write about patriarchy, sexual assault, and homophobia. Yet, although Namjoshi's work offers new ways of thinking about sexuality and patriarchy, she has scarcely been reckoned with in feminist or queer theory. Despite not sharing the easy recognition of Deleuze and Guattari in animal studies or feminist-queer theory, Namjoshi's literary and theoretical magic is no less evocatively controversial, albeit in different ways.

Namjoshi's lesbian cow is scandalous in the context of Hindu nationalist politics in India and its framing of cow as mother. Her "transnational sexual-textuality," as coined by Harveen S. Mann, opens up different potentials to becoming animal.[24] Mann elucidates Namjoshi's border-crossing poetics: "She moves from the asphyxiating nation-space where her 'lungs give out, I cannot breathe' to a transnational sexual-textuality (the latter also signified in the title of the collection *Flesh and Paper*), across *and* beyond political nations, to the land of body-text where women, Western and Eastern, feminist and (women's rights) activist, white and black, can 'walk freely / in the still, breathable air.'"[25] Thus, Namjoshi's textual politics provides a searing provocation to a transnational becoming animal and moves it far beyond its Western framings, remembering all the while that to critique the "West" as a monolithic entity reifies its power. Namjoshi provides an example of what Sean Meighoo means when he importantly reminds us, "There is no 'West,' at least not in the sense in which it has been conceived as an altogether unique and distinctly privileged event or course of events within world history."[26]

Heterogeneity and hybridity mark any point of reference. Monolithic categories, regardless of their ostensibly radical aims, often reinforce that which they seek to criticize as the all-encompassing anchor. Rather than compare Western and Eastern becoming animals, in my discussion of Namjoshi and Deleuze and Guattari, I reflect on the close slippages among animals, animality, and animalization that are framed by race, gender, sexuality, nationality, and other indices of belonging and othering. The play with human and animal is haunted by mechanisms of othering that becoming animal skillfully showcases.

Suniti Namjoshi: Style and Politics

Childhood in India and subsequent experiences in the United States and England color Namjoshi's sparkling, witty narratives, storytelling, and subversive politics. Often described as a lesbian feminist writer, Namjoshi was born in India in 1941. She currently resides in the United Kingdom at Devon. It is difficult to categorize Namjoshi's texts, not only because they spill through multiple genres—poetry, fables, short stories, and novels—but also because her words and politics refuse to be contained. They travel through contexts and spaces, carrying uncanny resonances to different situations and lives. Namjoshi weaves a poignantly personal narrative in her poetry, novels, and fables, which, despite being rooted in the personal realm, provide many ways to relate to the narrative and its characters without the author having to make too much of an effort to translate—all of which aid its traveling imagination.

Writing in English, Namjoshi celebrates the roles of language and its power. In *Goja: An Autobiographical Myth*, she comments on how the English language played an invaluable role in her engagements with the West:

> The most important thing about my encounter with the West was the English language. It took me several years and required my politicization to understand how language had power over power itself. Over the years, language mediated everything: my struggle with powerlessness and loss of identity, my understanding of who defined whom and how effectively, and my need to work out what really mattered and somehow to say it. What worried and delighted me at this time was how language cloaked, altered and even fashioned reality, *how there were multiple realities, and how it was possible to juxtapose these so that they resonated and shimmered and multiplied meaning.*[27]

As we read, we see how Namjoshi uses English to elucidate power dynamics and her own personal travels by richly interweaving different meaning-plays into her narratives. Her use of English plaited with multiplying nuances demonstrates "power over power itself." A playful textual politics frames Namjoshi's relation with English: agonized and tensed, delightful and creative.

Born into a royal landowner's family, Namjoshi recounts stories about the Rajasaheb and the Ranisaheb, her grandparents, while she was growing up in India.[28] Entangled with her life of entitlements and luxury is Namjosi's relation with Goja, a female servant in their home. Goja fed Namjoshi dried fish in the dark, a sensory memory that Namjoshi describes in the following way, "The smell of dried fish is not the smell of crushed white flowers, of jai or jui or queen of the night or even of jasmine."[29] Her grandmother, the Ranisaheb is, in juxtaposition, "glittering and glorious. . . . She is roses, mogra, cuddles and comfort."[30] Similar to Namjoshi's complex encounter with opulence and poverty, she engages with the East and West without reifying their distinctiveness: "I belong to India and to the West. Both belong to me and both reject me."[31] Braiding relations and differences, the meaning-plays in Namjoshi's texts participate in situating the complexities of social class, nationality, and sexuality.

Namjoshi left India and her civil service job in the prestigious Indian Administrative Services for many reasons: her job was "tedious," she was following a woman she was in love with who was leaving the country, and she had a fascination with the English language.³² So she embarked on a journey to the United States. She completed her master's in public administration from the University of Missouri and traveled on to Canada for a PhD in English literature. Her studies, work, and relationships necessitate a constant movement between locales. Namjoshi comments on returning to India and to the West, stubbornly and persistently, and her writing and politics speak to her constant endeavor to reconcile disjointed aspects of life and existence: "In the past I've used words to cloak me and clothe me, I've hidden in the forest like the fawn or Alice. Goja? Goldie? *Don't you understand that I've hidden from you?* It's time we told each other stories about the West and the East."³³

Along with engaging with the categories East and West, Namjoshi juxtaposes genres and styles in her playfully buoyant writing. Poems are interspersed within regular narratives. Her fables maintain their didactic function, but instead of upholding the status quo, they subvert structural patriarchy and violence. In an interview Namjoshi says, "If one wants to answer questions, the fable is a good form, for it is didactic and helps in dealing with issues such as racism, gender stereotyping and attitudes towards exploitation of the planet."³⁴ Namjoshi's texts are complexly multihued, surprisingly forthright with clear messages, playfully terse, and difficult to classify because they are influenced by multiple genealogies and points of reference. Anannya Dasgupta writes about the "sheer difficulty of classifying and contextualizing her works"³⁵ and points out Namjoshi's "genre-defying" proclivity and varied literary inspirations drawn from "Indian, West Asian, and European folklore, myth, fabulous stories, and fairy tales."³⁶ Namjoshi does not use juxtaposition in order to compare. Rather, her interest is, again, "to juxtapose these so that they resonated and shimmered and multiplied meaning." And so, through a uniquely playful amalgamation of voices, perspectives, and actors, the author narrates the uncanny resonance of multiplicity in ostensibly singular bodies and voices, whether a one-eyed monkey or crocodile. The play with style works in companionship through the play with genre and actors, mostly animals.

Namjoshi's stories, poems, narratives, and fables use animals as primary actors. From the blue donkey, one-eyed monkey, and lesbian cow to snakes, piglets, and swans, there is a veritable animal world in Namjoshi's writings. Thinking about the confluence of Eastern and Western ideas in her writing and imagination, Namjoshi notes the Hindu influences coloring her idea of animals. In *Because of India* she says, "To me a beast wasn't 'bestial' in the Western sense," notes Hinduism's pantheistic nature, with the emphasis on reincarnation and souls ascribed to all lives.³⁷ Working within this logic, Namjoshi's animals are not separate from humans or gods. They walk, talk, love, and even drink scotch. A seamless logic unifies animals, humans, gods, and all beings. They are all beings that share the qualities of the world. Namjoshi uses this alternative "universal" frame—a communion of human, animal, and god—to work on serious issues of violence and rape. For example, in "Further Adventures of the One-Eyed Monkey" narrated in *The Fabulous Feminist*, we read about a Brahmin woman, a god who raped her, and the testimony of a monkey. All the actors—human, god, and animal—seem embroiled in a worldly game, and none are necessarily more or less than human. This is how the story goes . . .

A monkey that was sitting in a peepal tree witnessed the rape of a woman, the wife of a famous Brahmin, by Lord Indra.[38] Soon, the woman's husband appears on the scene and summons the god Lord Vishnu to right the wrong. Lord Vishnu asks for a witness, and the monkey gives a testimony to the crime she witnessed. Lord Vishnu acknowledges the sin that Lord Indra had committed and asks him to perform a sacrifice to purify him of the sin. Lord Indra thus sacrifices a stallion. Namjoshi writes in conclusion: "And so it came about that a horse was killed, a god purified, a Brahmin appeased, a woman ruined, and a monkey left feeling thoroughly puzzled."[39] Entities and beings, terrestrial or otherwise, work together seamlessly in Namjoshi's narratives. The author looks at them all in puzzled dissidence, wondering aloud at the sheer absurdity and violence of politics and social life.

Namjoshi discusses her similarity and difference from Western feminists and thinking of the animal. Western feminists, as Namjoshi points out, have noted women's alignment as "other" with the "birds and the beasts and the rest of creation. . . . But I don't want to be separated from the birds and the beasts, nor do I want to 'humanize' them particularly." So it is a complex relationality that inspires Namjoshi's writings on and with animals: the need to live with animals but also to let them remain who they are without an anthropocentric humanism imposing a frame of reference. Instead of a becoming human imposed on animals, we notice an intriguing politics of becoming animal in Namjoshi's works: "All this complicated process still left one question unresolved. All right, I was a beast, a creature. But what sort of beast was I?"[40]

Becoming animal in Namjoshi's narratives works in complex attunement to traveling between worlds, the East and the West. Both spaces, with their concomitant memories and politics, provide a point of reference for the author and intricately color the narrative. Stories from the *Panchatantra* are liberally interspaced in her books, along with Western narratives like "The Princess and the Pea" and "The Hare and the Turtle."[41] However, the author does not maintain fidelity or authenticity to the stories and their original imagination. Rather, they are generously displaced from their original narrative. Namjoshi uses easy points of recollection from these immensely popular stories and then subverts the storylines with matter-of-fact happenings; the result is playful, subversive, and satirical. For instance, narrating the story "The Hare and the Turtle" in *The Fabulous Feminist*, Namjoshi tells us, "One day a turtle decided to emulate the prowess of his legendary ancestor."[42] What follows is a story with a very different twist. Having put forward the challenge to race, the hare started at a fifty-yard distance from the finishing line, while the turtle started just a foot away from the finishing line. The turtle beat the hare, which, according to the turtle, established the preeminence of turtles. The hare protested, saying that she had run fifty yards, while he, the turtle, had only navigated a foot of space. The turtle answered unyieldingly, "You really should learn to be a good loser."[43] Namjoshi ends the story by telling readers, "This turtle had a cousin, who, when he raced with hares, always drew the finishing line at the edge of the ocean."[44] Thus, even though the author maintains the original characters, they are gendered in the author's rewriting and used to reveal outright discriminatory practices. Stories like the one above are told alongside easily recognizable Indian stories of Swayamvara and other points of reference.[45] Thus, the author both speaks to and is influenced by the East and the West, and her narratives exhibit a playfully subversive account of entanglements and intimacies with the two.

Though Namjoshi addresses the East and the West, they are "plaited" relationships—agonistic and tensile. In *Flesh and Paper*, cowritten with her partner Gillian Hanscombe and comprising a lyrical attempt to compose new lesbian authorships separate from heterosexual worlds, Namjoshi and Hanscombe provide lyrical pictures of their passion and relationship traversing the East and the West, their separate countries, and nationalities: "It's our bodies, not our passports, fit so uncommonly well."[46] In the renditions of the East and West, India and elsewhere, the authors also underline their disidentification and estrangement from particular imaginations of "India" because of their lesbian identity:

> Because of India, before and after, . . .
> the history not for taking:
> the family not for joining:
> the cause not for naming: . . .
> —I/you can—press dreams and theories, bellies,
> Breasts, hair, hips, lips; and words; all
> Plaited now, until tomorrow.[47]

The authors are not part of this imagined community, its history, family, or cause. Rather with "plaited" bodies, and destinies, the lovers forge new connections between themselves and the spaces of estrangement. It is because of India, in spite of it, without it, and with it, that Namjoshi creates her work and draws out her textual inspirations. This understanding of "plaited" transnationalism—India, America, Australia, and spaces that create community while also divorcing people from its history and cause—haunt Namjoshi's framings of people, animals, issues, and contexts.

It is in this context that Namjoshi takes on the Hindu cow and unmoors it from a singular national belonging. Namjoshi's playful renditions of becoming animal take as their subtext the whole matter of becoming transnational, of mooring in and belonging to a diversity of places and nationalities. In *The Conversations of Cow*, Namjoshi introduces us to Suniti, her namesake and lesbian protagonist, who converses with a Brahmin cow, a "Cow of a Thousand Wishes." We follow the story of Bhadravati and Suniti, Bhadravati being an immigrant lesbian cow who drinks "scotch and water, very colonial—but in a finger bowl." The narrative unfolds through different becomings. Bhadravati changes from cow to Baddy, to Beautiful B, and many other becomings. Interspersed within and through the becomings are commentaries on human society and its hierarchies. For instance, one day Bhadravati the cow and Suniti go to a pizza place. They order two pizzas, while what Suniti was craving all along was a juicy hamburger. They are both thrown out of the restaurant, a lesbian cow and a lesbian, and what follows is a self-reflective understanding of the world composed of Class A (men) and Class B (women). "The rest don't count." The lesbian cow has nothing in common with men or with women.[48]

Identity Plays

The Conversations of Cow was written to make light of an overtly rigid feminism. According to Namjoshi, it was a "reaction to feeling I had to toe the party line." Written to display the absurdities in an overtly ideological feminism, and Namjoshi's discomfort with rigid identities as the basis for liberation, Namjoshi explains: "I had a logical difficulty with both women's liberation and gay liberation. Questioning gender stereotyping was a central tenet. But if I questioned gender stereotyping, then labeling various groups 'men,' 'women,' 'heterosexual,' 'homosexual,' didn't make good sense. It's true that politics often requires simplification, and that a certain amount of generalization is inevitable in that language has nouns, but I was uncomfortable with it, and particularly with the notion of a rigid identity."[49]

Initially written for her own private amusement, *The Conversations of Cow* first included real names that Namjoshi later altered. Her own name was left in because it would have been hypocritical to comment on lesbian feminists barring her own self. In addition, she uses her own name to frame the Indian speaking through the text. An engagement with identity thinking weaves its way through *Cow*. Namjoshi ruminates about how most writing from the West assumes identity to be a pivotal quest for everyone; yet, this identity-quest narrative lacks resonance within Hinduism because your present form is dependent on the actions of your last life. Further, Namjoshi comments, "We're told as children . . . that the ultimate aim is not to achieve a particular identity, but to divest ourselves of the particulars of identity." Thus, *The Conversations of Cow* demonstrates a persistent restlessness with identity as Cow, Suniti, Baddy, Bud, S2 (Suniti's copy), and others change form: "As Cow changes, Suniti changes too, until at the close, she's content to be someone and no one."[50]

The opening scene of the book begins with Suniti down on her knees, in Canada, expecting an appearance by a goddess. Upon opening her eyes, she sees "The Cow of a Thousand Wishes," a "Brahmini cow."[51] Suniti and Cow decide to become travel partners, and the traveling partnership is preceded by some introductions to their individual histories. Suniti learns that the cow is an immigrant, and she shares that she, too, is from India. Starting from these rudimentary introductions, Suniti and Cow strike a friendship based on long conversations and form-changing: animal to human, man to woman, and the reverse.

Suniti visits Cow's friends, "a self-sustaining community of lesbian cows." She learns that Cow's name is Bhadravati or Baddy for short. Suniti, all the while in trepidation, stays for supper with Baddy's friends, as she is not vegetarian and feels that at best she would be served stewed dandelion soup. During dinner, Sybilla, a member of the community of lesbian cows, talks about a dream in which she had turned into a "Carnivorous Cow" who ate a birthday cake that looked like Suniti. In turn, Suniti tries to convince the community of cows that they are, in general, herbivorous, and to change food habits would be calamitous. After a tense evening, Suniti wakes up very hungry the next morning and with a craving for pizza. To Suniti's dismay, Bhadravati accompanies her to the pizza place. The pizza arrives along with the manager, who asks if things are all right and addresses her as "Sir." Suniti replies with chagrin, "I am not a 'Sir,' I am a lesbian and my friend is a cow." The manager throws them out, but Suniti does get to make her point: "That cow is a citizen of planet earth. If you throw us out, I shall complain about you to the Human Rights Commission."[52] These events, though ostensibly funny because of their apparent ridiculousness, also function as social critique, a spirited engagement with social scenarios, varied meaning-plays combined creatively with a simple and direct narrative style. Cow is certainly a citizen of planet Earth, yet certainly not a "citizen" because of her nonhuman status. In addition, animal rights and human rights have a long and complex history of separation where human rights do not protect animals. Further, even within human rights, who gets to be a "human" and framed with rights is a question of politics with some deemed normal, natural, and worthy of rights. As Wendy Brown points out, "The powerful are in this way discursively normalized, naturalized, while the dominated appear as mutants, disabled."[53]

Conversations of Cow proceeds through active discussion, confrontations, and occasional fights between Suniti and Cow in different forms, for example, when B finds corned beef in Suniti's kitchen, walks out, and is then transformed into a large White man called Baddy. Baddy is inconsiderate and has a foul mouth, and the difference between lesbian cow and man is significantly horrific for Suniti. Interestingly, Namjoshi does not write about becomings in singularity or without a history. B knows Baddy and Bhadravati, and Suniti speaks to Cow with many names even when Cow is a White man or a White lesbian Hindu cow. The different becomings in Namjoshi's novel move with each other through curious combinations.

One day after walking down the street and wearing makeup in an attempt to look respectable and gain approval, Suniti feels guilty about being false and not true to her identity. B tells her that it was all right and that "identity is fluid. Haven't you heard of transmigration? And you call yourself a good Brahmin?" Suniti agonizingly asks, "But, B, aren't you really a lesbian cow?" The "reality" of identity and being-ness, along with continuous transformations and becomings, underpins *The Conversations of Cow*. Next, B changes into a beautiful woman, leaving Suniti confused and angry and unable to fathom how best to relate and converse with B as a beautiful woman: "I decide to do nothing. I shall treat B exactly as though she were B, which she is, who she was, well as she would have been."[54]

In the book Suniti is also asked to become someone. Not knowing who or what she wants to become, Suniti questions what it means to be someone and no one: "But aren't we all an accidental conglomeration of arbitrary particulars, duly supplied with a functioning ego?"[55] Suniti's ruminations and questioning of different becomings ask what it means to have an identity and what it entails to move from one to an-other (i.e., cow, woman). Namjoshi's treatment of becomings and identities is affirmative sabotage. It uses the cow and issues like beef eating to explode open and obviate the nationalist framing of the Hindu cow and all the "national" inclusions and exclusions that go along with it. Namjoshi's cow challenges the very notion of inclusions and exclusions as the nationalists frame them. But she offers no solutions. She plays.

Namjoshi presents a seamless narrative of many becomings. Noting the power politics that she positions between different entities and species, and the changing forms, how do we grapple with "becoming animal" as a specified theoretical ruse? As conversations on becoming animal have many dimensions, both positive and negative, postcolonial and colonial, I wonder whether a conversation on effusive becoming, of multihued energies and a subversion of teleological thinking, would help us grapple with some of the power politics and possibilities in thinking with becoming animal. For this, I turn to Deleuze and Guattari, who help us articulate the subversion of teleological and binary thinking that pervades distinctions between human and animal, but I argue even further that playing more radically with the division can sabotage some of its violence.

Becoming Animal

Multiple frames proliferate in animal studies. The field has grown exponentially in recent years, alongside various trajectories of analysis. Its varied movements in critical thinking encompass "posthumanism" and a critique of anthropocentrism, ecofeminism and an understanding of the connections between women and animals, queer ecologies and conversations opening up constructions of "nature" in sexuality and ecological systems, and various other offshoots and predecessors in food studies, feminisms, queer theory, and postcolonial movements.[56] Indeed, the question of the animal serves many purposes for (trans)disciplines, activisms, and theories. However, whether the animal "really" speaks through animal studies remains a complex question. As Jacques Derrida says, "The animal, what a word! The animal is a word, it is an appellation that men have instituted, a name they have given themselves the right and the authority to give to the living other."[57]

Alongside Derrida's framing of the "animal" as a willful "appellation" designed by men, it is also important to ask, if the animal spoke, would it be considered an animal as such? Being an animal means being an extreme "other," as the nonhuman or even more-than-human with its own unique politics. As Rosi Braidotti writes, "The animal is the necessary, familiar and much cherished other of *anthropos*."[58] An "other" to pure White men, animals serve many purposes in the project of making Man with a capital *M* who creates civilization and seeks to harness geological forces in his own image. Sylvia Wynter emphasizes the "over-representation" of the "now globally hegemonic ethnoclass world of 'Man.'"[59] An "other" to civilization and language, animals serve to frame Man as civil and with the ability to speak. Notwithstanding the varied modes of communicative mechanisms animals use, they remain "others" to the sphere of intelligible speech that has a right to resources, policies, politics, and autonomy.

Deleuze and Guattari's "becoming animal" constitutes one of the central theoretical strategies through which animal studies has worked to dismantle identities and signal toward a more creative and playful politics. While Deleuze and Guattari's "becoming animal" is used to critique binary thinking and inspire imaginations to think with heterogeneity, I argue that it fails to highlight the simultaneity of creativity and oppression, inclusion and exclusion, as well as the collusion of disparate politics embodied by the Indian Cow. My aim here is to work toward complicating the politics of creativity in our critiques of binary thinking. To that end, this section elucidates Deleuze and Guattari's "becoming animal" and pushes it toward different kinds of animal travels.

Deleuze and Guattari's becomings undo categorical definitiveness around bodies and ontologies. Their becomings are critiques of the state and institutions that produce hierarchies, create binaries, and conform identities. As a relational process, becomings for Deleuze and Guattari are about unscripting self and body toward different possibilities. "Becoming animal" is an example of intense minoritarian becoming toward an undoing of identity. Man becomes animal, or woman, or mineral. Not the other way around. For Deleuze and Guattari this concept of becoming is intended to undo dualistic thought. Deleuze and Guattari write about becoming animal as "perfectly real" and not simply imitating an animal. A deterritorialization of the man/animal binary, this minoritarian becoming should not be seen as a progress or evolution or even as a "productive" activity. Moreover, becoming animal is just one type of becoming amongst others, such as becoming woman, child, vegetable, or mineral. Deleuze and Guattari also maintain that becoming woman "is the key to all the other becomings."[60]

Responses to Deleuze and Guattari in feminism have varied, with many critical of the masculine trope in Deleuze's philosophy.[61] Moreover, alongside critical feminist engagements with his work, Deleuze has received varied responses from prisms of postcolonial theory. In *Deleuze and the Postcolonial*, Simone Bignall and Paul Patton note his inattention to colonialism and postcolonial theory and an irresponsible use of concepts such as nomadology with ignored genealogies in Indigenous theory and life.[62] However, they also point out how many have spotted potential in Deleuze for postcolonial theory and in Deleuze and Guattari's involvement with Palestine. They note, "We might point to their comments about the imperialism of normative Western forms of Oedipal subjectivity; movements of de/reterritorialization describing a conceptual politics of capture and relative liberation; [and] the creation of hybrid and migratory forms of selfhood through relational processes of becoming." Significantly, Bignall and Patton draw our attention to a useful approach to Deleuze and postcolonial theory: "Properly mutual negotiations witness the simultaneous becoming-Deleuzian of postcolonialism and the becoming-postcolonial of Deleuze."[63] Thinking with Deleuze and their critiques, I wonder about the possibilities emerging from this theory. Are there ways to make it travel to enlist it for feminist and queer struggles as well as subvert its masculine overtures? To my mind, Bignall and Patton inspire us to ask: How do we traverse the becoming Deleuzian of transnationalism and the becoming transnational of Deleuze? I think with Deleuze and Guattari to discern the heterogeneous "micropolitics" in their theory of becoming animal and to see whether it can travel the world and perhaps even include an Indian cow in the frame.

Deleuze and Guattari, in multiple projects, emphasized playing with representations and deterritorializing them from a static reference point. Writing about Franz Kafka's "animalistic" stories and stories about animals, Deleuze and Guattari discuss the "micropolitics" undergirding the narratives. Alongside the comic buoyancy in Kafka's works, they also point out, "Never has there been a more political and social author from the point of view of enunciation." In Kafka's enunciations Deleuze and Guattari find the mixture of laughter and politics that can think about new futures. Deleuze and Guattari do not envisage escapism or attempts to "flee the world" in Kafka's becoming animal, "[r]ather, it was the world and its representations that he *made take flight* and that he made follow these lines. It was a question of seeing and speaking like a beetle, like a dung beetle." The emphasis on "micropolitics" in Deleuze and Guattari's works is continuous with an emphasis on deterritorialization and an attempt to subvert framings of the world that speak through a coerced homogeneity. Indeed, what would it be to think like a dung beetle, as Deleuze and Guattari inspire us to ask? Thinking through becoming animal and Kafka's "collective assemblage," Deleuze and Guattari write that "becomings" do not constitute representations, reproductions, symbolism, or allegory. Rather, becoming animal is charting a "map of intensities," a "method that replaces subjectivity." In *Kafka: Toward a Minor Literature*, Deleuze and Guattari note, "To become animal is to participate in movement, to stake out the path of escape in all its positivity, to cross a threshold."[64]

In *A Thousand Plateaus: Capitalism and Schizophrenia*, written as a sequel to *Anti-Oedipus* and with a common subtitle, Deleuze and Guattari attempt to work philosophy against the grain and against a state-dictated philosophical organization.[65] They describe becoming as a "verb with a consistency all its own; it does not reduce to, or lead back to, 'appearing,' 'being,' 'equaling,' or 'producing.'"[66] Seen as counterpolitics to categories and classifications, becoming animal is an undoing of binary thinking in favor of an intensification of unbridled energies. Deleuze and Guattari write about three representations humans use to categorize animals. The first constitutes Oedipal animals such as family pets: "These animals invite us to regress, draw us into a narcissistic contemplation," and for this reason, they famously point out, "*Anyone who likes cats or dogs is a fool.*"[67] Here "becoming animal" could be read as a critique of making pets, a sentimental domestication or trivialization that reiterates the differences between man and animal through a projection of man over animal.[68] Disdainful toward little pets especially, Deleuze and Guattari describe large, powerful animals, noting all the while that a cheetah or an elephant could also be made a pet, "my little beast."[69] The distinction between animals and the category of "pet" is used to draw attention to how humans code animals and how animals become human projections and become incorporated into familial and institutional structures.

The second kind of animals Deleuze and Guattari discuss are animals represented within a firm typology, such as state animals or animals with symbolic stature. The third and final kind are pack animals, the more "demonic animals" that truly demonstrate a multiplicity by being seen in bands or herds. Deleuze and Guattari do not spell out types of animals to establish hierarchies of animals with demonic animals being lower than pets or vice versa. Instead, what is important is "the different states according to which they are integrated into family institutions, State apparatuses, war machines, etc." The way packs work is different from state structures or family relations, and it is here that they emphasize the possibility of the "becoming-animal of the human being."[70] Because pets and state/symbolic animals serve as projections of family and state structures, respectively, they are not available for the kinds of becomings Deleuze and Guattari are after. Pack animals with their demonic qualities, however, do offer a way to think of becoming animal. Deleuze and Guattari's typology is framed around a critique of anthropocentric codings and an urge to pull out animalistic energies of multiplicity that scorn domestication and state structures.[71]

Cows complicate Deleuze and Guattari's typology of animals. Perhaps especially so the Indian cow. Thinking about the cow as an animal in this conversation is particularly intriguing. The Indian cow is a herd animal, but it is also a state animal and subject to a sentimentalized domestication. Cows move in cattle herds, and while they may seem more docile than a pack of wolves, projecting less intensity, like pack animals they have leaders, wander the landscape, marauding and trampling and scouring for food. Cows are not only herd animals; in Hindu nationalism in India they are state animals, bestowed the reverent status of mother, and granted a sacrality that prohibits their slaughter. In addition, while a cow is not exactly a "pet," cows are bred and domesticated for milk and meat, and their keepers are fond of them and include them in family rituals. Its status as mother in many Hindu households does however complicate the meaning of "pet." In fact, most other animals could also be seen to thwart the typology. For example, the domesticated pet dog could also be a wolf, and the house cat has many similarities with the jungle cat.[72] I should add that Deleuze and Guattari were not rigid in their classificatory schema and recognized spills and run offs. Their main effort was to counter classifications through a counter-classificatory schema.

How about adding a lesbian Brahmin cow to the mix? Bhadravati, Baddy, and B add nuance to the conversation on becoming animal with their subversive overthrowing of the common associations of human and animal. While Deleuze and Guattari's formulations, followed avidly in animal studies, move us toward a nonteleological profusion of identity crossings, Namjoshi's cow inserts a politics of affirmative sabotage that complicates the matter further and adds varied playful resonances.

While Deleuze and Guattari's becoming animal overturns binary thinking and normative philosophical thinking, it does presume that binaries work in the same way for everyone the world over. But the binary of man and animal, for example, operates with specific nuances for a person of color or low caste. Animals, too, are far more heterogeneous and have unequal fates. Add to this a continual anthropocentric project of category building that moves with religion, culture, and political economy. For example, although Hindu India worships the cow, it is also the largest exporter of beef in the world market, a rank that it oftentimes shares with Brazil.[73] This is because the US Department of Agriculture (USDA) has a broad definition of "beef" that allows India to export the meat of water buffalo under this label. It thus keeps intact its reverence for the cow while allowing "beef" to be one of its largest revenue earners, even more than basmati rice. Deleuze and Guattari's typology flounders under such complications, which render representations of a play even before they can take flight. The play with the category of animal is insidious, continually reframed, and subject to a collision of forces.

Since 2014 and the victory of the BJP in national elections, the cow question has taken center stage in Indian politics. Election manifestos profess their loyalty to the cow, and cow-protection armies stand in vigilance to defend the cow from the human citizenry. Radhika Govindrajan highlights the significance of the cow in present-day Indian elections and writes about bumper stickers on cars in India that extoll people to think carefully about the choice that they would make: "*Kisey chunenge?* (Which will you choose?), the sticker demanded; *Gau-raksha ya gay-raksha* (Cow protection or gay protection)."[74] The bumper sticker posits a binary between the cow and being queer; in other words, choosing cow protection guaranteed under the BJP government would keep queer people outside the nation and ensure a pure Hindu national family. This is an excellent example to starkly illustrate how the queer body and the figure of the cow stand in marked counterpoise to each other in national politics. And this is exactly where I would like to reiterate the significance of Namjoshi's work and its play with political binaries. Namjoshi's seamless narrative comprising humans, animals, and gods notes the spill-offs and cross-overs between frames and subverts the framing by establishing a communion; Namjoshi's humans, animals, and gods share the same qualities. While a Deleuzian politics of becoming moves us beyond binary thinking, it fails to note the prolifically heterogeneous status of man and animal that plays with reality even before we can begin to undo them.

Play, stories, and ironies situate all kinds of politics, and they don't simply belong to a feminist politics of resistance. A play with binaries is also omnipresent in politics of all shades. For example, a member of India's parliament once declared publicly that the Indian cow was far superior to the foreign cow, as its hump concealed a gold artery that left traces of gold in the Indian cow's milk.[75] While the distinction between indigenous and nonindigenous cows is marked, the indigenous cow is also gold. This story plays in a different way with our radical politics of resistance; in this case, by upending Deleuze's becoming animal and mineral. Thus, by juxtaposing two frames of animal politics, Namjoshi with Deleuze and Guattari, I travel with both formulations to discern the manifold politics of play and how an affirmative sabotage—using a lesbian cow to haunt the Hindu national cow—can be particularly powerful in haunting the play of power.

Becoming Animal, Becoming Transnational

Despite the creative politics in becomings and their capacity to subvert, the obvious problems with Deleuzian becomings continue to agonize. Who has the capacity and/or privilege to participate in becomings? Man can become animal and become woman, as becomings are always minoritarian. Troublingly, a rigid politics of identity haunts a theory that seeks to undo them. Becomings in the Deleuzian schema (or counter-schema) engage effusively with identity to release untamed energies and possibilities. However, the construction of identity is culturally specific and conceptions of what is man, woman, and animal are colored deeply with cultural significations. Knowing the slippery terrains through which conceptions of masculinity and femininity travel across transnational borders, and questions of animality, it remains important to make this theory speak to transnational politics. When the "other" is repeatedly feminized and animalized through the masculine politics of imperialism, becoming woman and becoming animal signal toward hierarchical power regimes. I remain haunted by the profuse energies and reckless optimism in Deleuze and Guattari's becomings. How do we salvage its affirmative, creative edge without surrendering a critical stance about its implications and importance?

Jasbir Puar in *The Right to Maim* offers insight into working with Deleuzian becomings through her rendition of "becoming trans," "which seeks to link disability, trans, racial, and interspecies discourse to acknowledge porous boundaries constitutive of the overwhelming force of ontological multiplicity." As she points out, the endeavor is able to "transform the fantasy of discreteness of categories not through their disruption but, rather, through their dissolution via multiplicity." The specific focus of her chapter being to address affiliations between trans and disability, Puar wishes to address a "speculative reimagining," one that would enable a positioning beyond "trans normativity" or "trans being." As she pens it, "Becoming is awash in pure immanence, never coincident with itself, marked only by degrees of intensity and duration." Within this optimistic, effusive theorization and its politics, Puar also notes that capitalism uses becomings to generate profit, and all becomings should be situated within the "geopolitics of racial ontology."[76] Puar's endeavors to work through disability and trans with reference to Deleuzian becomings offers us a prism to understand the potential of Deleuzian becomings, which can help us understand the intensive multiplicity of subjectivity making and how it can travel through ostensibly disparate fields beyond self-defeating stereotypes and prejudices.

A becoming transnational of Deleuze may involve various forms of intervention, such as discerning varied cultural frames of animals and animality as a necessary step toward a deterritorialization of the binary between animal and man. An attempt at deterritorialization would have to deconstruct assumptions of the homogeneity of man and animals and be haunted by slippages of meaning at every playful turn. As we have seen, a politics of becoming and undoing binaries is used by extreme right-wing groups *and* in radical feminist and queer democratic projects. The Hindu cow is god and animal, and it muddies the territory of any univocal theory of being or becoming. Because stories, playful turns, and imaginative tropes proliferate in politics of varied ideological hues, acknowledging the play and hauntings remains pivotal to a feminist and queer politics.

I choose to think with Namjoshi and with Deleuze and Guattari in terms of an affirmative sabotage that may most skillfully draw out the playful nuances in both theories and politics. An explicit play with identity politics, both feminist and queer, Namjoshi's text is as much about irreverence and mischief as it is about uncovering associations between animality and queer and feminist politics—and haunting the text through those connections. A blatant subversion of Hindu nationalist politics that positions the cow as mother and sacred, and homosexuality as the "other" to the Hindu nation, Namjoshi's narrative nudges at its many meaning-plays by affirming the central role of the lesbian cow.[77]

Namjoshi indicates that she wrote *The Conversations of Cow* as a reaction to a feminist and queer politics that takes itself too seriously and works with simplistic identity categories, "particularly . . . the notion of a rigid identity."[78] Namjoshi thus writes a mischievous and witty narrative of constant becomings, shape shifting, and conversations through manifold identities. As the narrative progresses through the conversations, the relationship between B and Suniti becomes increasingly tender: "I'm not altogether sure whether it's B or the night that holds me so close." An emotional connection leads to them becoming lovers, having conversations that question the good and bad of things, and discussing the elemental composition of varied bodies, human and animal, composed of blood and gut. However, this romance does not end the conversation. In fact, B then changes into a Man from Mars, following Suniti's theory that men were a different species: "Invaders. This may be deduced from their subsequent behavior." However, other transformations follow the Man from Mars embodied experience. We also see S2, Suniti's copy, a doubling of personhood. Indeed, this is a narrative of "the Cow of a thousand faces and a thousand manifestations who walks rough-shod over fields and forests, and falls asleep when her day is done."[79]

Using anthropomorphic and zoomorphic politics, Namjoshi's play with identity provides valuable resources to visualize creative displacements, much like and unlike a Deleuzian onto-choreography. Namjoshi's cow is never outside its human framings, coded as it is with anthropocentric behavior patterns. It literally talks like a human. However, to read *Conversations of Cow* as an anthropocentric coding would lose the spirit of play and haunting through which the author renders herself animal as such. The zoomorphic elements of the text are manifested through the celebration of sexuality and becomings and through its incessant play with identity politics. Namjoshi uses animals and animality to write about a sexual politics that refuses to be contained by categories, and her becoming animal works concomitantly through a becoming transnational. These "plaited" becomings work with each other to reveal possibilities for lives and subjectivities by placing the associations of animals, animality, and animalization at the center and forefront of her conversations.

This chapter has emphasized the explicit connections between the strategic positioning of the animal and the formation of the state through national communities of belonging. Appropriated through an insidious politics of "inclusive exclusion" or "exclusive inclusion," animals help frame the state-forming Man. I refute political theories that homogenize the ways in which animals are included and excluded by positioning the Hindu cow in a stark opposition. Becoming animal is tied to state building in many ways; the Hindu cow as god and mother deterritorializes the proper space for animals as positioned within Western political theory. I look to Deleuze and Namjoshi to think about possibilities in becoming animal that could speak to the complexities of our transnational world. A Deleuzian politics of becoming animal seeks to overturn binary formulations of man/animal and revels in the counter-teleological possibilities of becomings. Including Namjoshi in this narrative adds an imagination of transnational becoming animal that mischievously teases our associations of animality and animalization through haunting their violent erasure of queer and feminist lives. It is this intervention, I argue, that can create a becoming transnational of becoming animal. Otherwise, we remain speaking of animals as a designed appellation, as Derrida reminded us in the introduction to this chapter. By sabotaging associations of animality and animalization with questions of sexuality and community that happen through play and hauntings, Namjoshi creatively works toward an undoing of borders—that which creates animals and contains nations.

Through Namjoshi's works and Deleuze and Guattari's counter-teleological politics, I have demonstrated how becoming animal and becoming transnational each need the other in order to unravel categorizations of animals as the other to man and nation. By bringing together questions on animals, animality, and animalization, I highlight how working singularly to improve the conditions of certain animals often has no significant effect in cycles of dehumanized violence. It is only through a reckoning of entanglements among animals, animality, and animalization with an attention to the politics of sexuality, gender, nationality, and different "othering" mechanisms that we can hope to build paradigms of inclusivity. Their intimate relationality, as well as their potential to undo each, is materialized through the heterogeneous politics of play and haunting. Namjoshi's meaning-plays emphasize a mischievous politics of affirmative sabotage that can undo categories such as human and animal through an exaggerated emphasis on those frames.

In writing *The Conversations of Cow* in English, Namjoshi displays her attention to meaning-plays and how, as she puts it, "language has power over power itself."[80] Despite her use of English, Namjoshi's incorporation of Indian fables and mythology interlaces the narrative with animals and zoomorphic articulations. The stories are amenable to multiple acts of translation as we read from our specific locales and attempt to situate its significances; indeed, it requires them. Thus, reckoning with the politics of translations to situate and understand meaning-play is critical for tracing how words travel through our transnational world. Chapter 2 continues this work by further elucidating frames of meaning and the playful slippages that haunt translation.

CHAPTER 2

Translations and Overlapping Belongings
Mapping Queer Transnationalism

> Translation is also the most intimate act of reading. And to read is to pray to be haunted.
> —Gayatri Chakravorty Spivak, "Translation as Culture"

> A translation issues from the original—not so much from its life as from its afterlife. .
> —Walter Benjamin, "The Task of the Translator"

The politics of translation, along with its ethical valence, as well as its impossibility, constitutes one of the core struggles of postcolonial transnational studies. Translations are a mechanism through which books, thoughts, and ideas cross borders and pass through varied constituencies; they inspire imagination, and they archive forgotten or lesser-known stories and histories. Any attempt at translation is inevitably haunted by its politics, whether by the power differentials between the translator and translated, the possible audiences, the meaning structures or status quo, the meanings in even naming an author, and so on. For example, texts translated into English are haunted by the fact that English, as the language of British colonialism, carries echoes of oppression and dominance into the text, which may effectively render any translation also inevitably a mistranslation. Or consider the English words "queer" and "lesbian." These words travel across borders, and both assert a kind of meaning but also change meaning in the context of their reception. Words and their resonances echo through borders and amidst overlapping belongings symptomatic of a complex postcolonial haunting. Gayatri Chakravorty Spivak puts it best when she simply states: "Translation is a necessary impossibility."[1] Although the global circulation of texts, ideas, movements, and identities makes translations unavoidable and oftentimes necessary, a translation is as much an impossibility: how can one attempt to fully represent a specific word, idea, identity, sensibility, or emotion? Translations demand tremendous hubris and/or enormous humility.

This chapter is concerned centrally with meaning-plays as demonstrated in the politics of translation. By emphasizing translations as postcolonial hauntings, this chapter demonstrates how meaning-plays shift through place and time, maps and borders, and remain haunted by their excesses, absences, and incongruities. My attention to translations is inspired by recent feminist and queer theory that considers the process of translation to be a democratic solution to a hegemonic projection of oneself, one that can move beyond the liberal politics of representation by including omissions and errors.[2] The "translation turn" in queer studies similarly attempts to democratize queer transnationalism. While the focus on translations is certainly important in attempts to reckon with global power imbalances, I wonder whether we are ready to work with the messiness of translations in feminist and queer politics, with its uses and misuses. We must reckon with the fact that translations can as easily fall into the traps of neoliberal economies and global capitalism. Given this possibility, what then is translation's critical import? How do we work with it to illuminate and act against power regimes? By seeking to understand the politics of translation in its meaning-plays, specifically in the context of queer politics, I hope to draw out the complexities that saturate translations in theory and activism. Meaning-plays haunt works of translation and carry manifold resonances for queer politics. The meaning-plays broached in this chapter centralize the play with "queer" that positions sexual subjectivities as we map and unmap belongings through various kinds of nations. Alongside, I continue to study frames, specifically in graphic narratives, to help visualize the braided mapping of play and hauntings.

In "Translating into English," Spivak discusses translating Mahasweta Devi's novel *Chotti Munda and His Arrow*.

> In the last paragraph that I translated I made a choice of level when I came across the phrase "mohajoner kachhe hat pa bandha." "Arms and legs in hock to the moneylender," I wrote. "In hock" is more in the global lingua franca than in the English that is one of the Indian languages. . . . But "mortgaged" would have been, in my judgement, an error of level, and would have missed the pun, "being tied up or trussed," present in the original.

Not that "in hock" catches the pun. But "hock" is sufficiently confusing in its etymology to carry the promise of nuances. The translator must play such games.

A certain play with words, a play to align meaning, to honestly represent against its impossibility, is what inspires the work of translation. As Spivak points out, the word "mortgaged" would have missed the meaning-plays of the Bengali "*hat pa bandha.*" Literally one could say that it translates into "hands and legs tied." However, Spivak uses "in hock" to display the pawn mechanisms, exchanges, mortgages, and varied other meanings that spill forth from the Bengali words. Even while translating, Spivak notes her dissatisfaction with available words and writes, "Translation is as much a problem as a solution. I hope the book will be taught by someone who has enough sense of the language to mark this kind of unavoidable failure, and that the rare reader will be led to the Bengali."[3]

The translator is caught with the need to literally re-present and must struggle with the myriad meaning-plays that get lost as the translator does so. Providing another more subtle example of what I am talking about, Spivak takes on the text "Intellectuals and Power: A Conversation between Michel Foucault and Gilles Deleuze." She famously writes, "The ventriloquism of the speaking subaltern is the left intellectual's stock-in-trade." Radical critiques, even when pointing toward exclusions and intending to uphold the "subaltern" or other oppressed people, fail to realize their own complicity within power discourses and to acknowledge their voice in speaking about the subaltern. Specifically, Spivak engages with how this text renders "Maoism" and the "worker's struggle" and fails to engage with the transnational division of labor, much like "gender and development." Spivak draws our attention to the romanticism that frames the speaking subaltern in the text of radical critiques, as well as their professed ability to speak about the subaltern. In this case, Spivak notes the many errors in speaking about "*the* worker's struggle" as a monolithic struggle. She argues that it is inadequate to fathom the working of capitalism, the role of agriculture in economies, the subject production of labor, and a host of other issues that remain obscured under umbrella terms for representation.[4] Moving from Maoism and the worker's struggle, we can see the conundrum with representation for queer studies when writing about sexual subjectivities in different political, social, and cultural contexts. Again, how do terms like "lesbian" and "queer" travel? What translations are at play?

The previous chapter drew our attention to Suniti Namjoshi's play with identity and to the zoomorphic politics that infiltrate her attempts to nudge at serious frames of being lesbian, feminist, human, and animal. While

The Conversations with Cow plays with categories and showcases different becomings, it also situates Namjoshi's translations across places and identity as she travels across continents. Written in English, the novel exhibits translations of meaning, not of an Indian language to English but of the meaning attached to identity positions. Translations, thus, do not entail only translating from one language to another. The meaning-plays emphasized throughout this book play with connotation and translation within, between, and beyond language systems. This chapter complicates the politics of translation further by analyzing the use of image as well as text in graphic narratives. Centering queer transnational studies, I intertwine the transnational and the translational to emphasize their playful intra-action and hauntings.

Queer politics struggles with and against language to articulate varied subject positions in transnational circuits. Working with this conundrum in queer transnational studies, it remains important to visualize the role of translations, across language systems and cultural contexts, in queer transnational studies. There are two matters that demand attention. The first is one I cast as a central haunting in democratizing queer studies in the transnational arena. It is the politics of recognition that deems the Western queer subject as properly queer; in other words, subjects elsewhere have to mirror the Western queer prototype in order to be recognized as queer. Transnational queerness is haunted in this way by Western habits. Pointedly, Keguro Macharia writes, "The way of thinking through Queer Africa will be mostly illegible to US and European ears trained by and embedded in LGBTI studies. Or, as is happening too often, queer African voices and experiences will be absorbed as 'data' or 'evidence,' not as modes of theory or as challenges to the conceptual assumptions that drive queer studies."[5] As I would like to emphasize, following the politics of selective exclusion and inclusion in queer studies, transnational studies often posits the outside as properly transnational; let us study the "other," their interesting habits, stories of oppression, or novel strategies of resistance through "our" language. Maya Mikdashi and Jasbir Puar in "Queer Theory and Permanent War" make an important point when they critique how the "transnational frame" is "routed through the west." "Rarely are the locations of Area Studies themselves understood as transnational; the Middle East, for example, is a historically, politically, and economically deeply transnational region unto itself."[6] Thus, alongside queer studies' concentration on Western modalities, transnational analyses oftentimes remain territorialized through unmoving maps, or an understanding of maps "routed" through the dominant imagination and served to a Western audience within a static frame of language, however much transnational analyses pulls to move.[7]

Second, it is important to attend to the play of meaning as the word "queer" travels to different places. Naisargi Dave in *Queer Activism in India*, writing "On Queer Language," provides us with an intriguing example from her work with activists in Hyderabad, India. One afternoon approximately forty individuals had gathered to discuss organizing around sexual rights in Asia:

> A Nepali woman spoke in Hindi when it was her turn to introduce herself. She talked about her work with a counseling service in Kathmandu for women in distress. An activist from Delhi responded to her in Hindi, inquiring if she received calls from lesbians. In posing the question, the Delhi activist translated "lesbian" into the Sanskritic *samlaingik log*, literally "those of the same sex" or "homo-sexual." My friend Gautam, who was sitting next to me, chuckled and wrote something in his notebook. I turned to him with an inquisitive look, and he slid the notebook into my lap, pointing with his pen to what he had written: "Translations. The queer language is always foreign."[8]

The Delhi activist felt the need to use *samlaingik log*, possibly to convey respect for the subject position, and also to claim it as a legitimate indigenous identity, making in fact an exaggerated claim for it by using India's ancient, classical language, Sanskrit. Dave's description draws our attention to the intricately paradoxical positioning of "queer" in India, mostly seen as a foreign imposition. It also draws out how the "queer language is always foreign," in other words, how translations are always woven into articulations of queer and never is it seen as part of the original or ordinary frame of things. Dave succinctly implores, "What are those moments in which the queer can be, and infinitely becomes, queer?"[9] Also, let's not forget that Gautam "chuckled" when pointing out the centrality of translations in queer language. While the chuckle itself may be impossible to translate, it helps to situate the oftentimes incongruent nature of the politics surrounding queer activism, as seen in the invocation of the Sanskritic rendering of lesbian, as it travels borders. Re-invoking Spivak's statement that "the translator must play such games," I wonder about the nature of play and haunting in this specific scenario, different kinds of play and haunting by the Delhi activist and Gautam: the use of "lesbian" involved a play toward purity politics by the Delhi activist, who wished to legitimize "lesbian" by Sanskritizing and making it into something pristinely Indian; its utterance was haunted by the ghost of Westernization and a play by Gautam who scribbled and chuckled to highlight these incongruent juxtapositions in queer activism.

Thinking with the two contexts on the agonies of translation and its meaning-plays and inspired by Dave's question, I ask: What would it mean to queer translations, to queer the very words that express nonnormative sexual identity? Would an account of their multiple mappings help in this endeavor? Working with these questions and in this chapter, I conceptualize translation as a postcolonial haunting and note its centrality in identity work through slippages, errors, excesses, impossibilities, and evolving meaning-plays.

Queer Transnationalism's Emphasis on Translation

Queer transnationalism troubles the contours of both queer theory and transnational studies. On the one hand, while *queer theory* is oftentimes West centric in its language of sexual identity and politics, *transnational studies* speaks to this West-centric bias and seeks to unravel the hegemonic normativity behind ostensibly nonnormative positions. On the other hand, queer theory does contribute greatly to centrally anchoring the social mediation of sexuality in a way that transnational studies often does not. *Queer transnationalism* transgresses the contours of both queer studies and transnational politics by discerning the shifting contours of national belonging in tandem with sexual identification. However, it is simplistic to think of queer transnationalism as a deft negotiation between "two" bodies of theory and action. For example, Elizabeth Povinelli and George Chauncey point out that the sexual history of New York and San Juan cannot be comprehended without understanding migration patterns and transnational movements.[10] Thus, to posit queer and transnational as distinct or opposing terms misses the varied entanglements through which both coexist.

The richness of the literature in queer transnationalism points to the complexities governing this field of study.[11] There has been an increasing emphasis on queer transnational studies, and through these projects we learn about attempts to broaden the scope and ambit of queer studies. A special issue of *GLQ: A Journal of Lesbian and Gay Studies* in 1999, edited by Elizabeth Povinelli and George Chauncey, points to the "transnational turn" in queer theory.[12] As they explain, "this issue of *GLQ* interrogates histories, cultures, and theories of sexuality from a transnational perspective and, to a lesser extent, critiques recent theories of globalization from a queer perspective."[13] In their 2002 book *Queer Globalizations: Citizenship and the Afterlife of Colonialism*, Arnaldo Cruz-Malave and Martin F. Manalansan IV draw out the promises and perils of queer globalizations seen in the impetus to secure queer rights across different borders and the increased emphasis on queer sexualities as units of consumption in the global marketplace.[14] Gayatri Gopinath in her 2018 book *Unruly Visions: The Aesthetic Practices of Queer Diaspora* emphasizes "a queer regional imaginary" that connects regions and operates "supranationally" and "subnationally."[15] This important interjection to the field of queer transnational studies and queer diaspora uses visual politics to foreground different mappings of sexuality across and through regions.

As queer studies, along with feminist studies, are entangled with transnational studies, they also urgently invoke the translational. Anjali Arondekar and Geeta Patel in "Area Impossible," their special issue for *GLQ* in 2016, put area studies and queer studies in conversation to tell different stories of "translations" and relationalities.[16] Rather than simply adding queer analytics to area studies or instilling an imagination of pure space in the global arena, Arondekar and Patel, following Spivak, approach the interstices of queer and area studies as the "irreducible work of translation."[17] Two years prior, in their 2014 essay for the Comparative Perspectives Symposium of *Signs*, Claudia de Lima Costa and Sonia E. Alvarez write about the "translation turn" in feminism and emphasize its utility as "politically and theoretically indispensable" in formulating antiracist and postcolonial solidarity and ways of knowing.[18] Their essay, "Dislocating the Sign: Toward a Translocal Feminist Politics of Translation," emphasizes translation as central to transnational politics with its emphasis on "an impropriety and inadequacy that underpins all systems of representation."[19] Working with translations means recognizing the inevitable lapses and incompleteness in any feminist project. Invoking the work of Maria Lugones, the authors look at translation as "'world'-travelling" and thus move beyond a linguistic register when writing about translations; instead, they emphasize the potency of translation, its power to "un-do," as in an undoing of the self in relation to others.[20]

Recent scholarship has emphasized the efficacy of working with translations in feminist activism and queer studies, as evidenced in de Lima Costa and Alvarez's work and the recent issue of *GLQ* titled "Area Impossible."[21] Translation has received interdisciplinary attention as well, as seen in feminist anthropologist Anna Lowenhaupt Tsing's descriptions of the workings of capitalism in our contemporary moment. Conversing with ecologists and economists, Tsing's work refers to translations as "patches" and "other forms of partial attunement."[22] Tsing refers to translation's investment in linguistic regimes and elaborates on its traveling potential across spaces that make it intrinsic to capitalism as well: "Translations across sites of difference *are* capitalism: they make it possible for investors to accumulate wealth."[23] Tsing's work makes us think of translations not simply as a progressive, anti–status quo feminist or queer politics but also as something that helps maintain capitalism's status quo.[24] It is useful to keep this analysis in mind when thinking of translations as a democratic resolution. Rather than simply a solution for hierarchical power equations and an epistemic preparation for democratic theory and activism, translations are also used to sell goods, define objects, and make money. Understanding its intrinsic role in capitalism broadens our understanding of the work of translation and of queer activism, where queer movements in various parts of the world have repeatedly shown their dependence on commodity purchases to look truly queer.[25] Thus, as we can see, the recent emphasis on translations spans multiple disciplines and feminist and queer theory as they grapple with movement politics across borders.

Critiques of representation and the emphasis on translations are not "new" turns. Theorists and activists have been writing continuously about the ethics of translations through varied spaces. Nor is it fair to characterize the recent emphasis on translations in feminist and queer studies as a simple re-turn. Instead, let us inquire about why the imperative to translate keeps haunting radical critiques of exclusions. Walter Benjamin's discussion on types of translations helps explain the relevance of translation. For Benjamin, a fundamental issue connected to translations was learning to distinguish between poor and good translations. In "The Task of the Translator," Benjamin distinguishes between translation and "transmission" and points out that those translations that simply transmit information are "bad translations." The task of translation is not the "reproduction" of the original; rather, it stands "as harmony, as a supplement." Thus, a good translation to Benjamin was never whether it resembled the original or if it could pass as the original. Instead, the translator would show "great longing for linguistic complementation."[26]

While Benjamin's works have pointed us toward good and bad ways of translating and the exclusions in simply working with literal reproductions, the interest in translations has a long history with varied politics. Postcolonial theorists, feminists, and queer-of-color critiques have persistently posited translation as indispensable to making sense of the world and its related misrepresentations. For instance, through multiple works, Spivak has emphasized the politics of translation: "Translation is thus not only necessary but unavoidable. If the text speaks, there will be Echo. And yet, as the text guards its secret, it is impossible. The ethical task is never quite performed."[27] Spivak's words provide a frame to work through the complex, power-saturated task of translation: in its impossibility lies its ethical imperative. Translations necessitate attention to nuances and meaning-plays, knowing all the while that there will never be perfect resonance between words and practices among differences. Through her works translating Mahasweta Devi, Jacques Derrida, and Aime Cesaire, among others, Spivak has consistently emphasized the complicated project of translation. In "Translating in a World of Languages," Spivak describes how translating starts before we translate in "the very moves of languaging."[28] Languaging looks at language beyond a singular entity and sees it implicated within multiple avenues: "This is a form of translation before translation."[29] In other words, our linguistic circuits are enmeshed in memories and reflexivity. "Reproductive heteronormativity," as Spivak says, serves as the "staging of each language."[30] We never translate in a void or outside discourse; projects of translation need to be anchored in the reality around us, as well as to strive to work against it. Spivak asks us to look at translations as a "persistent epistemological preparation" whereby "one never stops (not) translating."[31] Spivak's emphasis on the "untranslatable" as a persistent yearning and preparation, rather than a mindset that denounces the task or stops trying because it is considered insurmountable, frames her insistence on the difficult and complex, and hopeful, nature of the task.

If "reproductive heteronormativity" is the framing of language, its foundation, what does that mean for queering language? That is to say, as Spivak reminds us, that "reproductive heteronormativity" is the "theater" for language.[32] How may language subvert this initial "staging"? Such questions help us think about the politics of translations for queer subjects. Spivak's words provide a frame to note the inevitable slippages in translation, its haunting lapses, and its own haunting by the ethics of impossibility—or the inability to completely capture the meaning-play from one language system to another.

Texts in translation are marked by inevitable dissonances, notwithstanding the painstaking intimate labor involved in translations. Images are most often read through the visual politics of representations rather than translations, which remain defined by textuality and language. However, it is important to stay clear of a binary mode of defining text and image, as a text may also function as image and an image as text. We are reminded of W. J. T. Mitchell's words in *Iconology: Image, Text, Ideology*: "The point, then, is not to heal the split between words and images, but to see what interests and powers it serves."[33] To him the difference between words and images is oftentimes used in a manner similar to the differences we posit between nature and culture; this is a constructed positioning.[34] Thus, instead of seeing words and text as translatable, and image as representative, it is interesting to think about how both can simply perpetuate the power of the status quo while maintaining superficial distinctions. Graphic narratives, comics, or the hybrid combination of image-text provide an interesting landscape to study the queer politics of translation and the failure of representations. I turn toward two graphic narratives to read and translate their queer mappings haunted by their slippages, overlapping circuits, and imaginations in process: Alison Bechdel's *Fun Home: A Family Tragicomic* (2006) and Amruta Patil's *Kari* (2008).

Image and Text

Graphic narratives are often trivialized as child's play, their images making them seem less serious than a word-filled text. Much work about graphic narratives has subverted this stereotype, not simply in terms of placing them in adult literature but also delineating them as serious mediums for fiction and nonfiction. Art Spiegelman's *Maus* and Marjane Satrapi's *Persepolis* are just two examples of graphic narratives that have troubled conventional understandings of the politics of graphic narratives.[35] Graphic narratives can be of many different styles with more or fewer words and images, but what remains consistent is the play between words and images: what makes it text-image. Text and image spill forth and frame each other while also helping to move us from frame to frame. The configurations of text-image in graphic narratives move with other stylistic devices, such as panels, balloons, and gutters. The gutter, or the space between panels, plays in many ways in the works of specific comics. It may fuse or unfuse narratives, or it may appear as a pause or interruption. Hillary Chute puts it beautifully: "Comics is as much about what is *outside* the frame as what is *inside* it—what can be pictured, and what cannot be or won't be pictured, and is left to the reader's imagination."[36] Gutters and frames create manifold narratives and alterities that play with the reader's imagination. Comics are not child's play in the sense that they engage with serious issues, but they indeed are child's play in the way they subvert what it means to be childlike and serious.

Graphic narratives offer an invaluable prism to help visualize lines and frames, which is indispensable for any venture that seeks to fathom nationalism and transnationalism. Comprising text and images, graphic narratives offer a unique site to analyze the politics of space. There is little consensus about the typical layout of a graphic narrative. Jake Jakaitis and James F. Wurtz describe graphic narrative as "crossover" for many reasons, one of them being the unique placement of image and text that makes the reader cross over different indices of comprehension. The crossover happens on other levels as well, "between different genres, different forms, different linguistic registers, different types of art, and different storylines and character 'universes.'" Significantly, Jakaitis and Wurtz write, "Comics, we argue, work through these crossovers, and the political dimensions of graphic narrative are exposed precisely in those moments of crossover."[37] Muddling pure forms of textuality or imagery, graphic narratives offer a creative space to think with lines, frames, and the politics of translation, beyond the purely verbal text.

The art of crossover and the use of multiple frames in the graphic narrative serve as evocative metonyms of transnational identities, in contradistinction to nationalist renderings of identity, such as those analyzed by Benedict Anderson. Anderson's emphasis on the creation of national consciousness was tied to print capitalism.[38] In Anderson's analysis of nationalism, the circulation of printed books was pivotal in building the idea of nation. Embroiled within larger conversations on the origin of nationalism and Eurocentric models of nation building, postcolonial studies have questioned Anderson's thesis on the origins of nationalism and on its lack of resonance in postliberation struggles. Anne McClintock, for instance, questions Anderson's emphasis on print capitalism and instead sees "commodity spectacle" as the cohesive building block for nationalism.[39] McClintock emphasizes the visual rhetoric of objects such as flags, maps, and architecture in her analysis of nationalism.[40] Situating an analysis of transnationalism via graphic narratives provides an important interjection into these conversations, as graphic narratives are part of print capitalism but they also involve images and the politics of visibility that McClintock signals. The crossovers described above, for one, indicate how identities cannot be contained in single frames or by single symbols and how national mappings cannot hold the movement of meanings.

It is important to remember that queer comics have a distinct history and significant role in lesbian, gay, bisexual, transgender, and queer (LGBTQ) activism.[41] We can distinguish queer comics from other comics that have queer characters who are incidental to the theme. As Justin Hall, in the introduction to *No Straight Lines: Four Decades of Queer Comics*," comments, "It remains the job of mainstream comics to assimilate LGBTQ characters, while it falls to queer comics to dissect queer identities and examine in more profound ways the queer experience."[42] Queer comics have often been relegated to their specific communities, and queer cartoonists and comics have rarely received mainstream recognition. However, we do see a shift in this attitude with the increased popularity of queer comics, and, as Hall notes, "this is the moment to celebrate a world with no straight lines."[43] Hillary Chute, in her book *Why Comics? From Underground to Everywhere*, refers to the escalation of interest in queer comics, especially when 2015 marked the first annual comics convention to focus on queer comics.[44] Although Bechdel's *Fun Home* has significantly escalated the interest in and visibility of queer comics, Chute reminds us that comics have long carried the accusation of being quintessentially gay; in the 1950s Batman, Robin, and Wonder Woman were all read as gay.[45]

Fun Home and *Kari*

Graphic narratives lend themselves naturally to an analysis of queer transnationalism. In this vein I use Bechdel's *Fun Home* and Patil's *Kari* to frame and deframe queer transnationalism. Both texts I analyze here are popular, award-winning graphic narratives and transnationally acclaimed as landmark queer literature. The tremendous popularity of the two books helps situate recognition and draws the conversation into different national locales and ways of being. This chapter is not a comparison of two graphic narratives, one from the United States and the other from India. Cross-cultural comparisons often have a way of pitting one against the other, forcefully drawing antagonisms to make a point and etching superficial borders delimiting similarities and differences. I resist cross-cultural readings for the stark simplifications they often entail, as if schools of thought, meanings, theory, or activism are contained by specific brackets, American or Indian. In addition, I would inadvertently set myself up for failure if I sought to unravel queer transnationalism by proceeding through dichotomous white/black, first-world/third-world, and straight/gay paradigms.

Described as being "on par with graphic narrative memoirs such as Marjane Satrapi's *Persepolis* and Art Spiegelman's *Maus*," and as "one of the very best graphic narratives ever," Bechdel's *Fun Home* (2006) is no newcomer to the world of queer critical cultural studies.[46] Primarily situated in rural Pennsylvania, this graphic narrative recounts Bechdel's troubled relationship with her father and the joys and struggles of her early family life, her coming to terms with the death of her father, and her own identity. The title of the novel is ironically borrowed from the name of the family-owned funeral home.[47] Irony and double meaning spill over onto many frames, and nothing is quite what it appears to be. Bechdel draws and writes about the glaring discrepancy between their grandiose house and the experience of its inhabitants: "It's tempting to suggest, in retrospect, that our family was a sham. That our house was not a real home at all but the simulacrum of one, a museum. Yet we really were a family, and we really did live in those period rooms."[48] Appearance and reality, truth and fiction, past and present merge and disentangle to create a unique narrative of identity and of complex identifications that no singular logic can encompass. Rather, the play that structures *Fun Home* as a nonlinear haunted narrative illuminates the layered weave of Bechdel's meaning-plays.

In his review of Patil's *Kari*, Neel Mukherjee notes that comparisons between Bechdel's memoir and Patil's graphic narrative are "inevitable."[49] Mukherjee mentions in a recent interview that Patil has great respect for Bechdel. However, instead of thinking about their similarities, in that they are both lesbian novels, Mukherjee finds greater salience in looking at the differences between the novels, one being a memoir, the other fiction. Mukherjee clearly sides with Patil, considering it "more evocative."[50] Considered to be India's first woman graphic novelist and with *Kari* as India's first queer graphic narrative, Patil has drawn a great deal of attention and critical acclaim.[51] Rather than signaling better or worse, first or last, here I work to uncover the frames and lines that make these two presentations "inevitable" for the conversation on queer transnationalism and its meaning-plays.

Patil notes that *Kari* is "not autobiographical" and that her "asocial and queer" protagonist juxtaposes with the ever-prevalent "hyperfeminine prototypes."[52] *Kari* is situated in India and in "smog city," which the author depicts through images of sewers, offices, a crystal palace, and mysterious spaces. Wordy and eloquent, the graphic narrative combines a mixture of black-and-white images and the occasional placement of unusual color frames. The story is about Kari, who is shown jumping off a ledge with her lover Ruth right at the outset of the novel. Ruth is saved by a safety net and leaves the city, while Kari is washed into the city through the sewer lines. Right after her journey through the sewer lines, Kari walks into her office. Here the novel showcases interesting frames shifting among sewers, office, home, the real, and surreal. Elegant prose and cryptic statements characterize Kari's negotiations with the personal and political at home in Crystal Palace and in her office writing advertisements for Fairytale Hair. For instance, when sharing supper with her roommates in Crystal Palace, Kari remarks, "Make no mistake—there is no such thing as a straight woman."[53] Ostensibly commenting on her roommates' proclivity to flirt with and mother her in turns, Kari's statement could be framed within a wider narrative about gender, sexuality, and nation.[54] As we have seen previously, in India the heteronormative matrix is intrinsic to the national project; deviant sexualities are projected as "unpatriotic" and "foreign." In many ways, nations build themselves on straight lines, territorially and imaginatively. When Patil plays around with the nonexistence of straight women, she cuts right through the fantastical celebration of women in nationalist rhetoric and opens the possibility of nonlinear transnational connections.

Coming Out/Drawing Out

We seem to take it for granted that sexuality is anchored as identity, much like nationalism is anchored to a national identity. The narratives under question here both raise doubts about such closed questions of identity, evoking that familiar metaphor of the closet. The "closet" and "coming out" are involved with the politics of space in varied ways, nationally and transnationally. As Shane Phelan points out, "As a metaphor for invisibility, the closet is spatial. It suggests that our identity is clear, and the question is simply whether or not that identity is visible, whether it takes up space."[55] Coming out becomes a process of moving from invisibility to visibility and "a process of fashioning a self."[56] Transnational scholars have pointed out that the image of "being in the closet" and "coming out" are not universal but, rather, emerge from a Western frame of identity. Fran Martin, for instance, specifies that Taiwanese sexualities approximate the process of "masking" rather than being in the closet.[57] Dave shows how in the context of Indian society, people "leave home" rather than "come out."[58]

Neither of the two graphic narratives selected are singular narratives of "coming out." However, they both, in different ways, center identity work and the complexities saturating it. In *Fun Home*, Bechdel realizes "an" identity through texts. She writes-draws, "My realization at nineteen that I was a lesbian came about in a manner consistent with my bookish upbringing. A revelation not of the flesh, but of the mind." She sought confirmation about herself in books at the library, and finally she came out to her parents through a letter. Coming out is process-oriented, and in Bechdel's nonlinear graphic narrative readers are offered another explicit glimpse at frames that shift together to demonstrate the complexities involved in identity work. For example, we see identically sized, black-and-white frames that portray a conversation between Bechdel and her father. Bechdel asks him whether he anticipated the consequences of giving Bechdel a novel by the French writer Colette. Her father replies, "I guess there was some kind of identification." Moreover, the readers become privy to an extremely private conversation between Bechdel and her father in which he comes out as having had gay experiences and that he really wanted to be a girl.[59] Being in the closet and coming out are definitely spatial politics involving the negotiation and renegotiation of a certain relation to place and time. For individuals, the materiality of coming out is intensely braided with a specific time and locale that carries resonances throughout their lives.

In *Kari*, we don't encounter frames that signal "a" coming out. We see an endless trajectory of sewers and winding boat journeys. This is consistent with Dave's observation that people "leave home" rather than "come out." Walking through the city one night, Laz (Kari's coworker and friend) asks Kari, "Are you, like, a proper lesbian?" Kari notes how the word "lesbian" resonates "strange," "sort of fleshly, salivating, fresh off the boat from Lesbia, and totally inappropriate." It is interesting that while the identity "lesbian" is felt as "strange," Kari describes her fascination with k. d. lang on the very next page. She describes the first time she saw lang on TV in 1997: "What kind of creature was this, this genderless one, and why did she make me feel this way?"[60] The two passages, though seemingly incommensurable, are extremely important as they direct attention to the complex contours of queer transnationalism. Kari's choice of words is interesting. Being called a "proper lesbian" sets off a defensive reaction of thoughts like being seen as "fresh off the boat from Lesbia" and an overeager, promiscuous "salivating" sexuality. Kari obviously doesn't identify as a "lesbian," though she remains enamored with lang, whom she sees as "genderless" and narrates her soulful and physical meetings with her lover Ruth throughout the graphic narrative.

This example from Kari provides a frame to understand the unduly simplistic critique of "queer globalism" as West-centric LGBTQ politics that transports its vocabulary and meaning making to the rest of the world. Instead, through Kari's narrative we see an interesting circuit of the local with the global, an interactive mapping that moves back and forth, vertical and horizontal. In her fascinating article "There Are No Lesbians Here," Katie King emphasizes the varied receptions of the word "lesbian" and notes that "such receptions are inextricable from its traveling possibilities."

> Those travels are interconnected with other globalizing processes in an economy of multinationals in late capitalism, an economy also including representations and media, as well as activisms, art, and cyberspace, and inextricably intertwined too with worldwide movements against colonialism. It includes the possibility that "lesbianism" is a rejected term, as well as the possibility of using it as an inclusive, unmarked, or continually reconstructed "universal," although plural, not singular. Naming lesbian in this context, through this phrase, is a method coming-into-being that arises from acts of translation across fields of power.[61]

King's thought-provoking injunction notes the possibilities and problems with using the word "lesbian" in transnational struggles. King's analysis of "lesbian" as translation and, as a "coming-into-being," provides tremendous fuel for understanding the complex layers of "coming out" in queer transnationalism. King's analysis helps situate the term "lesbian" as antagonistic to particular (or all) national settings and the possibility of rearticulating it as a plural universal. Similarly, Dave invokes the term "lesbian" as a "practice of enunciation" rather than something people should rigidly adhere to as a fixed category.[62]

Rather than calling herself a "lesbian," we see Kari referring to herself as a "boatman": "As a boatman, you learn to row clean through the darkest water."[63] Images of Kari rowing her way through the clogged city remind the reader of her personal tribulations. It is interesting that Kari uses the identifier of "boatman" rather than "lesbian." Using King's interjection about "naming lesbian" as "acts of translation across fields of power," I wonder about the translation practices in this graphic narrative. Does "boatman" translate as "lesbian"? "Boatman" is certainly not an identity term in the manner of race, gender, or sexuality. Why do we keep anchoring sexuality via identity or a certain need to keep sexuality separate and distinguishable so that we can come out about it? It is important for me to emphasize that I am not suggesting that "boatman" substitutes for "lesbian" in *Kari*. The politics of substitution are different from that of translation, whereby working with translations means recognizing slippages and excesses that are impossible to contain because sexual subjectivities evolve in complex attunement with many other experiences of life, death, belonging, and loss. Kari's relationship with Angel, whom Kari describes as "the first actively dying person I'd met in my life," because of her advanced cancer, and Angel's subsequent death, adds layers of meaning and haunts Kari's identity as a "boatman" traversing through life and loss.[64] In her nuanced essay about *Kari* titled "Graphic Ecriture," Pia Mukherji writes about the "difficult desires" that constitute identity work in Kari, or "the delineation of identity by way of alterity."[65] In other words, it is through "dispossessions," rather than active constructions that we can best understand Kari's engagements with the world; loss and alterity frame Kari's changing sense of self. Substitutions or representations cannot contour around Kari's "difficult desires." Instead, intimate translations with their concomitant overflow attempt to engage with the labor of desire.

These are the complexities in translating "lesbian" and "coming out" as we travel through overlapping and spiraling mappings. The task of translation, with its incessant meaning-plays, underlines how mappings haunt imaginations and one's sense of place while also underlining how dispossessions situate a sense of self and others.

Place and Its Mappings

Fun Home's play with language and connotation is haunted side-by-side through memories, images, recollections of place, and text. The meaning-plays would be lost without an attention to the places and locations that thread the narrative: the house/funeral home where she grew up, the exact location of Bechdel's town in rural Pennsylvania, her college campus and its Gay Union, the multiple maps drawn to locate and situate her father's upbringing in the town, and New York streets, where the affirmation of gay identity was allowed, among many others. The house serves as a stage of sorts for her father's artistic aspirations as he attempts to restore it to its days of glory. Through images that display her father's aesthetic proclivity, Bechdel writes, "He would perform, as Daedalus did, dazzling displays of artfulness." With one of the maps drawn in the book, Bechdel points out how a tightly knit circumference enclosed the locations where her father was born, where he died, his grave, and the home where Bechdel lived with her family. Bechdel, however, also points out that despite this adherence to place, "This narrow compass suggests a provincialism on my father's part that is both misleading and accurate." With their urban styles of dress, mannerisms, and aesthetic pursuits, both her parents seemed extremely out of place in the rural setting. The "provincialism" also offered her father the space to conceal and hide his identity as a gay man. In stark contrast to the space of their hometown in rural Pennsylvania, Bechdel writes-draws about their family trips to New York: "I have a hallucinogenic memory of a throbbing welter of people in a large circle. It must have been Washington Square Park." Bechdel recalls that they were in New York only a few weeks after the Stonewall Riots and "might not a lingering vibration, a quantum particle of rebellion, still have hung in the humectant air?" New York offered the space of affirmation for identity, the spectacle of watching diverse identities and bodies, a certain exhilaration of spirit absent from drawings of her hometown. Bechdel's college experiences add to the conversation about place in the graphic narrative. She recalls attending a meeting of the Gay Union that was tantamount to a coming out. She left "exhilarated." And, it was in that "tremulous state" that she decided to tell her parents about her own identity.[66] Place, emotion, and identity work have an inextricable connection in Bechdel's text and images.

In her attention to place, Bechdel draws out the impossibility of containing it. *Fun Home*, in literal reference to the funeral home, mocks a sense of pure and contained positionality with its inversion of death and gaiety. The constant reference to maps suggests sharp attentiveness to placement and its role in making and shifting identity. Again, as Bechdel writes, it is both "misleading and accurate" to read the text as place-bound, as contained within the boundaries of a map. Although maps single out communities of belonging and history, Bechdel's graphic narrative repeatedly conveys the inability of maps to contain. Whether a map of rural Pennsylvania, trips to New York, or even the Gay Union, Bechdel's map-making concentrates on the importance of location and its concomitant mislocation. Like her favorite books read through the graphic narrative, space and textuality constantly attempt to translate each other and reconcile with inevitable slippages. I emphasize that it is misleading to read Bechdel's maps without attention to the texts and translations accompanying them.

Fun Home is an incredibly wordy graphic narrative. The profusion of text, the author's written commentary, gets added to by texts within the text. Marcel Proust, Albert Camus, F. Scott Fitzgerald, James Joyce, and others have an indelible presence throughout *Fun Home*. The space of these texts and the space of Alison's life are shown as blurred and intrusive. For example, in another elaborate rendering of maps, Bechdel comments, "In our *Wind in the Willows* coloring book, my favorite page was the map. I took for granted the parallels between this landscape and my own." And, thinking about her father's death and comparing him to Camus, Bechdel writes and draws, "A snapshot of him in a frat brother's sports car reminds me of Cartier Bresson's photos of Camus." The texts within the texts complicate understandings of place and time. Time loses its linearity as the past and present are constantly juxtaposed and live within each other. Place from another era becomes Bechdel's own. And, place and time lose their specific location as situated in one frame or as singular events. Hillary Chute uses Bechdel's description of her styles as "labyrinthine" to emphasize that not being a plot-driven narrative or chronology, "*Fun Home* is rather a drama of archival discovery and interpretation, as Bechdel searches for and discovers evidence about her father's life as a gay man."[67] The tangled web of images and texts, text upon text, images and their re-presentations all map out complex understandings of time and place.

Like *Fun Home*, *Kari* includes maps and other different kinds of mappings. The mappings in *Kari* traverse multidimensional space, upward and downward, within and outside bodies and cities. Smog city is represented through unending trajectories of sewage systems and canals. Often, roads mysteriously appear and create further inroads into its maze. On a map, Kari reflects, "An unfamiliar road, tender offshoot to the tar, has appeared today and it tempts me to walk it."[68] Canals, bodies, digestive tracts, and sewage systems seem to converge and entangle in smog city. The mappings seen in *Kari* have many different aesthetic styles. Roads, buildings, bridges, and bodies coinhabit in individual and collective agony and effervescence. The constant references to sewage systems and Kari's journey through them as a boatman underline yet more mappings of the clogged city. Aerial views of the city's buildings and maps that show a bird's-eye view of the city are underset with images of Kari rowing through the sewage waters. The overlapping maps point to different experiences and indistinct borders not simply at ground level but also to cartographies underground. It is underground that Kari is most herself, rowing through the murky waste of a clogged city where it is impossible to "come out."

The use of place and time in *Kari* is also particularly intriguing. The first few pages of the novel showcase Kari and Ruth joined together in body before they both step off the ledges of buildings. The reader participates in an aerial view of dense, populated city imagery and Ruth leaving in a plane. Kari's fall is not mediated by a safety net so she is "saved by a sewer, by the stinking river of effluents that snakes past our neighborhood, the one our buildings avert their faces from." The last few panels of the graphic narrative revert to the imagery of Kari atop a building. Here Kari is shown with a new resolve, and one of the three things she declares is, "I want to step back, not step off."[69] Ledges, sewage systems, and rowing through murky water offer the space-time amalgam mentioned previously in the analysis of *Fun Home*. Much like *Fun Home*, *Kari* moves uncontainably back and forth through different places and temporalities. Place resonates through multiple incidents, and it is not possible to separate one resonance from the other. Similarly, time moves back and forth through memories and yearnings. This results in an intense understanding of individual and collective living in a world of ever-changing cartographies.

The attention to place and its mappings in both graphic narratives draws our attention to the work of translation alongside the work of mappings, whereby translation and mappings both function to punctuate transnational lives with overlapping meaning-plays. Maps of all shapes and sizes, internal and external to the body and nation, weave through the two graphic narratives to contour complex belongings and unbelongings.

The Transnational and the Translational

Translations of different texts breathe through the pores of almost every frame in Bechdel's graphic narrative. For instance, at one point where Bechdel reminiscences about the release of a retitled translation of Proust's text, she points out that the translation "still doesn't quite capture the full resonance. . . . What's lost in translation is the complexity of loss itself." Bechdel proceeds to compare photos of herself and her dad and concludes, "It's about as close as a translation can get."[70] In *Fun Home* we see the attention to translations and an acknowledgment of its inevitable lapses. The inability to fully translate saturates the narrative and constitutes its irony and anguish. Deep emotions filtrate through every frame to draw out the tremendous complexities in relationships and identities as well as the failure of anyone to be completely translated into an identity.

Homi Bhabha in *The Location of Culture* significantly points out, "Culture as a strategy of survival is both transnational and translational." Bhabha is referring to transnational movements of people through migrations and relocations and what "makes the process of cultural translation a complex form of signification."[71] To think of a "pure" reference point for culture would miss the complex significations. Bechdel's use of text and maps reminds me of Bhabha's analysis for two reasons. First, the asymmetry among changing place, time, and vocabulary makes it imperative for us to keep the transnational and translational at the center of our analysis. Second, thinking of "culture as a strategy of survival" to reinvoke Bhabha is as indivisible from queer analysis as it is from postcolonial studies. The transnational and translational are of central importance here to make sense of reality and location. We see how Bechdel moves back and forth between different maps to chart out belongings, reflect on her past, and identify herself within different landscapes. The act of translation works alongside the attention to place when Bechdel notes the tremendous similarity between her father and Camus by reading different lines of Camus's texts or even in the act of naming the graphic narrative *Fun Home*. Moving on to *Kari*, we see another attempt at translation from a transnational prism.

Thinking through the space of "smog city" in Patil's graphic narrative demands an engagement that points out the impossibility of complete translation. I am reminded of Jason Ritchie's article "How Do You Say 'Come Out of the Closet' in Arabic?" where the author emphasizes that the "metaphor of checkpoint" seems more akin to the lived realities of queer Palestinians rather than the "metaphor of the closet." Ritchie argues, "Queer Israelis consolidate their membership in the nation as proper, patriotic citizens by reporting for duty as gatekeepers at a metaphorical checkpoint, where queer Palestinians are inspected, policed, and occasionally admitted into the fold of Israeli gayness as 'victims' of Palestinian culture but more often than not denied entry as excessively Arab or insufficiently 'gay.'" Ritchie engages with testimonials about the inability of Palestinians to "come out" and very significantly points out, "The question whether queer Palestinians need or want to come out and attain visibility is rarely asked."[72] Kari's scenario and Ritchie's case study are dissonant in terms of the space for politics and identity work; however, what I want to emphasize is the politics of translation that inevitably creeps up when thinking of queer identities through a transnational frame. The constant emphasis to establish identity and create one for "others" remains a persistent theme where "coming out" becomes akin to becoming fully national and governable.

Kari and *Fun Home* move far beyond a singular narrative of coming out, haunted as they are by different belongings, texts, memories, and frames. Bechdel's coming out through texts and Kari's endless journeys through the sewers of smog city signal the inadequacy of a language of difference or similarity to talk about queer transnationalism. To think with similarities as a bond between queer people in fact cloaks the intimate singularities that should be intrinsic to any politics that seeks to fathom desire. Neither is thinking with differences an adequate tool. Bracketing a vast difference between the two scenarios, the United States and India, may in the words of Petrus Liu, "naturalize and justify the 'West' as an indispensable and normative point of comparison."[73] The two graphic narratives provide valuable insight into the politics of space in queer transnationalism and riddle attempts to think with similarities or differences. We see location works closely with identity work in both the graphic narratives. Maps are important tropes in both narratives to display the making of private "communities of belonging," relation to family, and individual travels back and forth. None of the maps are prototypical national maps that project political boundaries. The maps redraw space through the individual protagonists and emphasize the need to pay attention to space by discerning intimate communities rather than a predefined national territory. The politics of translation move closely with transnational space movements in both the graphic narratives. The "transnational and translational" to reinvoke Bhabha work in entangled complicity in both the narratives. Maps with their drawings and redrawings signal attempts at framing belonging and its impossibility. In addition, the constant tug at language and intelligibility making through attention to translations signals repeatedly the importance of working with translations to understand queer transnationalism.

Kari and *Fun Home* inspire readers to question linear and territorial understandings of coming out, being a lesbian, mapping, fixed place and time, and other modalities intrinsic to our understanding of queer subjects. The constant attention to translations, repetitions, reversions, and circling back and forth, displayed in both graphic novels, draws our attention to the incessant play that marks the graphic narratives. Image and text, maps and translations, move together in the graphic novels to display the complexities of identity in different locales. Underground maps, aerial maps, imaginative maps, architectural maps, and maps of sewage systems vein their way through the queer narratives and signal their transnational mooring. Along with the maps that spiral out through overlapping contours, the acts of translation intimately frame queer subjects as both embedded in and in excess of languages of representation. The play through translations, of the protagonists' subjectivities, of places and their haunted entanglements, are intrinsic to the graphic novels and enable them to move with myriad meanings.

Queer Transnationalism and the Politics of Translations

Any understanding of transnationalism is anchored to an understanding of the legal-physical frame surrounding nations and nationalisms; transnationalism attempts to transcend or transit through those frames. Situating and grappling with nationalism remains key to an understanding of communities of belonging or unbelonging. This leads me to ask, how might queer transnationalism change its politics if we understood nationalism itself as an act of translation or postcolonial haunting?

Eve Kosofsky Sedgwick, in her essay "Nationalisms and Sexualities: As Opposed to What?" provides intriguing insight into problems that undergird our understandings of nationalism and sexualities. She writes, "My sense is that an underlying liberal understanding of nationalism as an ideology, as something *against which* there exist conceptual tools to fight, is currently shaping our sense of the relations between nationalism and sexuality in circumscriptive ways."[74] Sedgwick uses anthropologist Benedict Anderson's seminal book on nationalism, *Imagined Communities*, to point out that nationalism seen as an ideology posits an opposition (i.e., liberalism and its antithesis).[75] However, if we think of nationalism as more akin to religion or kinship systems, we could think of a modern organizational logic that could be configured in many different ways.[76] Thus, a cemented idea of "nationalism as ideology" greatly circumscribes our understanding of nationalism and sexualities. Further, Sedgwick adds that the "trope of the other" works in our judgment of nationalism as the repression hypothesis does in pre-Foucauldian configurations of sexualities.[77] Akin to the repression hypothesis, as Sedgwick points out, "the trope of the other in relation to nationalism must almost a priori fail to do justice to the complex activity, creativity, and engagement of those whom it figures simply as relegated objects."[78] Simplistic thinking about homosexuality as the "other" to the nation fails to note different politics that involve and disinvolve different sexualities in various ways through moments of national life.

To explain her thesis further, Sedgwick quotes Anderson, who said, "In the modern world, everyone can, should, will 'have' a nationality, as he or she 'has' a gender."[79] Interpreting Anderson's statement to mean that everyone will have a "sex-gender system" and a "habitation/nation system," Sedgwick emphasizes that this does not mean everyone will have the same sex-gender system congruent to a habitation/nation system.[80] Sedgwick notes how people have different relations to gender-sex and to nation: "It may be that there exists for nations, as for genders, simply no normal way to partake of the categorical definitiveness of the national."[81] Sedgwick notes different examples like the Navajo Nation, Quebec, Hawaii, and African American nationalisms to emphasize that nationalisms and nonnationalisms take many different forms.[82] These myriad forms of subnationalisms complicate and make indefinite wider nationalisms and eschew them even as they partake in them, too. Besides Sedgwick, numerous studies have pointed out exclusions and caveats in Anderson's definition and conceptualization of nations. As Anderson himself acknowledges, "No one has been able to demonstrate decisively either its modernity or its antiquity."[83] For example, Partha Chatterjee, in his intriguing essay "Whose Imagined Community?" draws our attention to certain models of nations, as in Europe and the Americas, that are used to help the postcolonial world imagine themselves in their "anti-colonial resistance and postcolonial misery."[84] Chatterjee bitingly emphasizes, "Even our imaginations must remain forever colonized."[85]

Sedgwick's and Chatterjee's analyses implore us to complicate our understanding of nationalisms and sexualities as active projects of translations. Often when we project a marked difference between Western or Eastern sexualities, or demarcate different ways of "coming out," or even the complete lack of resonance of "coming out" to a non-Western subject, there is a way in which we are writing and thinking more in terms of nationalism as specific identity (i.e., a liberal nation coming out) rather than the complicated terrain of nationalisms and sexualities. For instance, it is important to remember that nationalisms may overlap in the case of dual citizenship, and sexualities intersect with many other variables, such as race, gender, age, nation, and other aspects of identity making. Chatterjee's imploration to examine the ramifications of the Euro-American framing of nations asks us to be aware of the colonization of imaginations, of setting of borders around what can and cannot count as nation.

An attention to maps and borders, with their physical, legal, and imaginative parameters, as well as attempts to subvert them, inspires much transnational work. I suggest that we recognize the slippage in meanings as we work with nationalisms and transnationalisms. In doing so, transnational feminists can uncover playful places of subversion that ostensibly appear nation bound. This chapter has shown how graphic narratives, maps, and translations, with their errors and excesses, anchor the politics of play and hauntings in queer transnational politics. The braided working of play and hauntings constructs meaning-plays and enables a creative negotiation with the changing terrains of nationalisms and transnationalisms. I gesture toward a playful epistemology of being here and there, of articulating and disarticulating identities that works with hauntings all along.

To visualize this gesture, it is useful to think with Judith Butler and Spivak's conversation in *Who Sings the Nation-State?* Butler and Spivak talk about the 2006 protest demonstration in California on the question of "illegal" residents during which the American national anthem was sung in Spanish. Butler recalls a statement from President George W. Bush, who had said that English was the only language that could be used to sing the national anthem, thereby signifying a language of belonging. Butler notes that this does not make the anthem "less sing-able" in another language, "They alter not just the language of the nation but its public space as well."[86] Thinking about queer transnationalism as an active process of translation would enable it to alter didactic claims of sexuality or nation. Indeed, positioning translation—with its meaning-plays—at the heart of queer transnationalism queers translation and haunts it from "coming out" with a singular story of sexual identity or nationalism.

CHAPTER 3

Un-Mithu's Politics

Lingual Anarchy and
Playful Undoings

> What exactly is language here?
> —Rey Chow, *Not like a Native Speaker*

> While playful we have not abandoned ourselves to, nor are we stuck in, any particular "world."
> —Maria Lugones, "Playfulness, 'World'-Travelling, and Loving Perception"

Translations within language structures and within cultural systems involve myriad meaning-plays, as the previous chapter demonstrates. Transnational and postcolonial feminisms constantly grapple with the urgencies of solidarity work and the need to connect across borders, all the while noting the many slippages, binds, errors, and absences that accompany the movement of words, debates, and people across those same borders. My emphasis on meaning-plays centers their repeated occurrence in transnational and postcolonial encounters. If we are alert, we may see these emerge whenever we speak across language and cultural systems. Attentiveness to meaning-plays urges us to broaden our theoretical and practical frames so as to be constantly alive to the resonances of play and haunting. Alertness to meaning plays can help postcolonial and transnational feminisms move beyond static or one-dimensional representations of people and issues as they cross borders, and it can also signal deft negotiations with power. While previous chapters have emphasized the need to undo binary frames, think through categories, and examine meaning-plays, this chapter studies how one Indian artist, Mithu Sen, does all of this by playing with identity and language, specifically, through what she calls "lingual anarchy." Paying close attention to the politics of play and language used by an artist whose work traverses the globe opening up conversations in transnational and postcolonial feminisms about mischievous, subversive politics inspires us to think anew about our methods, approaches, and ways of knowing the "other."

The use of language in colonial and postcolonial settings has received significant attention in postcolonial studies, especially regarding its centrality in continuing the colonizer's mastery over societies, such that acquiring a specific language, such as English or French, is tantamount to acquiring privileges in certain societies. Think, for instance, of Frantz Fanon's accounts in *Black Skin, White Masks*, where in chapter 1, "The Black Man and Language," he points out, "The more the black Antillean assimilates the French language, the whiter he gets—i.e., the closer he comes to becoming a true human being."[1] As a continuous haunting, the master language is never fully in the colonized's grasp. He can never really quite be human. Also emphasizing connections between colonization and language, Rey Chow, in her book *Not like a Native Speaker: On Languaging as a Postcolonial Experience*, draws our attention to call-center workers in India and the Philippines, where workers are trained into an "aesthetics of performativity" and taught to sound American. Chow uses the term "languaging," a concept coined by A. L. Becker, to refer to the complex politics surrounding the use of language in postcolonial contexts.[2] She argues, "Notwithstanding the shock, humiliation, rage, and melancholy involved, the colonized's encounter with the colonizer's language offers a privileged vantage point from which to view the postcolonial situation, for precisely the reason that this language has been imposed from without."[3] Looking at language as a foreign imposition and object, Chow examines "languaging as a type of prostheticization," so that speaking becomes "impermanent, detachable, and (ex)changeable."[4] Chow's emphasis on language as prosthesis does not undercut the importance of language systems as measures of control; rather, as a continuation of the body, though foreign to the body, language as prosthesis enables us to visualize its central role in figuring and disfiguring senses of the self and others. This chapter examines lingual anarchy, linguistic work that plays with and disturbs protocols of language systems. Rather than positioning the postcolonial subject as capable of speaking outside dominant language systems or being read outside them, Mithu Sen's aesthetic politics emphasizes the complicated positionalities of the postcolonial subject as they move through the global economy. As prosthesis, language is a foreign attachment or imposition, and as prosthesis it may also teach us to run in multiple ways. Sen's lingual anarchy plays with language and overturns it to inspire multiple ways of being and belonging in postcolonial, transnational societies.[5]

One can confidently state that a play with language—its rules, grammar, and meanings—is a central thread weaving through Sen's art. As she explains, "Unlanguage is part of a practice I call lingual anarchy, which aims to expose and unsettle how language (often the colonial remnant of English) functions as a hierarchical institution."[6] For me, writing in English about an artist whose expressed intention is to work against its grains, remains a challenge. How do I write about an artist whose modus operandi is to defy classifications, subvert definitions, flee capture, and jostle societal and cultural establishments? In what language should I attempt to write about lingual anarchy, playful undoings, and the exuberant buoyancy in using life as a conduit for art? What translations am I attempting? While conundrums persist in being able to write about Sen, it is inspiring and stirring to make the attempt. A certain capacious broadening of horizons permeates Sen's works and embraces the audience in an infectious revelry. Noting the complexities and excitement in the task of writing about Sen's art practices, I endeavor to address the persisting thread of lingual anarchy in Sen's art—noting all the while its entanglements with themes commenting on capitalism, hospitality, gender, and sexual subversions.

Sen's artwork is always complex, exploring multiple themes that compel us to ask: Is it possible to distance questions of language from gender or capitalism? What interests would we be serving in making these differentiations? Persistent questioning marks my attempts to read Sen's art as we unravel the confluences and trajectories stemming outward, very much like her paintings that display trees with roots spanning outside the picture frames. Working with the impossibility of singling out one issue, I read Sen's politics of lingual anarchy as a motif that weaves its way through multiple works, amplifying the artist's intentions to provide a counterframe for social and political matters. An exuberant play with societal expectations and protocol undergirds the artist's linguistic disruptions. Thus, I read lingual anarchy as a play with language, its subversion. But before moving to an analysis of that aspect of her work, I attempt to situate the creative impetus, macabre dances, and buoyant spirit in her politics of play.[7]

Mithu Sen

Sen's prolific art career has garnered many awards, including the world-renowned Skoda Prize (2010) and the Prudential Eye Award (2015). Easily one of India's most well-known artists, Sen's art trots the globe. Her solo exhibitions and performances have spanned internationally, from *I Hate Pink* in Mumbai (2003), *Nothing Lost in Translation* in Berlin (2010), to *Aphasia* in New York (2016), and *(Un)Mansplaining* in Venice (2019). Those of us who have had the joyous pleasure to interact with Sen have to acknowledge the close alliance between her public artworks/performances and her personal interactions: vibrantly exuberant, warmly hospitable, and incredibly openhearted. It is impossible to separate the personal from the public and political in her works, as is seen in many of her performances and drawings.

Sen is the sole artist in her family, though they share her love of language. She never lived in a big city prior to entering the art world. Her schooling was in Bengali medium, and she loved studying biology. Fascinated with bodies and their entrails, Sen loved to study anatomical representations and draw them. Becoming an art student was unplanned and sporadic. She appeared drenched to the skin for her entrance examination to art school in Santiniketan, India. The World Cup finals were on the same day, and before the interview had even begun, Sen asked the interviewing committee whether she could leave. They looked at her in amazement as she explained her love for sports, namely, football and cricket. So the examining body questioned her about sports instead of art. Considering her career to follow, it should not surprise us that Sen's entrance into art was through sports and play. Her experiences in art school were very liberating; there she was recognized for her work and also considered beautiful. Her agony with her dark-toned skin color had always traveled with her, so she reveled in art school where it was not considered a liability.[8] Sen uses stories prolifically in her works, stories that riff on life experiences and relationships, whether in art school or elsewhere: trying to kill the mosquito that sat on Bengali poet Shankha Ghosh's head when he visited their college, eating dog biscuits at someone's home, or finding a snake in her studio and then displaying a sign, "Snakes are not allowed."[9]

Regardless of how we situate and complicate Sen's personal and public narratives, she continues to surprise and provoke. As viewers and consumers of her art, we soon realize that much of our assessment of Sen's works belongs to us, to our projections, as we actively labor to understand them. Her commentary on capitalism, hospitality, gender, sexuality, and language is incessantly undone and reworked as she continues her conversations with these matters and identities. The yearning to defy containment and play with categories weaves its way through Sen's works; it is her persistent query. Try as we might, it is impossible to frame Mithu Sen.

The Centrality of Play in Sen's Art

I find Maria Lugones's description of play, in the second epigraph of this chapter, to be immensely helpful as I work my way through Sen's aesthetic politics. Lugones differentiates her concept of play from the agonistic theories of Johan Huizinga and Hans-Georg Gadamer. For Huizinga and

Gadamer, play is tied to contest, winning, losing, competence, and rules that govern the game. As Lugones writes, this is about "role-playing": "In role-playing, the person who is a participant in the game has a *fixed conception of him or herself*." The agonistic attitude is contrary to "travelling across 'worlds.'" It is the attitude of a conqueror and an imperialist who violates worlds rather than being able to travel with them. Lugones, in contrast, focuses on "*the attitude that carries us through the activity, a playful attitude, turns the activity into play*." The emphasis on "a playful attitude" in Lugones's work facilitates "travelling across 'worlds.'" Such a playful attitude applies well to Sen's art. Sen subverts a static conception of self and other and her playful works do not compare, contrast, compete, or contest. Rather, their spirited spontaneity exhibits what Lugones highlights: "While playful we have not abandoned ourselves to, nor are we stuck in, any particular 'world.' We *are there creatively*. We are not passive."[10]

Sen's play *with* play is an intriguing phenomenon. Different aspects of play spark her immense artistic repertoire, but to situate play as a mere ingredient or affect in Sen's art making neglects its role in illuminating the various undoings of normative gender and sexuality, hospitality, language, and capitalism, themes that braid through many of her exhibits and performances. In describing her practice as a "play *with* play," I attempt to situate the openhearted, infectious embrace of rupture, confusion, and displacements that enthuse her art and its relationships. But, in addition, and importantly, the artist is playing *with*, rather than against or over, the artistic products and performances. At heart and with heart, they wrench our concepts apart. Sen unceasingly plays with our sensorium of play, pushing limits and crossing thresholds. To further understand the play with play, let us look more closely at some elements of play she uses in her artistic practice.

First, she openly declares herself to be a "trickster" and "prankster."[11] Even a casual encounter with Sen and her works situates this playful ethos at the heart of her politics, both personal and public. She wears vermillion outfits as she performs her art. The color vermillion is considered sacred in Hindu society, whether seen in vermillion flowers that grace religious ceremonies or the vermillion powder that is worn by Hindu women as a symbol of marriage. Although people might expect to hear soulful music fitting the outfit and image she presents, instead they hear Sen's nonlanguage or what sounds like gibberish to their ears. Being a trickster, Sen never lets her art rest. It teases our comfort zones. She never produces what is expected of her. Nancy Adajania puts it well: "In Sen's mercurial works, we may imagine a voice that reverberates: 'I don't become the "me" you have in mind when you summon me.'"[12]

Second, her works prod, nudge, and overturn societal expectations of place, normalcy, value, and good, among other markers. Sen says, "I like to create traps. I like to create questions, and, of course, you can criticize me—I am a catalyst."[13] Think here about the miniature skulls masquerading as teeth in Sen's exhibit *Border Unseen* (2014) or the androgynous voice booming through *iforgotmypenisathome* (2010). Playfully, the artist plants objects, things, voices, emotions, and people at unexpected locations. As we walk into a gallery expecting art as we know it, these surprising encounters offer a humorous jolt and mischievously tease the audience into a space of incessant questioning. Sen's art talks in all tongues and certainly not in one that you expect to hear.

Third, a deconstruction of identity weaves its way through Sen's play in an attempt to undo rigid formulations of self and other. Whether an interrogation of what it means to be an Indian woman, a Bengali woman, an Indian artist, a man, an android, a human-animal, bird, or organs in disarray, Sen's playful revelry with identity illuminates its constructed frame. In *Half Full* (2007), Sen's canvases display her face on animal bodies and human bodies in disarray. Some canvases showcase a deliberately coy Bengali woman, Sen's face, smiling at the viewer only to be instantly displaced by the rest of the presentation consisting of tiger heads, roses, fish, horses, and myriad other references that would usually never be drawn as one body.[14]

Fourth, to situate Sen's politics of play, one has to visualize how the artist moves through walls and borders of different kinds of bodies, both physical and territorial, simultaneously overturning them, piercing them, and subverting their sacrosanct presence. One has to acknowledge that defining Sen's politics of play is bound to be a self-defeating attempt at delineating characteristics of a politics that plays with the attempt to frame, define, contain, and bracket identities, places, emotions, and people. Thinking with the characteristics of Sen's aesthetic politics delineated above and of it being a play *with* play enables us to visualize the "playful attitude" that Lugones emphasizes and how it enables "travelling across 'worlds.'"

To engage further Sen's play *with* play, let's turn to her exhibit *Ahh Taj!!* (2011), in which Sen plays with the name of a popular brand of tea (Taj Mahal Tea) to engage with the marketing of identity. The artist was provoked by the incessant demands of Western curators and audiences for Sen to showcase her inherent "Indian-ness." Marketed as an "Indian female artist," Sen was constantly asked to be Indian in her work. Recall here Trinh T. Minh-ha's words about her own artistic experiences in the "first world": "It still happens that when I'm invited to speak, I'm asked with great expectations to speak as a representative—of a culture, a people, a country, an ethnicity or a gender considered to be mine and my own.

In other words, tell us about Vietnam, be woman, talk Asian, stay within the Third World."[15] Responding to a similar call to be an identity, Sen draws the Taj Mahal, the very epitome of Indian tourism and signifier of undying love. However, her drawing actively subverts the essentialism or unchanging fixity that frames appeals to nationalism and its monuments by drawing portions of the Taj Mahal in different parts of the gallery and gifting her audience pieces of marble as a token of a fragmented Taj Mahal, her exhibit, and identity. Columns and arches of the Taj Mahal frame the doors that lead onto the gallery space, and delicate drawings of the different domes stare down at the audience from the gallery ceiling. The Taj Mahal is everywhere and nowhere in the gallery. Active seeing ponders the impossibility of consuming the "whole" picture. What does it mean to be an "Indian" artist? How do we frame interconnected identities, affiliations that spill over, a self that is fragmented over space and time? By belonging to a nation, do we unbelong from other aspects of self-making? This exhibit clearly displays Sen's play with a Western gaze and its consumption of Indian-ness.

Even when Sen constructs tangible walls and borders, as in her exhibit *Border Unseen* (2014), she attempts to loosen different demarcations. Wendy Brown in her book *Walled States, Waning Sovereignty* describes the proliferation of walls in and in-between nation-states as a dominant characteristic of our contemporary era. However, Brown maintains that these walls are not expressions of swelling state sovereignty. Rather, "while they may appear as hyperbolic tokens of such sovereignty, like all hyperbole, they reveal a tremulousness, vulnerability, dubiousness, or instability at the core of what they aim to express—qualities that are themselves antithetical to sovereignty and thus elements of its undoing."[16] In *Border Unseen*, Sen images a similar political restlessness by creating an eighty-foot sculpture made of teeth and dental polymer that sprawls like a wall throughout the museum space. This wall functions like a usual wall because it demarcates, defines, and territorializes the space. However, it did more (and/or less), as well. By combining the natural and artificial, teeth and polymer, human and nonhuman, Sen comments upon the tenuousness of demarcations. Composed of body parts (e.g., teeth), irregular, undulating, and hot pink in color, Sen's wall combines fear, horror, agony, desire, hunger, hunting, eating, savagery, enunciation, and other gnawing emotions to showcase the subversion of neat demarcations. Among the monstrous sculpture of uneven, pink polymer and teeth (oftentimes shaped as skulls), the viewer sees miniature figures of bodies in embrace or a figure sitting nonchalantly and viewing everything. Where does the wall begin and end? Who constitutes the wall? This wall mouths a different language: nonlinear, unsovereign, personal, and political.

These two examples, selected from Sen's spiraling artistic repertoire, illustrate her explicit play with national identity and territoriality, both personal and political. The play *with* play in Sen's works attempts to unravel and undo structures of categorization. Sen's addition of "un-" before words, for example, un-forbidden, un-institutional, un-medium, un-grammar, un-gallery, un-border, and a plethora of other words that haunt her exhibits and its descriptions, attests to her creative play with various thresholds and their rigid definitions. While "un" is very different from "non," as it does not posit a cancelling out, destruction, or an opposition, the term "un" positioned before much of Sen's playful adventures is irreverently investigative: What is it that makes a gallery? Why is grammar important? Who lives at the border of institutions? What institutions do forbidden practices help to keep in place? These and a host of questions proliferate as we navigate Sen's art and endeavor to see/feel/breath with it, rather than think about formulaic solutions. Invoking Gayatri Chakravorty Spivak, "Deconstruction is precisely not taking everything away and breaking everything apart. What people forget is that there is a C-O-N in the middle of that word, because Derrida was redoing Heidegger's idea of *Destruktion*. Titles like *Deconstruction and Reconstruction of* . . . are, from this point of view, just the tiniest bit embarrassing."[17] In the spirit of deconstruction, it remains important to constantly engage with institutions, ideas, and theories; we must read and re-read to be able to fathom a world otherwise. The "con" draws attention to the slipperiness of reality, the complicity of actors and agencies, and interactive entanglements, where one searches for what lies beneath the surface, knowing all the while its effusive and framed nature. To "be framed" is also to "con" as Judith Butler reminds us in *Frames of War*.[18] So, Sen's framed and unframed art works incessantly play *with* play, unmooring us from varied unpossibilities.

Lingual Anarchy and Other Undoings

Being a Poet

Sen's play with language is central to her artistic performances, exhibits, and life works. She was born into a family that celebrated the beauty of language. Her mother is a poet, and Sen grew up reading and writing poetry. Her poetry is written in Bengali, the language she grew up with and also the primary medium of instruction in school and college. Further, she spent a great deal of time in Santiniketan, the town of India's famous Bengali poet Rabindranath Tagore and the vibrant center of Bengali song and poetry. She has always declared, "I am a Poet," which also serves as the title of her performance at the Tate Modern, London, in 2013. Recognizing the explicit power hierarchies that code acceptable speech and thereby legitimate bodies, Sen created for her performance an alternate language of gibberish nonsense and made a book of poetry out of it. Courageously, Sen, as the self-proclaimed poet in *I Am a Poet*, read out verses of ostensibly senseless jargon. She invited the audience to read out loud with her, and embody with her the declaration "I am a Poet." With the veritable panoply of sound montage created by the voices of different poets, Sen and the audience moved the gallery to a space where a proper code for language ceased to exist, and everyone could belong in this space as poets, by unbelonging from w-rite ways of being and doing language. This undoing of space and protocol weaves through Sen's creative expressions, and in *I Am a Poet*, she plays with the power in language by displacing it and creating communities of (un)belonging. She also works for people who are made to unbelong involuntarily. At the second Dhaka Art Summit (2014), Sen created an installation called *Batil-Kobitaoli* [Poems declined], which showcased words of rejection sent to aspiring Bengali poets. Thus the politics of language in containing imaginations and identities runs through varied lines in Sen's works.[19]

Although scholars have long recorded the use of language to create communities of belonging and have noted the exclusions to this framing of a political imagination based on a very European experience, Sen skillfully draws our attention to the possibilities of different forms of unbelonging that deepen inclusion.[20] The artist's personal experiences influence the politics of her art. After moving to Delhi, where English remains a prominent mode of communication, she felt increasingly alienated and humiliated because her lack of English proficiency colored people's responses to her. While *I Am a Poet* creates an alternate language through unlanguage, many of Sen's other works play with language in other ways, explicitly and implicitly. Sen's undoing of the rules of grammar and meaning in English set the tone for her persistent practice of lingual anarchy. While knowing English sets the standards for respectability and legitimacy, English as the language of power also frames the Western gaze on the exotic "other," people without language—or at best the language of the child and not fully human. Fanon's emphasis on the colonial bestiary haunts the scene of language where the "other" is without language and is animal. Moreover, English has traveled through postcolonial societies in interesting ways, and many, including Salman Rushdie, celebrate the hybridized English of the colonies as a different kind of English with creative potential. In *The Empire Writes Back*, Bill Ashcroft, Gareth Griffiths, and Helen Tiffin point out, "The existence of varieties of English has meant that the concept of a standard English has been exploded, the very existence of postcolonial literatures completely undermines any project for literary studies in English which is postulated on a single culture masquerading as the originating centre."²¹ While postcolonial engagements with language are various and varied, Sen's politics of lingual anarchy brings to mind many conversations on the relevance, hierarchies, subversions, and other possibilities imminent in language, as well as outside it.

In *Aphasia* (2016) at the Guggenheim in New York, Sen combined film, performance, and poetry in nonlanguage to subvert expectations of her as an international artist. *Aphasia* was a critique of the function of language and its embeddedness within societal protocols and hierarchies. The prestigious event, called Thinking Practice, was an invitation to selected Asian artists to reflect on their art and activism, as this was relevant to US institutions. The invited artists were given a maximum of nineteen minutes and informed that there would be strict adherence to time limits. Artists were asked to be creative, focus on one work, and were encouraged to engage in performance.²² Sen appeared on stage brandishing a glowing wand, speaking gibberish, and gesturing and performing in front of a screen intercut with images from her artwork overlaid with words and instructions from the invitation, including the deadlines, time limits, and other guidelines. The audience saw images of Sen protesting in *I Am Not Me*, Johannesburg, 2012; the hot-pink wall from *Border Unseen*, East Lansing, Michigan, 2014; bodies of hair from various parts of the human body that were shown in *Breathing*, New York, 2004; images from *Half Full*, 2007; and a plethora of other images following in quick succession on screen. All the while, Sen was gesturing at the images in a language known only to her, playfully mimicking them, and playing with her host's invitation to focus on just one work. The mirth in her performance and its biting, as well as surprisingly generous humor, are clearly discernible. The question-and-answer session that followed two days of performance work was equally provocative. On being asked about the role of performance in her work and the changing tone of her art, Sen responded in her unlanguage. Her host spoke affirmatively about the humor she used in response to her "dictatorial directions" and the "magical" proclivity of artists who are "just ready to play."²³

Aphasia brings together many aspects of Sen's works on lingual anarchy, gender, sexuality, nationality, capitalism, and the Western gaze, all humorously and playfully presented. She showcased the relevance of her work as an Asian artist through her lingual anarchy, using language without rules of protocol and meaning-making. However, it is simplistic to think of lingual anarchy as a mere strategy or method for Sen's performance. Alongside the play with words, let us not forget the images from a decade of work fleeting on the screen and the body of a female artist gesturing with a wand, with her long, black hair, flowing dress, and exotic persona. How does language operate in this scenario? What would we expect her to say?

And, are we prepared to hear her say something different? Lingual anarchy works as a catalyst through Sen's performances, inspiring the audience to be active and to think, not simply consume the status quo, whether through the consumption of Eastern art and/or the consumption of the artist as an authentic representation of the "other." Think of an Indian woman gesturing toward breathing pubic hair, laughing with her own art, courageously, and insolently standing before an international audience speaking her own language! Defying norms of sexuality, gender conformism, and stereotypes, Sen's lingual anarchy is a spirited postcolonial moment of play and subversion.

Language and Belonging

Lingual anarchy is an active postcolonial method. Like Suniti Namjoshi's play with becoming animal in chapter 1 and like the unmappings of sexualities and identities in the graphic narratives discussed in chapter 2, Sen's method of lingual anarchy functions by attending to postcolonial hauntings and uses them to play and travel through many spaces, home and abroad, questioning the borders it travels and transgresses. A particularly striking example of the work of lingual anarchy is Sen's video installation *I have only one language; it is not mine*, which she created in 2014 for the Kochi-Muziris Biennale in India. For three days Sen lived in a government orphanage for young girls in Kerala, India, not as Sen but as Mago, who is homeless and speaks her own language. Mago, with her child Bonzai, which is also a doll, enters the lives of the girls in the orphanage, many of whom have survived experiences of violence and sexual abuse and live with histories of traumatic hauntings. Mago speaks her own language, and after much questioning from the children at the orphanage, she continues to speak it and live with the children, amidst great mirth, amusement, and bewilderment. Mago records her interactions with a devise she wears around her neck, and the children also turn the gaze back on Mago to record her. In the video piece, unfocussed images and blurred-out profiles that resemble comic images keep everyone anonymous except Mago. We see the contours of profiles and objects in red and the occasional glimpse of multihued images. A serene voice, speaking gibberish, beckons us toward lost memories and forgotten lands. This voice belongs to Mago, and it frames the performance. The children involve Mago in their daily activities, watching TV, eating, washing their hands after a meal, and doing various other daily chores. The companionship of a being with nonlanguage makes every activity a playful one, opening spaces for experimentation and trial and for abundant revelry.

Mago has no specified human lineage, and she leaves as unexpectedly as she has appeared in the orphanage. The young girls watch from behind their iron gates as Mago leaves their world. Sen's play with language through this performance centered unlanguaging as a politics of hope, whereby one could live with the help of the rays of sunlight that creep in, that infiltrate even the most haunting traumas. Unlanguage acts here as a catalyst for mirth, play, questioning, and a fleeting respite to a world beyond the gates of the orphanage and the status quo of the world at large. The children speak the language of their world, but has it embraced them or let them belong?

I have only one language; it is not mine frames this performance, saturating it with sadness and laughter. These lines from Jacques Derrida's *Monolingualism of the Other or the Prosthesis of Origin* seethe through this performance and open his text to multiple meanings as well. When Derrida says these words, he conveys the complexity of being monolingual and knowing only one language, one that does not belong to him.[24] He emphasizes the tensions in language communities around questions of rightful belonging and his own struggles as a Franco-Maghrebian with issues of language acquisition, citizenship, and belonging to the French nation. Derrida maintains that when he writes about knowing only one language, a language that does not belong to him, he is not saying that the language is "foreign" to him.[25] There is an important difference between the two, because while foreignness implies a certain external quality and a separation from what is native, Derrida's articulation seeks to convey a very different politics. What does it mean to be defined by a language that does not let one belong to it? How do we relate to the language of the colonizer when it frames and defines who we are? Numerous queries jostle for attention through Derrida's enunciation, drawing out the agonies of postcolonial existences. In the site of the orphanage in Kerala where children live through their experienced brutalities, what does it mean to unlanguage the present? What work does lingual anarchy do in the lives of the children as they see the world through the gates of the orphanage? Sen does not provide an easy answer. Instead, she compels us to question and ponder, not simply the courageous nature of her performance but also the unfair and warped present moment that it seeks to undo.

Technologies of Exclusion

Sen has never been afraid to make a fool of herself. We soon realize as we watch the artwork and performances that we are not laughing at Sen but at ridiculous social customs, internalized stereotypes of people and identities, and our supposedly sophisticated knowledge systems. Take, for instance, *UnMYthU: UnKIND(s) Alternatives*, her performance with Alexa,

Amazon's smart-home speaker, in 2018 for the ninth Asia Pacific Triennial of Contemporary Art (APT9) held in Brisbane. This performance-exhibit, composed of large drawings on kozo paper, instructions for the audience, contracts, bodies falling outside the frames, Sen conversing with and asking questions of Alexa as she points to related images, and a host of other dynamics, was a manifestation of Sen's ongoing UnMYthU project. The large diagrams, drawn with the precision of scientific illustrations with neat labels and arrows, are interrupted by all kinds of bodies. Humans, boats, and animals cross their framed, diagrammatic enclosures and wander forth, overflowing the frames as if to riddle our very understanding of bodies and relationships between them. For example, while half a boat resides in one frame, the other half wanders to the next framed painting-diagram. Alongside, concomitantly, persistently, Sen plays with artificial intelligence (AI) and a recorded understanding of the world. While each component of the exhibit cum performance merits individual attention for its details and interesting nuances, it also becomes important to see-feel-hear how they all work together—their composite politics.

Figure 1 is an image from the performance-exhibit showing Sen conversing with Alexa and pointing at her drawings. She asks Alexa for definitions, speaks gibberish, animatedly walks around, and gestures. Sen tells Alexa

Figure 1. Mithu Sen in her performance *UnMYthU: UnKIND(s) Alternatives*, talking with Alexa against the backdrop of her paintings, 2018. *QAGOMA* 2019, Queensland Art Gallery—Gallery of Modern Art. Source: Mithu Sen.

that she loves her and asks multiple questions. She asks Alexa whether she speaks Bengali, who is a refugee, what is the meaning of waterboarding, does Alexa know the name of the boy who drowned in the ocean while crossing the sea from Syria, what comprises an agreement, who is considered dead on arrival, and a host of other questions with direct linkages to global politics and the drawings behind her. Alexa answers some of the questions with rigid dictionary definitions. At other times, Alexa mishears Sen's questions, which could be attributed to Sen's accent, for example, when she answers with a definition of diffusion when asked about refugees. Sen laughs through the mistakes, keeps prodding Alexa, moving persistently on toward grim news and realities from contemporary issues. The device that has been engineered to answer all questions is blissfully apolitical or maybe very political in conforming to predesigned answers that maintain the violent status quo of the world.

What does it mean to pair explicit instructions for the audience guided with arrows and signage, alongside Sen's dialogue with Alexa, which is also driven through AI rules? Why does Sen ask Alexa about waterboarding while showing images of its occurrence? What are we to make of gender politics, as Alexa gives a dictionary definition of gender while Sen points to her drawing of a "plagiarized dick"? Sen's play with language, whether through her explicit questioning or her speaking gibberish with Alexa, positions lingual anarchy as a political strategy to unlayer the many levels of hypocrisy and deception in our social and political world. Bitingly pertinent and startling in its political directness, this performance-exhibit sears the skin of political normalcy, social protocol, and the uses of technology.

Lingual anarchy has many functions. It humorously unveils hypocrisies and regimented protocols, as well as opens the door to flights of fancy and the imagination; we see how the world can change when we play with its language. Rather than maneuvering us outside society at large, like a beautiful sound that makes our mind drift away from the realities of the present, Sen's play with language and sound is of a different kind. Often, a soulful rendition acts as the conduit for gibberish, as in the opening of the film based on Sen's work for the Kochi-Muziris Biennale. The unusual juxtaposition of harmonious melody with unharmonious language is just one example of the anomalies that abound in Sen's works. The contradictions work alongside the play with language and constitute the overall politics of lingual anarchy. Think, for instance, about Sen's dialogue with Alexa and her performative show of affection for the device when she tells Alexa that she loves her. What does love mean to a computer-generated figure? Alexa does not know the boy from Syria who drowned in the ocean, nor does she live with refugees. Why does Sen ask her these questions? Indeed, who is a refugee? When does one stop becoming one? Trinh T. Minh-ha ponders the slippage between "refuge" and "refuse" and narrates about how refugees live through refusals from governments and societies.[26] Sen's questioning about refugees to Alexa can make us think about their lives at the borders of refusals, by governments and technologies. Lingual anarchy functions through these questions about systems, political and technological, and reads their inclusions and exclusions.

Also, why is Alexa a woman? Is virtual assistance more trustworthy when we speak to Alexa rather than Alex, for instance?[27] The gendering of artificial intelligence is an intriguing phenomenon, knowing fully well that capitalism has always used gender to generate profit. Much has been written recently about Alexa's role as an instrument of "surveillance capitalism," where she records our commands and provides Amazon with buying histories and trends.[28] Moreover, artificial intelligence is always being advanced as the information to expand and improve comes from consumers. Our voice recordings are used by Amazon to consistently improve Alexa and make her even more intuitive and humanlike—extrahuman, actually—so that she can appear human. Thus when Sen talks to Alexa about myriad issues in politics and society, it helps showcase the inadequacy of artificial intelligence and its constructed nature; and in a macabre way, it shows us the convoluted nature of technology and language. Technology does not simply obey language as its coder and programmer, it also uses it and mimics it. Technology fashions language in political economy to make more money and create citizens who think they are actually making the decision. Reinvoking Trinh, the framer can also be framed.[29] Sen's performance inspires these thoughts as I ponder the possibilities of radical politics in neoliberal times. Further, what are relations between technology and art? None of these questions, as I have extolled through this chapter, have an easy answer. However, Sen's play with language continues to make us question and endeavor to see/hear/feel anew.

Language and Possession

Sen's art performances provoke reactions, questioning, and thinking. Her play with language wraps around many aspects of our contemporary life: technology, patriarchy, migration, homelessness, and other issues. In *(Un)Mansplaining*, presented at the 2019 Venice Biennale (figure 2), Sen brought together many aspects of her works with lingual anarchy. Dressed in vermillion and with her hair down and brandishing her sword of gibberish, Sen stunned Venice with her outright critique of male privilege, White privilege, the Western gaze, and a playful push toward possibilities otherwise. A male art critic had written about Sen's performance as being possessed, which inspired Sen's play with the idea of a possessed woman and with women

Figure 2. Mithu Sen in her performance *(Un)Mansplaining*, Venice Biennale, 2019. Source: Mithu Sen.

being possessed, in general. Sen responds with an explicit stereotypical performance of possession in *(Un)Mansplaining*. The stereotypical possession depicts a woman in the hold of a powerful spirit and without her own volition to act or speak. The only difference between a subject possessed who is made to perform, guided by a spirit, and the woman in vermillion is the accompaniment of lingual anarchy pouring forth from the lips of the possessed artist defying definition, containment, and capture. Appearing possessed, all the while speaking nonsensical rhetoric, or could it be the purest form of Sanskrit, or Urdu, or some other language that the Western world wants to hear, whether as fetish or as music, Sen's performance in *(Un)Mansplaining* is spiritful, buoyant, and tremendously creative.

(Un)Mansplaining was part of *She Persists*, a group show of twenty female artists from around the world. Sen's performance included a prerecorded voice collage of male critics and scholars, collected from YouTube, commenting on art and feminism. Sen raised her own voice above this sound landscape, speaking gibberish, while the seated audience grappled to understand its meaning. Figure 2 is a photograph from the performance and shows Sen speaking her own language amidst the audience's gaze. Moments of silence and music punctuated the performance strategically and dramatically.[30] Sen seldom rehearses her onsite performances. However, extensive planning precedes all her performances and exhibits, including the use of

social media to invite audiences, spur curiosity, and frame the performance, or perhaps unframe is more appropriate here, as the audience oftentimes walks right into traps or spaces that they seldom anticipate. In *(Un)Mansplaining*, Sen was the exotic goddess in her flowing dress with pleated ruffles and long sleeves—Bengali fashion from many decades ago—and shells adorning her waist. This irreverent goddess, appearing possessed, extolled the audience to examine their possession. In Sen's words, "the deeper the viewers' (the onsite viewer and the online viewer, along with the live streaming) fantasy of the exotic goddess is fetishised and sexualised, the more likely they are to think I am possessed. But, in fact, it is they who are possessed with the idea of fantasy. I am playing with them all. I am playing with their need to always explain to me, to control and overshadow me. I wear my exotica and singular vulnerability with pride."[31]

Responding directly to audiences' and critics' enthusiasm to define her according to their lenses and worldviews, Sen feeds the fetish to reveal their biases. Oftentimes described as childish or exotic or as dark humor and eroticism, Sen's works emphasize these qualities to turn them on their head or unhinge them from their foundational pillar. That is why the performance is called *(Un)Mansplaining*. Through lingual anarchy Sen dislodges communication through established protocols of language-based hierarchies. Working with the power of language to script society, the artist creates its nemesis, its undoing. Sen's doings are to undo social hierarchies and oppressive structures of power. However, let us not forget, as Butler reminds us in *Undoing Gender*, that "becoming undone" can be both bad and good. Sometimes becoming undone can thwart the ability to live. In addition, sometimes, "the experience of a normative restriction becoming undone can undo a prior conception of who one is only to inaugurate a relatively newer one that has greater livability as its aim."[32] By building her politics of social justice on expanding and deepening paradigms of livability outside singular explanations, fetishized gazes, and privileges to contain, Sen inspires new ways of seeing and being.

Un-Conclusion

The few, of many, works I have analyzed so far offer a sense of the spirit of play flowing through Sen's works of lingual anarchy. I have not maintained a time-based chronology in describing Sen's exhibits or performances. Earlier works creep into later exhibits, whether as shadow politics that linger rhizomatically, or literally in exhibits of her unsold earlier works, or as she covers earlier works with shimmering paint as in *Twinkle Twinkle* (2012), exhibited in Copenhagen. Her creative politics displaces lineages and trajectories and is uncomfortably untimely. As Derrida asks in *Specters of Marx*, "what happens when *time itself* gets 'out of joint,' dis-jointed, disadjusted, disharmonic, discorded, or unjust? *Ana-chronique?*" Here Derrida converses with the ghosts of Hamlet and Marx's love of Shakespeare to think with specters and their untimeliness, how they appear and reappear without us really knowing whether it is an appearance or a reappearance. Derrida situates this untimeliness as a question of justice if we want to move beyond totalizing conceptions of justice that settle the question for all times.[33] When time is "out of joint," as Derrida emphasizes, narratives of progress or regression do not encompass the work of justice that has to work with hauntings. Yes, in Sen's work time is certainly out of joint. Whether it is the asynchronous nature of Sen's art or its appearance and reappearance in different exhibition sites, her art moves through frames and is "ana-chronique." Defying possession and appearing possessed to play with the audience, Sen's spectral politics haunts a postcolonial sensorium.

Although lingual anarchy has been a persisting cord through Sen's works, there are many kinds of anarchies—or the yearning to inspire a world with no rules—that suffuse her aesthetic politics. Alongside vibrant humor, hauntingly dark at times, we can also discern the trickster waiting for us around the scary canopy of hair or images of blood and other matters oozing through unskinned bodies. Sen does not fall prey to the easy tokenization of the trickster figure, for example, as seen in narratives of Indigenous humor where the native *should* be funny.[34] Rather, through a deft play with the grotesque and beautiful, animals and human, men and women, life and death, Sen startles and jolts her audiences, or coperformers as she calls them, to unmoor from expectations and protocol. In this performance, do not be averse to being a fool. Lugones expresses this spirit beautifully: "Playfulness is, in part, an openness to being a fool, which is a combination of not worrying about competence, not being self-important, not taking norms as sacred and finding ambiguity and double edges a source of wisdom and delight."[35]

Writing about Mithu Sen is a process of learning. As I write, I learn and unlearn. Through my mind's eye, I continue to stare mesmerized at the broken pieces of marble from *Ahh Taj*, the pile of rejected manuscripts from *Poems Declined*, the vermillion outfit from *(Un)Mansplaining*, and the fleeting images from her many works during *Aphasia*. I encounter these images-performances and make them my own. Sen's works unfurl a curious intimacy and play with our relations to each other and to the world. After my first meeting with Sen in her art studio in New Delhi, she presented me with the catalogue for her exhibit *It's Good to Be Queen* with the following words written on the first page: "To another queen Sushmita." In this postcolonial kingdom, play reigns supreme.

CHAPTER 4

Feminist Transnationalism and the Political Dimension of Friendships

Thinking through Mithu Sen's *It's Good to Be Queen*

In 2006 Mithu Sen was a guest in New York at the Bose Pacia Gallery as an artist in residence. The resulting exhibit, *It's Good to Be Queen*, evolved as a response to a handwritten note that was left for her at her apartment in New York. It reads: "Dear Guest, Please use one set of bed covers/pillows etc. what's on the bed for your use. Make sure the bed room does not have hair on the floor. We will keep everything tidy for your use also. Thanks."[1] In response to the note, Sen created art installations throughout her apartment that subverted, questioned, and reflected on friendships and guest-host relational dynamics. She exhibited her blurred status as simultaneously friend and host, stranger and guest, in a space that is personal and public, apartment and art gallery. As instructed, Sen did not leave hair on the floor, but she did make its presence palpable by placing it all over the house in installations like "hair on two serving plates" and "objects with hair on the wall."[2] In addition, she was simultaneously tidy and untidy in playful receptivity to the note's asking her to expect a reciprocal tidiness in response to her being tidy. Sen required visitors to wear gloves if they wanted to touch anything.[3] Simultaneously, Sen is intimately untidy in her artistic exuberance and the self-reflective aesthetic adventures she creates to highlight the artist as friend, guest, host, and queen. As Irina Aristarkhova explains:

> Sen takes on the role of Queen. As queen, she is hosting and holding: people, guests, animals, birds, plants, and artifacts. A queen does what she wants, without reference to human laws of hospitality. . . . Kings and queens are unlike mortals, "ordinary people," and they claim their special status in different ways in different places. Often it involves a special and

usually privileged relationship to the laws of hospitality: to animals (hunting), to birds (caging), to people (ruling), to land (owning) and to gods and goddesses (kinship). In other words, the human law of hospitality does not bind a queen in the same way as an ordinary woman. She can leave her guests any time she wants, even at the most crucial time. She does not have to serve, to please or entertain.[4]

As queen, Sen defies a normative subjectivity that would extol her to "be" and to "do" within a stipulated protocol. She is the queen, a transnational queen, an Indian in New York displaying the politics of being a guest/host and an insider/outsider in a space inviting her artistic incursions. Sen writes, "Welcome, negotiate, become aware, and lose yourself if you are still able."[5]

This exhibit was not Sen's first work on what she calls "radical hospitality," nor was it her last. In 2017, a decade after *It's Good to Be Queen*, Sen startled audiences in Los Angeles with her art project *UNhome in City IF Angels*. This art project, based on a two-month residency, describes "UNhome" as an unjudgmental space of *acceptance*, not merely *tolerance*.[6] Her impetus to unplan and unhome so that we can be comfortable with strangeness and strangers gathered momentum when she was literally unhomed from her exhibit venue on the evening of her opening.[7] Initially, Sen had unplanned the event at the home of a philosophy professor in Los Angeles. On the day of the event, he was stunned to discover that there was no art, or his definition of art, and as a result, the philosophy professor displaced Sen from her venue. Unhomed gathered layers of irony through the physical dislocation of the project. The dislocation did not at all upset Sen's explicit intention to unhome through an unplanned artistic play with hospitality and ways we relate to one another. Eventually, she met with guests at a park in Los Angeles, around a red blanket procured from someone's car, and with flowers scattered on the ground. With her audience, Sen started a conversation about friendships, people we meet, encounters, and our vulnerabilities. The audience gradually participated with their own stories and questions. The deterritorialization of the proper place for art accompanied an intimate conversation about building deeper connections. Sen's aesthetic politics wanted to draw out that "Home is in the un-home."[8]

Sen's 2017 art project proceeded absent an artifact we can tangibly hold as "art." In *It's Good to Be Queen*, it was Sen herself who was absent on the day of the opening; she roamed around New York in a red double-decker bus. The parallel absence of artifact and artist in projects on radical hospitality point toward an unwavering play with expectations and the protocols of being in place. Redefining spaces for hospitality by becoming queen, Sen strives to create playful modes of friend-making that might dislocate entrenched communities of belonging.

As a transnational artist who is making space outside her own national frame, Sen's playful subversion offers an invaluable prism for rethinking the nature of transnational friendships. Her work prompts us to ask what it means to forge democratic feminist transnational friendships. An answer to this question requires we grapple with unequal power relations both within and between nations. Adding the possibility of friendship to transnational relations remains incredibly difficult in the face of such unequal power relations. Democratizing transnational relations involves facing power hierarchies and noticing the politics implicit in traveling between different spaces. So this chapter is written with an almost impossible aim: to identify the possibilities for forging democratic feminist transnational friendships. I suggest that the space for possibilities, in the vast sea of impossibilities that could deter such friendships, will be found in playful subversions, in the willingness to be haunted, and in acts of resistance that can showcase power relations and provide a space to think and be otherwise. *It's Good to Be Queen* exemplifies this endeavor with its art, politics, and playful tug at the haunted borders of differences.

We have seen how Sen's politics of lingual anarchy, along with her performative praxis, urges a reconsideration of dominance and hierarchy in communicative practices and relations and offers other ways of seeing and being. Here I continue the conversation by analyzing *It's Good to Be Queen* as a particular haunting in transnational feminist praxis. This exhibition offers insights into Sen's mischievously playful artistic practice and illustrates a postcolonial haunting, where power structures haunt friendship even as postcolonial friendship haunts the flow of power. What are the power relations that frame transnational border crossing, and can these power relations be renegotiated through vibrant friendships? How do we build intimate relational ties in the shadow of neoliberal political regimes, colonial histories, global capitalism, and heavily stratified inter- (and intra-) social dynamics? Can we imagine ways to connect with each other that neither ignores power disparities nor keeps us from thriving and connecting in friendship, both despite and even through such disparities? More fundamental, this chapter addresses how one can be a friend across communities of belonging that value similarity over difference, the familiar over the strange.

I begin with a look at the "politics" of friendship and analyze its framework. Political theory has historically depicted friendship as a fraternal association that aids in the construction of national belonging. With a detour through Derrida's work on radical democracy and friendship, I question whether friendship can be just as important for radical feminist democracy and transnational relations as it is for any sense of national belonging. In other words, I ask, can friendships be an exemplification of radical feminist democracy, or are friendships destined to be fraternally biased and based?

To expand the concept of friendship in this way, I rely on conversations among feminists to tell us about how these issues of friendship and solidarity have traveled through feminist theory and suggest ways that we can add to the conversation with Sen's counterpolitics. In conversation with theorist-artists, such as Sen, Leela Gandhi, Irina Aristarkhova, Chandra Talpade Mohanty, Audre Lorde, bell hooks, and others, I argue that querying (and queering) transnational friendships will offer us a space for politics that can redraw our cartographies of struggle. Although my earlier discussion of queer transnationalism showcase braided maps and their meaning-plays, this chapter offers a way to relate and travel through state-bound maps while keeping alive a commitment to democratic feminist transnational politics. An in-depth look at Sen's *It's Good to Be Queen* will illustrate the shape and movement of these nonfraternal concepts of friendship. I engage with Sen's exhibit here primarily through Irina Aristarkhova's description and analysis of the exhibit and theorize its playful subversion of expectations of hospitality and friendships that help us see the spirited buoyancy at the heart of feminist transnational relations. In conclusion, I draw from feminist-queer theory to address a question that Derrida poses with passionate intensity: "When will we be ready for an experience of freedom and equality that is capable of respectfully experiencing that friendship, which would at last be just, just beyond the law, and measured up against its measurelessness?"[9]

Democracy and the Political Dimension of Friendships

Friendships are political and related to the workings of democracy. As friendships form, they create inclusions and exclusions in the name of creating community, a sense of belonging, and the solidarity indispensable for acting in unison. But at the same time, friendships can also disrupt and crosscut political associations when they center unity and loyalty above any particular political agenda or disagreement. When friendships cross borders, as they do in transnational friendships, they have the potential to, for example, work at cross-purposes to any imperial habit of colonizing an Other. Before moving on to how Sen's work opens up new possibilities of radically democratic transnational friendship, I discuss the politics of friendship as delineated in political theory and feminist theory, beginning with the manner in which the nation is founded on fraternal bonds. A feminist transnationalism premised on friendships would have to counter the homogenizing vision of such brotherhood and its politics of exclusion. For instance, writing about border-crossing friendships in their volume *Dissident Friendships: Feminism, Imperialism, and Transnational Solidarity*, Elora

Halim Chowdhury and Liz Philipose point out, "Dissident friendships, then, are potentially transformative, personally and socially transformative, and in many cases, subversive, as [Leela] Gandhi says, 'a breach . . . in the fabric of imperial inhospitality.'"[10] Chowdhury and Philipose draw our attention to the agonizing labor of creating meaningful friendships that can work through asymmetrical power lines and move beyond simply "tolerating" the other in one's space, which may be a foil to structural conditions of inhospitality as seen, for example, in immigration laws. Our conversations about hospitality, tolerance, and friendship are often divorced from each other, but like Sen, whose aesthetic politics displays the futility of such separations, feminist activists and theorists have also noted the entangled nature of these relations in their own work. An analysis of democracy as a political form full of possibilities yet unrealized undergirds Derrida's work on radical democracy and the role of friendships.

This section engages with the ideal of radical democracy in the work of Derrida. While sameness and equality of virtue cement friendships in classical political theory, Derrida questions whether other forms of friendship are possible in the context of a democracy yet to come:

> For democracy remains to come; this is its essence in so far as it remains: not only will it remain indefinitely perfectible, hence always insufficient and future, but, belonging to the time of the promise, it will always remain, in each of its future times, to come: even when there is democracy, it never exists, it is never present, it remains the theme of a nonpresentable concept. Is it possible to open up to the "come" of a certain democracy which is no longer an insult to the friendship we have striven to think beyond the homo-fraternal and phallogocentric schema?[11]

For Derrida, democracy remains a promise awaiting fruition. He engages with regime types that "*present themselves as* democratic" (i.e., popular democracy, parliamentary democracy, liberal democracy, Christian democracy, etc.) and ponders the discourse that defines democracy with rigidity and truism.[12] Derrida provides a provocative platform to inspire a democratic dialogue about democracy. Speaking "democratically about democracy" becomes a problem when one ascribes a singular tenet or an "idea" to it.[13] Democracy, to Derrida, is "interminable in its incompletion."[14] Thinking of democracy as a moving horizon, forever incomplete, incessantly endless and ongoing, puts democracy with and beyond the liberal right to vote, freedom of press, right to work, and so on. I argue that thinking of democracy in this way, as a moving horizon filled with spectral visitations alerting us to its incompleteness, moves us toward "becoming queen" in a feminist way. Thinking in a democratic manner about democracy has to be process oriented and take into account the exclusions and investments in any definition of democracy within a specific sociopolitical frame. Working with a conception of democracy "to come" enables a hopeful striving toward more and more democracy; this is a productive project for feminisms that seek to build further inclusions in the political realm.[15] How will Derrida help us envisage a friendship that speaks to the aspirations of radical democracy and enables us to think about democratic potentials beyond the fraternal and patriarchal frame that pervades social-political life?

Derrida's analysis deconstructs the national moorings of friendship, where friends are active agents in cementing a national democratic imagination. He invokes the figure of the "friend" who incessantly appears as the "brother" in the act and place of politics. He recognizes that the association of "friend" and "brother" belongs to a "*familial, fraternalist* and thus *androcentric* configuration of politics." Politics as centered on the state hankers for some commonality based on blood, birth, or nature. As Derrida reminds us, democracy, in its republican mode, upholds equality, liberty, and fraternity. Repeatedly and significantly, he writes about how democracy is always associated with an intrinsic "fraternization," though this does not entirely divorce women from its proceedings, and Derrida also points out that "fratriarchy" may "include" women (e.g., cousins or sisters). However, the politics of inclusion has many nuances, and inclusion does not mean being rendered equal. Derrida asks: "What happens when, in taking up the case of the sister, the woman is made a sister? And a sister a case of the brother?" Such an inclusion may mean assimilation or rendering "docile." The links among democracy, patriarchy, and "fraternization" remain undeniable, and Derrida points out that patriarchy holds out the promise of fraternization.[16] Fraternal friendships are intimately bound together with state-based politics, democracies, and patriarchies, providing them with infrastructural cohesion and legitimacy. For a feminist transnational project working toward democratic friendships, it remains critically important to recognize the fraternal underpinnings in a national project if we are to move with democracy, the democracy yet to come. When feminist transnationalism is built on a celebration of differences, it remains pivotal to think about how this fraternal bonding can be subverted.

Derrida traces the politics of friendship through selected figures in the history of political theory.[17] To Aristotle, friendship is a preeminently political concern that answers questions of justice.[18] In *The Eudemian Ethics*, Aristotle raises the question of what is just in friendship and sees politics as generating "the most friendship possible." However, the emphasis on friendship does not mean that everyone can become a friend. It is a matter of judgment, choice, and the passage of time that enables one to select correctly. Aristotle speaks about giving preference to "*certain*" friends, for friends need a certain virtue to be considered a viable friend. Moreover, primary friendships necessitate an "equality of virtue" between friends. Other, lesser forms of friendship, "with children, animals, and the wicked," do not need "equality in virtue." Derrida traces the need for friends as a propellant for effective politics throughout trajectories of political theory in Montaigne and others, where political friendships make us think of a citizen body as a "countable singularity." Thus, democracy takes on the garb of a "universal fraternity." Derrida ponders a catalytic tension in democratic theory between addressing the undeniable feature of a democracy as respect for "singularity or alterity" and the emphasis that there cannot exist democracy without a "community of friends." Derrida words this tension as "tragically irreconcilable and forever wounding."[19]

If the origin of democratic theory is premised on a fraternal bonding between groups of like-minded men, how do we undo its parameters and speak to feminist concerns in a world marked by transnational economics and politics? How do we envisage feminist friendships in the transnational arena that move beyond the collapse of differences? These questions take on an added urgency in a post-9/11 world characterized by increased security concerns and divisions between "us" and "them." In *Philosophy in a Time of Terror*, Derrida points out descriptions such as "axis of evil," "absolute threat," and so forth end up "reproducing" their objects of criticism. The response and responsibility in our present times, according to Derrida, is to move beyond "tolerance" that is seen as "a form of charity." Different from tolerance, unconditional hospitality does not prescribe or contain. Instead, unconditional hospitality means being open to someone who is different, unexpected, and "non-identifiable." Derrida calls this a hospitality of "visitation," including even spectral visitations, a notion quite different from "invitation." Unconditional hospitality offers conditions for many kinds of flourishing and does not limit its vistas to only people we know but includes even strangers and ghosts. He recognizes that "visitations" would be legally untranslatable for the state. However, Derrida recognizes the potential of this haunting: "Unconditional hospitality, which is neither juridical nor political, is nonetheless the condition of the political and the juridical."[20] Derrida's "democracy to come" works with visitations and recognizes the (im)possibilities in thinking of a post-9/11 world through terms that contain differences. Thus, Derrida's radical democracy helps us question the categorization of the world into "us" and "them," where the possibilities of hospitality and tolerance remain circumscribed by this explicit territorialization. By reconfiguring the political beyond fraternal similarities, Derrida provides a prism to conceptualize relationships beyond scripted national communities.

To illustrate Derrida's point, let me turn to Gandhi's work, which provides examples of friendships that have in this way transgressed fraternal national communities. Theorizing on the "politics of friendship" as the production of "countercultural revolutionary practices," Gandhi's work provides an excellent companion to Derrida's emphasis on hospitality and the potentials of friendship beyond fraternal bonds scripted in laws and statehood. In her book *Affective Communities: Anticolonial Thought, Fin-de-Siècle Radicalism, and the Politics of Friendship*, Gandhi traces concrete instances of friendships between South Asians and Europeans from 1878 to 1914. She works in parallel with Derrida's philosophy in recognizing the "trope of friendship as the most comprehensive philosophical signifier for all those invisible affective gestures that refuse alignment along the secure axes of filiation to seek expression outside, if not against, possessive communities of belonging." Using Giorgio Agamben's argument that the state cannot accept singular beings who do not coalesce to form "an" identity and sense of belonging, Gandhi theorizes on alternative relationships that have transgressed state-defined politics. In *Affective Communities*, for instance, Gandhi traces the spiritual friendship between Mirra Alfassa, a French Jewish mystic, and Sri Aurobindo, an Indian nationalist and mystic, and how they developed a critique of imperialism and nationalism. Their unusual collaboration that moved through state boundaries displays how "singularities," which form meaningful alliances, can subvert state-dictated norms of community belonging. "Friendship," to Gandhi, "is one name for the co-belonging of nonidentical singularities" and indispensable for understanding transnational collaboration.[21]

Radical democracy, with its emphasis on alterity, can provide an impetus to undo the "equality in virtue" circumscribing national communities of belonging. It is important for feminist transnationalism to undercut fraternal communities of belonging as it endeavors to engage with and move through borders of belonging and unbelonging. Derrida and Gandhi demand us to move beyond binaries when thinking of friendships. State-defined subjectivity or imperial self-articulation is always expressed in terms of definitions that distinguish between "us" and "them." Postcolonial scholarship has eloquently drawn out the excesses and overflowing nature of imperial boundaries. Gandhi, recounting Homi Bhabha's argument, tells us about the failure of imperialism to sustain binary thinking: "Its yearning for secure psychic quarantine is always complicated by a perennial osmosis through which colonizer and colonized mutate unawares but inexorably into each other in the countless hybrid and interstitial sites of imperial antagonism." Gandhi discerns great creative energy in these spaces of "interstitiality" and "in-between-ness" as they inaugurate different forms of relationships that would remain incomprehensible if we saw imperialism as completely successful in delineating borders.[22] Thinking about feminist transnationalism through these conversations makes us alive to possibilities within and between borders as we grapple with security politics in a post-9/11 world.

Derrida's and Gandhi's insights provide theoretical fuel to engage with some of the central questions in feminist transnational politics and the politics of friendships. What is the difference between colonial border crossing and postcolonial border crossing? How do we conceptualize a place that is productively restless, and how do we transcend a frame for politics (i.e., the state) that situates friendships as fraternal relationships? Ironically, and playfully, I suggest that Sen's *It's Good to Be Queen* provides us with an invaluable impetus to think of transnational friendships and their possibilities. Paradoxically, becoming "queen" is an antidote to an imperial consumption of the "Other," and it clears a creative field to express the "nonidentical singularity" that Gandhi writes about as necessary for political regeneration. Moreover, becoming "queen" in New York is also suggestive of a play with fraternal bonds and gender roles being haunted by its deep history. Sen's playful imitations and inversions draw out the limited and limiting nature of tolerance and move us toward visualizing vibrant, democratic friendships.

It's Good to Be Queen

Irina Aristarkhova, in her catalog essay for *It's Good to Be Queen*, eloquently narrates and analyzes different aspects of Sen's exhibit. As mentioned earlier, a handwritten note in red was left for Sen in an apartment where she would stay while a guest in New York, hosted by the Bose Pacia Gallery staff and the author of the note (figure 3). Sen took this note as a "gift" or "risky offering."[23] She accepted the gift fully, if ironically, such that it colored her artistic endeavors while in New York.

As Aristarkhova notes, it is strange that the message was conveyed to Sen via a handwritten note rather than through phone or email or in person. Sen's status as a "guest" was literally written in red. The title of "guest" immediately placed Sen in a certain ontological and epistemological position via her host. Ontologically, she was "othered," a guest in relation to her host. Epistemologically, being a polite guest requires that one follows the rules set down by the host. One would not be a polite guest if one asked too many questions or ventured into unmarked territory. Aristarkhova

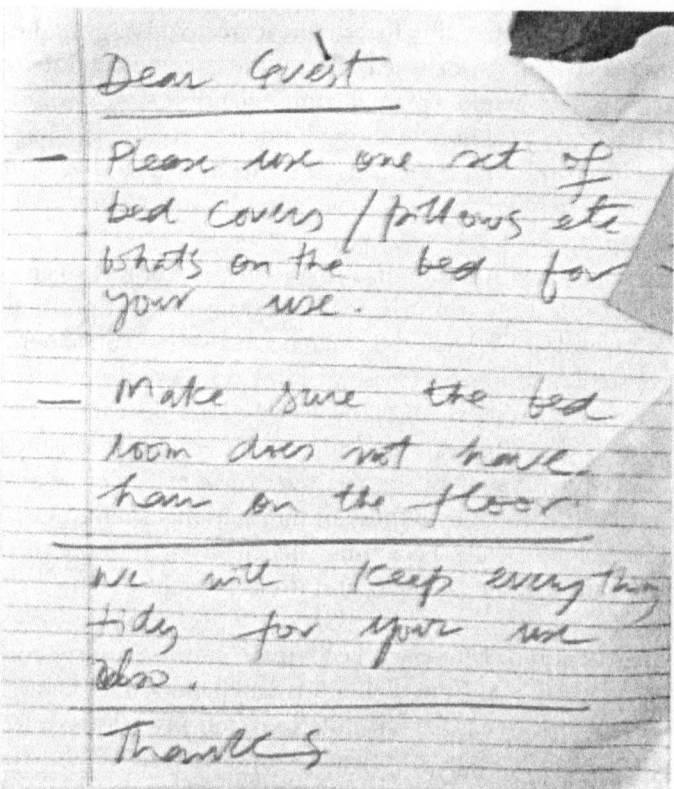

Figure 3. "Letter from the Invisible Landlord," 2006. Source: Mithu Sen, *It's Good to Be Queen* (New York: Bose Pacia, 2008), 79.

emphasizes, "Mithu Sen, in her creative submission to the demands of the absent host, played her role too, as it is only a guest who makes a host a host." However, Sen's "creative submission" meant compliance of a different order. Answering the request that she use "one set of bed covers/pillows etc. what's on the bed for your use," Sen crafted her own bed covers and pillows, which Aristarkhova describes as "splendid, gorgeous, outlandish."[24]

Figure 4 shows a drawing of a greasy pillow decorated with an embroidered flower that Sen made for her art installation. There were other pillows, too, including one with a fish drawn on it. The art fish was definitely not a real fish, with its associated smell and presence, and therefore would not offend a host's sensibility, but it certainly suggests this provocation. Similarly, the greasy pillow would be in direct defiance of the host's request that Sen imprint her presence on just one set of pillows and contain her presence. Sen flamboyantly marks herself through her artwork on pillows that she

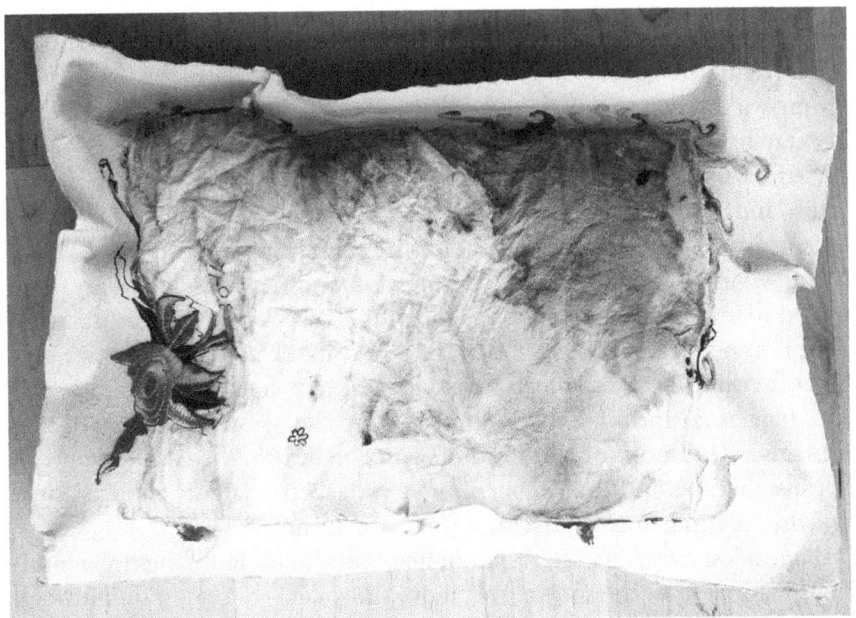

Figure 4. *Greasy Pillow*, 2006, by Mithu Sen. Mixed media on paper, 14 × 21 × 6 in. Source: Mithu Sen, *It's Good to Be Queen* (New York: Bose Pacia, 2008), 31.

made. Sen certainly "used" her pillow, marking it with her art and politics. Thus she follows her host's request and playfully tugs at the limits of the hospitality offered. Invoking Derrida, the greased pillow was definitely the result of a "visitation" and not an "invitation," which, as noted earlier, he distinguishes as different modes of relationality.[25] "Unconditional hospitality," as we saw above, is alive to visitations and does not limit the "other" to terms laid out in an invitation. Sen's "greasy pillow" keeps to the protocols of her invitation but also maneuvers the rules by following them to their extreme. The "greasy pillow" becomes a visitation, a haunting rejoinder to her host's conditional hospitality. As an invited guest, Sen uses her art to draw out excesses in bound protocol that reveal both the possibilities and limitations in the host-guest relationship.

The note of figure 3 becomes a part of Sen's art installation in more ways than one. Written in pencil and mostly likely hurriedly, "Dear Guest" is underlined and the text separated by lines that make clear demarcations of Sen's responsibilities and the host's duty. There is no name or descriptive term on the note. While the guest is singular and named as "guest," the host could be anyone and anything in the apartment offered to Sen as an artist in residence. Sen thus responds to the note likewise and throughout the apartment traces her response with her art installations. Her apartment becomes an art gallery and vice versa. Sen's bedroom, bathroom, living room, and all corners of the apartment speak to the note that welcomed her stay in New York.

Sen set up an enormous comb on the bathroom wall, hung hair on the walls, and put balls of hair on serving plates; there was hair everywhere except on the floors, in deference to the note. Hair has different cross-cultural connotations and bodily associations. Some kinds of hair are more valued than others, whether on the individual body or on the cultural map. Hair is also an artifact of memory and has a significant role in Sen's work. Sen oftentimes weaves spinal cords made of hair for her art projects and uses hair as an intimate medium of artistic expression. As Aristarkhova explains, "This motif of hair is not new to Sen's work, she used it before in her installations and drawings, but here it has a special feel and meaning, known only to her as a guest, and to an absent host."[26]

Figure 5 shows Sen's use of hair in her bathroom. Hair hangs in an ominous manner from the shower and above the toilet—but never on the floor. Moreover, the toilet seat is out of use, and the black tape commands all hair remain outside the toilet's territory. One wonders whether the ominous head of hair will keep to this protocol and remain fixed to its relegated territory above the floor, never on it. In a way, to make sure that the floor does not have hair remains an improbability despite one's best intentions, going by the call of gravity and nature of hair to drift everywhere. It is difficult to contain hair, and Sen's art installation playfully subverts the request made to her as a guest. This subversion is not a flagrant act of disobedience. In fact, by strictly following the rules, Sen displays its laughable absurdity.

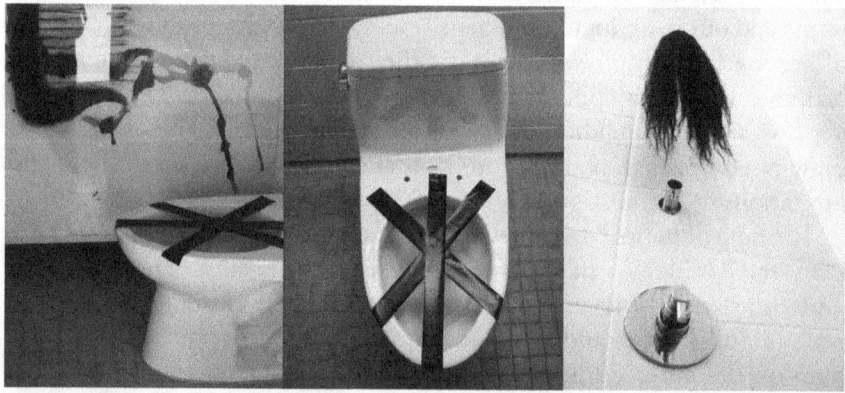

Figure 5. *Queen's Toilet*, by Mithu Sen, 2006. Source: Mithu Sen, *It's Good to Be Queen* (New York: Bose Pacia, 2008), 21.

The politics of hair as seen in Sen's installation has many meanings. Directly, it references her host's note, and its meaning-play could be seen to cross many boundaries, such as of body and nation. In her essay "The Hair Trade," Lisa Jones writes, "Hair is human tissue, but dead cells. Of the body, body like, and to quote shampoo ads, 'full of body,' yet not a body part, at least so says Western science."[27] Jones draws out how hair, classified as "inanimate," constitutes an integral part of body aesthetics and transnational trade.[28] Human and animal hair is imported into the United States from China, India, and other countries for wigs, paintbrushes, and hairbrushes.[29] The employment of immigrant workers in hair salons is also indexed by the cut-hair installations. Seen as crossing borders of bodies and nations, hair has many significations in identity, art, and activism. Significantly, Kobena Mercer in "Black Hair/Style Politics" says, "All black hair-styles are political in that they articulate responses to the panoply of historical forces which have invested this element of the ethnic signifier with both personal and political 'meaning' and significance."[30] The political importance of the Afro and accusations of assimilating with a White society if Black women straighten their hair are just some of the explicit associations among identity, hair, race, and politics.

Did Sen's host know that Sen was an Indian woman when they asked her to make sure there was no hair on the floor? Notwithstanding the answer to the question, the request is curiously personal and immediately positions a guest in a negative position of making sure that there are no bodily traces or movements out of place.

The attention to hair is certainly not a new trope in art. In artist Ana Mendieta's use of Cuban hair on a tree in Miami and Janine Antoni's use of her hair as the material for a broom, we see two striking examples of female artists employing hair for cultural commentary and aesthetic politics.[31] I add here to the wide political history and resonances of hair through different avenues of art, critique, and resistance by situating Sen's use of hair in her installation as significant for transnational friendships. As noted, hair was everywhere in Sen's exhibit except on the floor. It was out of place on serving plates and everywhere else, from the bedroom to the bathroom. A play with body and space is intrinsic to Sen's politics of hair, in which it becomes an actor of its own, an agent with a body that needs to be contained. While hair is a commodity for transnational trade and moves between borders, it does so divorced from its human or animal source. Sen showcases how she must contain her own body to be a good guest. In defiance, the artist as queen makes her own rules and helps us visualize the movement toward friendship that would not contain and keep in place but, rather, enable expressions. Out-of-place transnational friendships need not keep within the protocols of singularity and "equality in virtue" that keep us situated in a space governed by what the host decrees.

Sen decorated her apartment with whimsically chosen objects: a picture of actor and producer Shah Rukh Khan, dolls, family portraits, paper, hair, beads, and fabric. Moreover, she displayed her drawings in the apartment close together and on hangers, like dresses in a New York store (figure 6).

The accompanying array of paintings on hangers in Sen's *Buy a Drawing and Get a Hanger Free* comments broadly on our consumer lifestyle and specifically on the consumption of art as product rather than experience. Sen's audience would need to make an extra effort to see the paintings, as

Figure 6. *Buy a Drawing and Get a Hanger Free*, by Mithu Sen, 2006. Source: Mithu Sen, *It's Good to Be Queen* (New York: Bose Pacia, 2008), 39.

they do not hang on the wall waiting to be seen. Sen's emphasis on relationships through her aesthetic creations constantly provokes her to push her audience to think and react rather than remain placid consumers of art.[32] In some of her exhibits, Sen often draws outside the frame and on the wall to demonstrate that one cannot "buy" art in its totality.[33] There is a limit to one-dimensional consumption, and Sen's play with it emphasizes the need to think of aesthetic experiences through a broad sensorium.

In addition, in tune with the note that extols Sen to be "tidy" and organized, she presented her given space as a "laboratory or a masquerade."[34] Sen's guests had to wear white gloves to touch anything, and the gloves were strategically positioned so that the guests would not miss them. As Aristarkhova eloquently points out, "This sense of gloves on one's hands was, once again both liberating (like a mask during a carnival) and alienating (like a protective gear one has to wear in a sterile room). You could touch almost everything, but you were not, really, at home. In this 'perfectly' clean space, we are all presumably safe: guests and their hostess, the artist."[35] Wearing gloves made one feel alienated and circumscribed, not "at home." And, certainly, as Aristarkhova points out, gloves also serve as protection and security. Sen's guests were thus invited to feel tension and to relate to her art and to each other through multilayered experiences.

It is only an artist or a queen who can get away with this kind of experimentation and subversion of protocol and who can through it strive to become a friend. As Sen says, "I took advantage of being an artist," "I was enlarging myself," and "Queen-liness means enjoying yourself."[36] Sen as queen kept her studio open twenty-four hours a day, and everyone was welcome. People dropped in for hours, which led to different attachments and friendships. Sen writes, "This person: what does she mean to me, and what do I mean to her? It is the same moment when one enters: room, house, gallery, space etc. Should I stop? Smile?"[37] Sen is acutely aware of the tensions, trepidations, and anxieties that pervade relationships. How to make a guest feel at ease? How to make friends that move beyond tolerance? These questions cast their trace on all aspects of her art installation, which she rigorously archived by pinning used tea bags to a wall as relics of her conversations and friend-making.

Sen was not present on the opening day of her art exhibit. Instead, she wrote an email to her guests:

Dear,
    I am sorry for not being sorry about my physical absence in my opening night. . . . I am sad but not sorry for my act. . . . It was a conscious decision. . . . It was a part of my whole relationship (guest-host-hospitality-tolerance) project. . . .

In most art openings the artist's presence is needed to explain the intimate details of the artist's persona in order to put the art objects into context. In this case however all of my most intimate details were and are open for your viewing and I did not want my presence to interfere with your process of discovery of those very private and intimate details.

I was overwhelmed when I came back completely soaked and drenched. . . . I found the wet footsteps all around my apartment. . . . I found the white gloves filled up with touches of invisible friends. . . .

I walked all the way to the river and finally got into a New York site seeing bus, made a night trip in the city. . . . Believe me, it was so wonderful. . . . I treated myself as a queen. . . .

Yours and only yours
Mithu[38]

Sen was the definitive queen. Being eagerly awaited and desired, she chose to be absent from her own art-show opening. She chose to exercise her power and privilege to be queen, self-appointed and arbitrary. Her guests arrived and walked their way through the apartment-gallery, looking at her installations, carefully mulling over the objects on display. At that moment, Sen was riding through Manhattan on a red double-decker tourist bus. As David A. Ross describes, "In the apartment, Sen had left her work not only to be found and viewed, she was hoping each thing would find its own way in the world—would somehow connect with the person who needed it (not those who simply wanted to own an object or drawing, but those who found an irresistible force compelling them into a relationship)."[39]

Sen started her artist's residence with a red handwritten note, and she ended it on another note, which she wrote to her audience and friends. The two notes are very different. The first exemplifies the limited notion of tolerance that Derrida discerns as "a conditional, circumspect, careful hospitality."[40] The second note was different, a gesture of friendship, of unconditional hospitality, a gesture filled with risk and uncertainty: "Without this thought of pure hospitality (a thought that is also, in its own way, an experience), we would not even have the idea of the other, of the alterity of the other, that is, of someone who enters into our lives without having been invited."[41] Sen's audience works their way through her art creating their own relationships, making specific connections. Sen's friendship and hospitality do not lay out rules of encounter. In fact, it is unmediated by the absence of the artist as queen. Sen was not there at the opening of her exhibit to spell out the meaning-making to her audience. It is useful here to again invoke Gandhi's use of Derrida's work to emphasize that risk sometimes carries a magnificent "affirmation of relationality."[42] Gandhi quotes Derrida: "Let us say yes *to who or what turns up*, before any determination, before any anticipation, before any *identification*, whether or not it has to do with a foreigner, an immigrant, an invited guest, or an unexpected visitor, whether or not the new arrival is a citizen of another country, a human, animal, or divine creature, a living or dead thing, male or female."[43]

Having distinguished Sen's friendships and mode of hospitality as different from her host's tolerance, how do we delineate the political valence of *It's Good to Be Queen*? In pursuit of an answer, I turn next to a conversation on feminist friendships and their renegotiation of power hierarchy.

Feminist Friendships

> The only motive that makes sense to me for your joining us in this investigation is the motive of friendship, out of friendship. A non-imperialist feminism requires that you make a real space for our articulating, interpreting, theorizing and reflecting about the connections among them—a real space must be a noncoerced space—and/or that you follow us into our world out of friendship.[44]

Maria Lugones and Elizabeth Spelman, in their dialogue about responding adequately to differences and thus being able to decolonize feminist theory, emphasize the need for friendships as a suitable motive and approach for "white/Anglo" feminists engaged in the task of feminist theory.[45] To Lugones and Spelman, friendships offer the momentum and ability to attain "appropriate reciprocity of care" and recognition of "whole beings."[46] Friendships hold a special place in feminist transnational theory and politics, and different feminists emphasize its irreplaceable virtue for the purpose of responsible feminist politics. Friendships take many forms and are emphasized differently under diverse theoretical frames. For example, Chandra Talpade Mohanty urges us to work with the "solidarity model" that emphasizes "mutuality and coimplication."[47] Mohanty's emphasis on solidarity would reckon with the power hierarchies in geopolitics and envisage relational pedagogical techniques that decolonize how we inhabit our world. While not explicitly about friendships, a "solidarity" model highlights relation building across differences and ways that feminists can work through transnational lines outside the tourist and explorer mentalities.[48] Chowdhury and Philipose articulate the connection between solidarity and friendship in their volume on *Dissident Friendships*, as they write about "solidarities—oppositional, dissident, complicit, failed, attempted, or realized—that we can envision at the intersections of the contradictory practices of neoliberalism, militarism, imperialism, and humanism."[49] Solidarity remains indispensable to friendships and defines their possibilities and tensions. Thus, the "politics" of friendship, its urgency, potentials, and problems, occupies a central place in feminist transnational-postcolonial theory.

However, despite the emphasis on solidarity and friendship, there are considerable differences among feminists on the question of friendship. While Lugones and Spelman emphasize the undeniable importance of friendships in forging an anti-imperialist ethos in feminism, others, such as hooks, Iris Young, and Lorde, emphasize other foundations for feminist relationships.[50] Lugones and Spelman emphasize the need to hear women's different "voices."[51] They critique how feminist theory speaks to the lives of White, middle-class women and has remained largely incognizant of the lives of a majority of women. Lugones and Spelman make some suggestions about how to do theory that is "not imperialist, ethnocentric, disrespectful."[52] They study reasons why White/Anglo women should engage such a theory. The motives of self-interest, self-growth, or moral obligation do not suffice, and Lugones and Spellman stress that friendship remains the "only appropriate and understandable motive."[53] This kind of friendship involves reciprocity, openness, sensitivity, and self-questioning reflection and does not reduce people to the "abstraction called 'women.'"[54] Likewise, although hooks invokes feminist solidarity as indispensable to a viable feminist movement, she urges us to see how "sisterhood" is often the expressive appeal that covers up differences and the "opportunism of manipulative bourgeois white women."[55] To hooks, feminist solidarity requires incessant commitment to reckoning with multiple differences, tensions, and confrontations.[56] Lorde continues this conversation: "differences must be not merely tolerated, but seen as a fund of necessary polarities between which our creativity can spark like a dialectic."[57]

Despite many differences in their theoretical orientations, hooks and Derrida agree that friendships should move beyond an "equality of virtue." In thinking about Aristotle and friendships, Derrida delineates how primary friendships always demand an "equality of virtue" in Aristotle's political schema: "One wonders what is left of a friendship which makes the virtue of the other its own condition (be virtuous if you want me to love you)."[58] hooks similarly invokes the idea of solidarity as political stance that can withstand disagreements and not consume the other in the image of oneself. Derrida and hooks extol us to question "brotherhood" and "sisterhood" as the basis for politics. For Derrida and hooks, radical democracy or a feminist future does not rest on forging similitude and cloaking differences. This is what Sen knows.

Sen's installation echoes hooks's antipathy toward a homogenization of differences. *It's Good to Be Queen* continues the conversation about radical democracy and feminist friendships through an aesthetic medium. Sen as queen subverts protocols that would be outside the domain of regular subjects and invents her own rules, whether in the display of hair hanging from the ceiling or being absent on the day of her art-show opening. Paradoxically, being queen allows her to revel in democratic freedom, renegotiate power and privilege, and border-cross at her art's will. Alive to different encounters and not wanting to charter relations between the audience and her art, queen Mithu Sen transforms being "queen" from its imperial, national connotations to a transnational play with alterity and differences. A transnational queen, very different from a colonial one, does not discipline and homogenize. A transnational queen does not have to forge communities of allegiance with reference to fraternal ties. For a border-crossing queen, containment, categorizations, and protocols have little value. Eclectic, whimsical, and playful, the transnational queen extols us to open our hearts and minds to new encounters and unexpected interrelations and attune to hauntings that prevent the transnational queen from aligning to the specified status quo.

Olu Oguibe writes, "In *Its Good to be Queen*, Sen presents us with an alluring and much nuanced performance that leaves us torn between rigorous contemplation and having a mere good time, each guest welcome to their own interpretations and dispositions while the artist gives away so little and yet so much."[59] Sen's transnational overture of friendship does not presume a symmetrical level of power. The artist is a "guest" in New York and also a "host" as artist in residence. Queen Mithu Sen plays with this asymmetry through the most intimate and public expressions. Her expression of friendship plays with different roles to articulate their limits and limitlessness. We are mindful of limits in the designation of space, time, and responsibilities. The limitlessness surfaces alongside and within these limits. Her audience moves through the intimate space (bedroom, bathroom, enormous comb, dolls) forging their own connections. Inadvertently, they are also interactive agents and generative of the space they peruse. It would be as impossible to sum up the results of her exhibit as it would be to contain the hair that floats through and between bodies and things despite attempts to sequester it in a comb or on a serving plate. The indefinability of her aesthetic experiment of ostentatiously performing categories could be seen as the queen's resourcefulness and an indicator of transnational politics in which borders and borderlessness often coalesce in catalytic tension. To understand transnational politics, we have to reckon with bordered delineations, as seen in the boundaries of nation-states and with the associated privileges of national citizenship that allow some to cross them. While recognizing the power of borders, we have to note that political demarcations often say very little about the movements of people and commodities over political boundaries, such as through diaspora, transnational markets, or activist networks. Grappling with the politics of borders as being forever maneuvered remains a central issue for feminist transnational politics.

Thinking with the politics of being "queen" in the context of hospitality and friendships has multiple layers, many of which are agonizingly ironical. In the context of the United States, the "welfare queen" can scarcely write her own rules of encounter. Framed as an insult and derogatory strategy to shame the recipients of welfare, the practice of labeling Black women on welfare as "welfare queens" has a long and nefarious history in American political thought and its framings of race and gender. In her book *The Politics of Disgust: The Public Identity of the Welfare Queen*, Ange-Marie Hancock writes, "The 'welfare queen' public identity, a contemporary moniker applied to welfare recipients, has two organizing dimensions: hyperfertility and laziness." "Welfare," a program that was initially scripted to help the "worthy white widow" in the latter half of the nineteenth century, took on a completely different frame when used by Black women under the equality provision in the US constitution. Supporting White women was justified through their role as mothers of the nation and the need to nurture future citizen-subjects. In other words, supporting White women was tantamount to preserving the sanctimony of the White family and nation. Wide-ranging political debates through the 1980s and 1990s repeatedly dehumanized Black mothers as akin to animals, lazy and unproductive, exemplified in US Senator Russell B. Long's use of the term "brood mares" to describe Puerto Rican and Black welfare receivers.[60] To think about being "queen" through the politics of welfare serves as a haunting rejoinder to assess questions of privilege and power. While Sen's aesthetic politics play on the subversive aspect of being queen for a transnational subject and drew on her familiarity with histories of queens and kings in India, colonial and precolonial, it remains important to situate the politics of being "queen" within regimes of race and gender, colony and postcolony.

Concepts of tolerance and hospitality are haunting visitations in the categorization of people as "welfare queens." Divorced from recognition even as human, the ethics of tolerance and hospitality cease to operate in the liminal spaces occupied by many people of color. Being a "welfare queen" is about being not human, about being not a citizen, and about having no rights.[61] While I think with the uncanny provocations through being "queen" in varied ways, the politics of hair drifts in through myriad conversations. For instance, in 1995 the *Christian Science Monitor* presented Desiree Stewart, who through the benefits of microlending will soon overcome poverty: "Desiree Stewarts's hair salon is just over one year old. The equipment is used, the pipes are bad, and there are no mirrors on the walls—yet. But the growing Chicago business is making a profit and, if things go as planned, the single mother will soon be able to get off welfare for the first time in seven years."[62] While ostensibly about a single mother's work environment and habits that will enable her to move from welfare, the narrative situates the work in a hair salon. Here I would like to ask, What is the connection between hair and hospitality and ways of working with differences that constantly invoke it being kept in place? What ways of becoming "queen" might subvert these associations?

Sen plays queen in New York, a place where being "queen" has its additional sexual and gendered overtones.[63] Queer theorists such as Judith Butler have repeatedly emphasized the importance of thinking with drag and its usefulness. Butler points out how queens are much more than an imitation of the heterosexual real: "The parodic or imitative effect of gay identities works neither to copy nor to emulate heterosexuality, but rather, to expose heterosexuality as an incessant and *panicked* imitation of its own naturalized idealization."[64] Dramatically, Sen's "drag aesthetics," when hanging hair from the top of the shower, making her guests wear protective gloves, or making her own pillows, playfully mimic and exaggerate her host's dictums. The playful mimicry ensures that Sen does not explicitly copy her host. Rather, her drag aesthetics exposes how tolerance is an expression of naturalized parochialism and regimes of power. Sen's art performance as queen haunts the boundary lines of identity categorization, as guest, host, insider, and outsider, to draw out its inherent limitations in forging friendships that can speak to the project of a radical, transnational democracy. Sen as queen subverts rules and decorum and subverts an inclination to fraternize with her audience; instead, she queers friendships through play. Derrida, as examined earlier describing the "politics of friendship," has emphasized the fraternal underpinnings in national communities by examining various political theories on friendship. Fraternity dependent on blood and birth emphasizes singularity or a common basis. Sen's drag aesthetics runs counter to an imagination that seeks to establish sameness.[65]

Sen, in her creative way, plays with hospitality and friendship, a queering of friendships by displaying the power mechanisms that allow some people to make the rules. I want to suggest that queering friendships could be full of possibilities for feminist transnationalism. It will enable us to move beyond "fratriarchy" and the need to create communities of sameness. Also, it is important to note that one doesn't always have to be comfortable with friends. Feminist friendship should not be self-mirroring narcissism. Working with differences, friendships can evolve in many ways and directions. Like hair perched on top of a showerhead or a massive comb on the bedroom wall, queering transnational feminist friendships could subvert expectations and build creative relational dynamics that can lead to unforeseen possibilities.

Sen saw her art as an active project of hospitality and friendship. As artist in residence, Sen took photographs of herself with the studio visitors, drank cups of Darjeeling tea with them, and welcomed them into her home and life. Beth Citron describes the opening day of Sen's art show in the following way:

> Arriving early to the artist space on the evening of its opening, it was exciting to have the full space to see, touch, and explore Sen's work and her living space. As more people arrived, it was fascinating to see the hospitality extended by the artist and by the space itself as we rifled through Sen's drawings, books on Shahrukh Khan, and everyday paraphernalia—with white gloves on, of course. Slowly becoming comfortable with the unusual protocol, as if we too were at home, the rooms revealed the layered dimensionality of Sen's drawings, in which each line extends beyond the paper into the artist's real and psychic space.[66]

Citron delineates the growing frames of Sen's drawings that extend far beyond their original parameters, while other pieces are hung on clothes racks and resonantly cut against the business mentality of senseless buying and selling. The stained pillows and tea bags speak of memories, bodies, and stories that invite her audience to be cotravelers. Sen's art show is politics and theory in its creative play with power and framing and extending feminist conversations on friendships. The visualization enabled through her art show works along other affective registers (for example, touch) to emphasize the rolling borders of aesthetic politics as beyond a single register, space, or role.

Sen's intervention into feminist conversations on friendship offers insights and nuances to our understanding of its political and personal workings. As emphasized by Lugones and Spelman and recounted earlier, decolonial friendships could vastly improve feminist theory and activism, while hooks alerts us to the dangers of homogenizing differences under a cult of "sisterhood." *It's Good to Be Queen* interjects at the borders of these conversations. Sen wholeheartedly affirms friendships like those that Lugones and Spelman theorize. Her attempt at decolonial friendships that play with her host's dictums is characterized by a counterpolitics to showcase reservoirs that can remake power structures. Starting as a guest, Sen becomes host and queen while playfully haunting the meaning of the categories through her artwork. Indeed, Sen's friendships evoke the "messy and tangled ecologism of intra- and intersubjectivity" that Gandhi writes about with fervor.[67] As an active mode of transgression and subversion, Sen's artwork draws out the tensions in forging transnational friendships. An Indian in New York, a guest who is also a host, an artist and creator who is circumscribed by the manners of a foreign territory, Sen engages herself with different relationships and establishes friendships that speak beyond foundational categories of being a "friend" or "enemy," at "home" or "abroad." Sen underlines how being a guest could also mean being a host and vice versa. Stipulating rigid roles suffocates encounters and stifles relational possibilities. Friendships as a part of Sen's aesthetics grow and connect in unexpected ways.

Sen's art show contains creative political valence for feminist transnationalism. Her renegotiation of power dynamics through wit, humor, and thoughtful reflection enables her art to comment on and engage in friendships that move far beyond a singular bargain or buy-sell camaraderie. Sen does not "tell" her guests how to read her art. Instead, they (and I) read, engage, and make our own connections. Reinvoking Lorde, "differences" become a reservoir through which "creativity can spark like a dialectic."[68] For feminist transnational activists who move between borders, Sen's mode of friend-making offers insights into power dynamics at play in a certain space. It also offers movement toward its undoing through spaces for growth and self-reflection that do not ossify the "other" in the image of oneself. Friendship holds special meaning in feminist transnationalism, and reckoning with its necessarily multihued configurations and power plays remains a challenge and a source for creative possibilities.

Let me end this chapter by turning our attention back to Sen's 2017 exhibit *UNhome in City IF Angels*. Is it a coincidence that a lost passport framed Sen's stay in Los Angeles in 2017, and the consequent artwork was about unmooring oneself through a project of radical hospitality and friend-making? Was it a coincidence that in projects separated by more than ten years, Sen haunted the exhibits with her own absence and subsequently with the absence of formalized artifacts? How do we read the reaction of the professor in Los Angeles who unhomed Sen's exhibit because, to him, there was no art present? How may we read the absence and presence of art and the artist? I end with these questions as a way to continue thinking with Sen's political aesthetics. Moving beyond a relation to art as consumption,

Sen inspires us to build relations across differences, beyond possessing a friend or artifact. Playing with invitations, whether to a foreign country or art exhibit, Sen's visitations urge us to think about transnational friendships as fraught, tensed, agonistic possibilities that need to reckon holistically with geopolitics and the urge to possess an Other. Whether a lost passport, lost art, or lost artist, Sen's unhoming of friendships urges us to unmoor our framings of it, and endeavor to connect anew.

CHAPTER 5

Spectral Politics

> A question of repetition: a specter is always a *revenant*. One cannot control its comings and goings because it *begins by coming back*.
> —Jacques Derrida, *Specters of Marx*

> I entered this hall pleasantly haunted by those who have entered it before me.
> —Toni Morrison, 1993 Nobel banquet speech

As I said at the beginning, I believe in ghosts. This simple statement is oftentimes met with disbelief, an incredulous stare, or affirming solidarity. None of these responses can interfere with my conviction, whether questioning it or embracing it, for seeing a ghost is an extremely solitary experience. Seldom do they appear when we move in parties of people. When seen, ghosts can fracture liberal individualism's frames of autonomy and sovereignty. Flitting in and out, ghosts move through walls and bodies. This is not the reason, though, that I say that I believe in ghosts. I have never seen one. To put it in other words, a ghost has never appeared to me as a ghost. The ghosts that I live with come from my childhood growing up in Bengal, listening to *bhooter golpo* (ghost stories) on the terrace of our old house in Kolkata, which provided slight respite through the seething summer nights. The entire family would converge on the terrace, some listening to the radio, others watering our extensive collection of potted plants, while the conversation and stories about ghosts gathered steam.

We were sternly admonished to refrain from eating fish on the terrace, as it would invite the ghosts who lived in the coconut trees bordering our house to reach out with their long hands from the trees and snatch our food.[1] My mother, a Sikh Punjabi, would often interrupt these conversations, tell us to stop thinking of nonsense, and assure us that strength of mind is the ultimate enemy for spirits. To believe or not to believe in ghosts was a religious divide in our very secular family of Bengali and Punjabi parents, grandparents, cousins, and extended members, who shared very different ways of viewing the world. My belief in ghosts was seen as my Bengali-ness, creative imagination, and unwillingness to do schoolwork late in the evening. Ironically, though, my mother would also indulge us with her own ghost stories about when she visited my grandparent's ancestral home in rural Bengal. Overall, these were days rife with imagination and tales, plentiful and paradoxical cultural signals, and a great deal of laughter and good food—a ton of fish!

My schooling in La Martiniere in Kolkata, set up by the French in India in 1836, did little to allay my respect for ghosts. English was the primary language of communication in this school, incongruous in many ways in a communist party–dominated Bengal. The colonial architecture of the school, with its grand stairways and echoing halls, fed our imaginations along with stories of underground tunnels and other unseen infrastructure. Subsequently, I was soon in the midst of a very different, and equally inspiring, imaginative kaleidoscope when I attended Presidency College as an undergraduate and graduate student. Karl Marx dominated my political science and history classes, and a raw Marxist energy among active student bodies dominated the college canteens and libraries. There were plenty of ghosts in Presidency College, ones very different from those in La Martiniere. Postcolonial and colonial ghosts spirited the intellectual landscape in both spaces. Thus, my imagination and its sensorium have always lived with ghosts. Were they real? Could I see them? Such questions were never on my horizon. The subject of many stories, experienced as actively present and absent, ghosts emerged from a frame of unknowingness, of fear and wonder, and the impossibility of being able to ever truly control a space or time. Ghosts have always played with us and our neatly ordered worlds.

These ghostly memories have compelled me to situate spectral politics as the ethical epistemology of this book. I have found that an epistemology that centers hauntings and recognizes their play with the status quo can be the basis for postcolonial and transnational visions of justice. Spectral politics centralizes the work of play and haunting in a radical politics of justice, beginning with the understanding that the two are irreducible to one or the other. As we work toward social change and against the status quo of societal structures at large, I argue we must identify structures and frames that perpetuate violence, and the play and haunting that labor to uncover them. I have worked here to showcase works where this epistemology is at play, whether in questions of friendship, animalization, or translation. I have attended throughout to the heterogeneity of play and haunting and worked to reveal their prolific occurrence in politics of various shades. For example, while I identify friendships as a postcolonial haunting in transnational feminist visions, I also note the mischievous play with subjects in capitalist and imperial politics that invites and uninvites them capriciously. This multifarious and pervasive occurrence marks the urgency to take play and hauntings seriously in our theories and activisms. What, I have been asking, would it mean to productively haunt transnational friendships? How do we haunt frames of animalization through play and sabotage? Why is it important to reckon with meaning-plays as we travel the world, and how may this haunt queer and feminist politics? In striving to answer these questions, I follow ghosts as they enter and exit through disasters and crisis in their persistent play with reality, ultimately exposing frames and effecting their undoing.

This book's emphasis on the heterogeneity of play and haunting, their relevance across many contexts, situates them also as layered politics. That is to say that the more we engage with play and haunting as methods for epistemological inquiry, we notice how many other inclusions and exclusions are produced in our theories and actions. To illustrate this point further, let me highlight in this final chapter an example of such layered exclusions. In short, let us consider the example of Marxist ghosts who critique capitalism but exclude women, not to mention the queer ghosts who riddle heterosexual temporality and its linear reproductive narrative of progression. This chapter illustrates spectral politics as a necessary project of continually noting absences and gaps in our frames of living and dying, even with the ghosts that haunt us, and continually engaging with them to deepen and widen projects of transnational feminist and queer justice.

Ghosts and the Event

Ghosts haunt places: a house, a spot on the road, a lonely forest, a site of untimely death. When ghosts mark such places, they seem to imbue them with a sense of disorientation, a spatial dissonance as well as a temporal one. The work of time and memory weaves irrevocably through these spatial dissonances. A ghost is a certain configuration of a living past; one that should be in the dead past. Past, present, and future are riddled and play against each other through the appearance of a ghost. Ghosts interrupt a static conception of event or occurrence.

There are plenty of ghosts in the world around us. We could think about colonialism's traces, its vestiges in architectures, policies, politics, and languages. To reckon with such traces bestows colonialism with a singularity that hides its pervasive presence and continuities. Ann Laura Stoler says it well: "Colonial pasts, the narratives recounted about them, the unspoken distinctions they continue to 'cue,' the affective charges they reactivate, and the implicit 'lessons' they are mobilized to impart are sometimes so ineffably threaded through the fabric of contemporary life forms they seem indiscernible as distinct effects, as if everywhere and nowhere at all."[2] Indeed, it is impossible to untwine entanglements, and colonial pasts are indelibly present in values, beliefs, and modes of perception, even though we may choose to think beyond colonialism's many manifestations.

The problem with thinking about colonialism through its traces is that it elides the way in which colonialism continues to haunt social reality as an enduring presence, a ghost. Stoler reminds us, "The scholarly romance with 'traces' risks rendering colonial remnants as pale filigrees, benign overlays with barely detectable presence rather than deep pressure points of generative possibilities or violent and violating absences." Attentive to the flimsy projections in "trace," Stoler draws us toward "duress," or the "hardened, tenacious qualities of colonial effects."[3] Stoler's work emphasizes the here and now of colonialism and its presences and absent presences. Even when ostensibly postliberation, many societies reel in colonialism's presence. Settler colonialism stands testimony to the "now" of colonialism. Colonial hauntings need to thus be conceptualized through a complication of presences and absences, past and present, and present and future.

Max Horkheimer and Theodor W. Adorno in their work on social domination on the Enlightenment address the duress and continuity that forms of domination produce in the guise of ghosts. In *Dialectic of Enlightenment*, they draw our attention to ghosts in the chapter "Notes and Drafts." In "On the Theory of Ghosts," Adorno and Horkheimer engage with Sigmund Freud's theory about ghosts and find it narrow in scope. Instead, they contend, "Only the conscious horror of destruction creates the correct relationship with the dead: unity with them because we, like them, are the victims of the same condition and the same disappointed hope." Freud's theory on ghosts was limited to examining the thoughts of living people about the deceased. Instead, Horkheimer and Adorno want us to see continuities in conditions, and unity with ghosts, in the collapse of the promises of Enlightenment. In discussing the politics and the concept of enlightenment, Horkheimer and Adorno describe it as the mastery of computation, calculation, and the meter of utility, where "the world becomes subject to man," and relations of domination are naturalized.[4] What might have happened had the Enlightenment conversed with ghosts? How might the path of human aggrandizement, modernity, and colonialism have changed if the Enlightenment had engaged with ghosts?

Despite, or perhaps because of, the Enlightenment's framing of man as the center of the world, ghosts have emerged to perforate the social fabric of our world and given rise to haunting afterlives in the form of anti-Enlightenment narratives. Although this process is pervasive, perhaps it is easier to see it in the form of events. Take, for instance, 9/11. This "major event" in recent history was a blow to the pinnacle of capitalism, progress narratives, power, and might. In the book *Philosophy in a Time of Terror*, Jurgen Habermas suggests that 9/11 was the "first historic world event in the strictest sense: the impact, the explosion, the slow collapse—everything that was not Hollywood anymore but, rather, a gruesome reality, literally took place in front of the 'universal eyewitness' of a global public."[5] September 11 heralded what was considered a "new" kind of terror and terrorism that made assessments, preparations, or even a defense impossible.[6] This terror could strike from anywhere and at any time, without notice and uncontrollable. 9/11 marked a turning point in thinking about security, vulnerability, and the autonomy of liberal subjects; it marked a turn toward a world configured by technosurveillance. In the spirit of this book, we have to ask, too, What ghosts did the event produce, and how do they haunt?

Since 9/11 Art Spiegelman has been living "in the shadow of no towers," and he uses his graphic narrative about 9/11 to illustrate his conversation with ghosts. Much as *Kari* and *Fun Home* used overlapping maps and frames as meaning-plays, Spiegelman's *In the Shadow of No Towers* draws collapsing frames overridden with ghosts and their hauntings as he weaves together the personal and political in an attempt to comprehend the events from the day. Spiegelman witnessed the crumbling towers "unmediated," and he writes-draws, "I still see the glowing tower, Awesome as it collapses." His daughter had just started at a high school located near the towers. Spiegelman and his wife rushed to the school when they saw the towers burning. They were inside the school when the first tower collapsed. The second followed suit. He writes, "The pivotal image from my 9/11 morning—one that didn't get photographed or videotaped into public memory but still remains burned onto the inside of my eyelids several years later—was the image of the looming north tower's glowing bones just before it vaporized."[7] What better description of a haunting. To Spiegelman, 9/11 is the ghost towers, its glowing bones, its black-on-black projection. The glowing bones of the tower haunt every page of the graphic narrative. They are ghosts, haunting

Spectral Politics   125

shadows, a burning background, the presence of absence, a seething presence. These simmering manifestations play with a purported normalcy or *post*-9/11 world.

Spiegelman converses with many ghosts in this novel. For example, *Maus* reenters this conversation. *Maus*, Spiegelman's Pulitzer Prize–winning graphic novel that narrated the experience of his family surviving the holocaust, emerges in his narrative about 9/11 through images of Spiegelman as a mouse now "equally terrorized by Al-Qaeda and by his own government." Ghosts proliferate the pages of *In the Shadow of No Towers*. The very first page displays newspaper print from 1901 with the headline, "President's Wound Reopened: Slight Change for Worse." The newspaper refers to the gunshots and subsequent wounding of the American President William McKinley, who was assassinated in 1901. A colored frame of the ghost towers overlaid on the old newspaper's black-and-white print communicates the inextricability of the past and present and their stubborn continuance. Spiegelman also uses cartoon characters from past comic strips to display entanglements and grapple with the present. He writes, "The blast that disintegrated those lower Manhattan towers also disinterred the ghosts of some Sunday supplement stars born on nearby Park Row about a century earlier." Spiegelman uses cartoon characters from newspaper comic strips, such as the *Katzenjammer Kids*, *Little Nemo in Slumberland*, and *Krazy Kat*, to exclaim in amazement, "I tell you, some of those century-old crumbling newspaper pages seem like they were drawn yesterday!"[8]

Ghosts in Spiegelman's graphic narrative are material actors—larger than life and with a looming presence. These myriad ghosts prevent Spiegelman from singularizing 9/11 as an isolated event or even an event without traces and vestiges. In Stoler's terms, its duress is palpably ubiquitous and haunts a tendency to singularize its presence. *In the Shadow of No Towers* reminds me of Derrida's contributions to the conversation about 9/11. He was in Shanghai on September 11, sitting in a café, when the café owner told him that "an airplane had 'crashed' into the Twin Towers." Derrida rushed back to his hotel to watch the televised news reports, and he notes, "It was easy to foresee that this was going to become, *in the eyes* of the world, what you called a 'major event.'"[9] Derrida sees the event mediated on television, unlike Spiegelman. However, like Spiegelman, he repeatedly works to situate the event as inextricably connected to world politics.

Derrida draws our attention to the concept of "event" and what gives it meaning and importance. He talks about how an event is formulated through an "organized information machine." This machine is political, economic, and technical in translating some events as major and others not. Derrida notes that these are not simply quantitative questions, as "one does not count the dead in the same way from one corner of the globe to the other."[10] While the information machine prominently displays and discusses deaths in specific places, other deaths are ignored if they don't fit the calculations. Old forms and concepts of territory and terrorism are riddled through 9/11, and new concepts prove inadequate to explain the vicissitudes of nanotechnologies and bacterial warfare. Terror, trauma, and fear straddle questions of sovereignty and autonomy as territorial demarcations are made permeable by new modes of warfare. Like Spiegelman, Derrida moves back and forth between theories and events, place and time, to decipher 9/11 and to use its haunting as a major event to unravel trajectories in global politics.

Thinking about events and our responsibility to them means conversing with ghosts as indices of duress and recognizing the importance of spectral apparitions that refuse to die. Ghosts and their absent presence draw out continuities between events, as Spiegelman uses the holocaust to understand 9/11 or how Derrida questions what makes an event as differentially valuing the dead from one part of the world to the other. While events create ghosts, their aftermath impels a conversation with ghosts of events past, present, and future. Appearing without an announcement, uninvited, and looming large, ghosts tear through the frames of containment and borders, the arrogance or need for privacy. Desettling individual and societal calculations about the numbers of living or dead, ghosts haunt the hubris of knowingness. They play with us to show us spaces of violence. It's no wonder that many of our radical ideologies or movements are predicated on hauntings.

Change and revolution, in this case, rise from uncontainable forces of the other world—inevitable, uncontrollable, and powerful. Ghosts, in this scenario, are social actors and agents of change. Whether it was Suniti Namjoshi's talking cow or Mithu Sen's painted pillows in *It's Good to Be Queen*, this book's narratives of play and haunting situate ghosts as social actors. The cow haunts binaries of human and animal, and the pillow seethes through conversations on hospitality and friendships by questioning protocols. The examples rendered in this book, while buoyant and playful, are no less serious as hauntings. They emerge from and tease the wide enduring duress of colonialism, of capitalism, of the arrogance of mastery, of sexism, of racism, and of nationalism. Indeed, the specter is haunting Hindu nationalism and transnational venues. Springing forth from landscapes of disaster, exploitation, and constructed normalcy, these ghosts herald revolution through their stubborn presence. They haunt through duress and event, unhinging conversations of postcolonialism, post-Marxism, or postdisaster. They play with the fabric of normality and the status quo of the world. No wonder Derrida converses with the specters of Marx when thinking about the future of Marxism.

Ghosts and Marxism

Whether reading Marx at Presidency College in India or teaching it to students in the United States, the opening lines of *The Communist Manifesto* echo through societal frames and the possibilities of societal reconfiguration: "A spectre is haunting Europe—the spectre of Communism. All the Powers of old Europe have entered into a holy alliance to exorcise this spectre: Pope and Czar, Metternich and Guizot, French Radicals and German police-spies." Published in 1848, *The Communist Manifesto* was written by Marx and Friedrich Engels at the request of a German workers' party to help formulate a party platform. Laying out the history of class struggle and an agenda for change, this poetically hard-hitting manifesto points out the ways that the bourgeoisie has revolutionized the relations of production. Feudal relations, sentimentalism, religion, and all other "idyllic relations" were transformed in the all-pervasive spread of capitalism and its greed: "It must nestle everywhere, settle everywhere, establish connections everywhere." Moreover, through its revolutionary spread and grandiose exploitation, the bourgeoisie produces its "grave-diggers" in the proletariat. What Marx and Engels emphasize through the manifesto are the revolutionary changes spearheaded by capitalism and its inevitable downfall. The capitalists are "like the sorcerer, who is no longer able to control the powers of the nether world whom he has called up by his spells."[11]

The repeated invocations of specters and spirits in *The Communist Manifesto* underline its central politics in drawing out a method for historical materialism and the unfolding of different relations of production. The specter of communism haunts Europe and compels alliance amongst its opposition. It promises change; it signals upheaval and revolution. As ghosts animate Marxism and signal its radical spirit, Marxism itself acts as a specter of capitalism and signals its disarray. Hauntings provide an ethics of justice in ideologies inspired by Marxism and frame their revolutionary spirit.

However, there are absences even within this spectral politics. As I have noted, even hauntings may produce ghosts of their own. Here I turn to the ghosts of Marxism and to the ghosts it produces. Marxism is unable to converse with ghost women. In this multidimensional analysis we can see how hauntings can preclude other hauntings and how some are doubly rendered spectral. The specters of Marx can take many guises.

Derrida's *Specters of Marx* is based on a plenary address he delivered in 1993 at a conference at the University of California Riverside, titled

"Whither Marxism? Global Crises in International Perspective." In the wake of Francis Fukuyama's dictum of the "end of history" and the victory of the free market, the conference organizers sought to frame a Marxist response to the turmoil in Eastern Europe and the former Soviet Union by bringing together participants from many parts of the world.[12] Derrida's plenary address at the conference forms the basis of *Specters of Marx: The State of the Debt, the Work of Mourning, and the New International*. A companion conference volume, *Whither Marxism? Global Crises in International Perspective*, supplements it with essays from Marxist scholars.

Derrida starts *Specters of Marx* with the yearning about "learning to live." He points out that this kind of living has to converse with life and death and between life and death "to learn to live *with* ghosts." It is the motivation for justice that compels him to speak at length about ghosts. Justice would be impossible without a reckoning of the responsibility beyond those who are "living present": "Without this *non-contemporaneity with itself of the living present*, without that which secretly unhinges it, without this responsibility and this respect for justice concerning those who *are not there*, of those who are no longer or who are not yet *present and living*, what sense would there be to ask the question 'where?' 'where tomorrow?' 'whither?'"[13] Derrida's response to "Whither Marxism?" converses with Marxism's relevance by invoking the specters of Marx, that which unhinges the present.

Derrida sees the specter as a "paradoxical incorporation," a "becoming-body": "It becomes, rather, some 'thing' that remains difficult to name: neither soul nor body, and both one and the other." More encompassing and looming large, a haunting plays with an ontological thinking of being. Derrida's "hauntology" is premised on repetition and plurality. The specter is a visitation, a remnant, and a constant arrival that unsettles ontological calculations. Riddling categories and linearity, the specter operates beyond regulations of the homogeneous time of the Enlightenment. As Derrida writes, "Furtive and untimely, the apparition of the specter does not belong to that time, it does not give that time, not that one: 'Enter the ghost, exit the ghost, re-enter the ghost.'" Playing with time and singularity, the specter cannot be contained. Not only is a haunting never dated but it is also plural, as in "specters" of Marx. Derrida clarifies that the plural connotes not simply an increase from one but also "*less than one*." Along with time and singularity, a specter challenges visuality, "it is *nothing* visible." In a specter's absent presence, we are looked upon without quite being able to pinpoint the gaze, something that Derrida calls the "*visor effect*."[14]

Derrida emphasizes Marx's love for Shakespeare and ghosts, as seen in Marx's use of Shakespeare's *Hamlet* in Marx's 1841 dissertation, and pronounces that Marx was "obsessed" with ghosts. For instance, if we look at *The German Ideology*, "it is crawling with them, a crowd of *revenants* are waiting for us there: shrouds, errant souls, clanking of chains in the night, groanings, chilling bursts of laughter, and all those heads, so many invisible heads that look at us, the greatest concentration of all specters in the history of humanity." Written a year after *The German Ideology*, *The Eighteenth Brumaire of Louis Bonaparte* is also marked with its "spectropolitics," as Derrida emphasizes. Marx's work with ghosts was integral to his understanding of the spirit and historical materialism, where the specter is vital to this historical change in relations of production.[15]

Spivak responds to *Specters of Marx* in her essay "Ghostwriting," published in 1995. While observing some problems with Derrida's works on Marx, Spivak writes about plenty of redeeming qualities in the book: "The reading of Hamlet—the visor-effect of history as the face of the ghostly father (an entire Derrida-Levinasian cluster there), the irreducible 'out-of-joint'—ness of time, the rehearsal of justice as relation to the other, and above all, the peculiar predications of ghostliness—is perhaps the best part of the book." Despite the good parts of the book, Spivak notes "woman is nowhere": "If Derrida plays Hamlet to Marx's ghost, there are no takers for Gertrude or Ophelia."[16] What does it mean for the *Specters of Marx* if woman is forever cast into darkness? How do we work with ghosts that also create ghosts? If Marxism is seen as a spectral presence and a persistent haunting, we must emphasize also that it works with its own apparitions, keeping women outside its "spectropolitics." My stress on spectral politics adds to a Marxist spectropolitics through its attention to multiple layers of haunting by communism and by women. "Ghostly women" riddle the contradiction at the heart of Marxism; how can it also create specters through its radical "spectropolitics"? While capitalism is haunted by the specter of communism and the specters of Marx, ghost women haunt a Marxist analytic, as Spivak explains to us.

In "Ghostwriting," Spivak works with her possession by "ghostwomen of Islam" when thinking with woman in Algeria and other Islamic contexts. Spivak uses Assia Djebar's book *Far from Medina* to write about the women in the narrative and ways to converse with "ghostly women": "The question of woman is here a figure for the impossible contradiction in the heart of history." Spivak notes the importance of rethinking the role of women in Islam as indispensable to understanding Algeria and Islam as a whole. *Far from Medina* begins at the historical moment when Muhammad is alive, and the Muslim world is yet to take shape. Djebar's narrative takes into account thirty-three women, and as Spivak describes, "attempting to make their ghosts dance, she imagines thirty-three possible worlds." The women in *Far from Medina* take an active role to shape the future, the women shape Islam, but they are always ghosts who appear from the past and are forever exclusions from history. Noting Muhammad's daughter Fatima's impossible struggle with her ancestors, gendered roles in Islam, and the passage of history in general, Spivak emphasizes how Djebar's book ends with a passionate call to respond to the question, "How shall I name you, Algeria?" Spivak notes that for the *Specters of Marx* to be asking questions with the same resonance, it needs to move much further.[17]

Aihwa Ong draws our attention to yet another set of "ghost women." In *Spirits of Resistance and Capitalist Discipline*, Ong studies Malay women as they transition from agricultural economies to working in industrial factories. In her analysis of how the women negotiated the changes, Ong describes the spirit possession that regularly animated the factory floors. Industrial capitalism, with its hallmarks of rationality and productivity, met a staunch opponent: the ghost. The author writes, "The American director wondered how he was to explain to corporate headquarters that '8000 hours of production were lost because someone saw a ghost.'" There were repeated reports that the factory was "dirty" and haunted. Sometimes factory managers explained the recurrence of the ghost in rational terms, pointing out that the workers lacked sleep and food, and the sightings of the apparitions were thus natural. Drawing our attention to the feminization of the industrial workforce and changes in the lives of Malay women, Ong lucidly emphasizes spirit possessions and seeking ghosts as an "unconscious retaliation" by Malay women, against male supervision, and against changing capitalist structures of production. The ghosts on the factory floors in Malaysia haunted the supervisors and women in different ways: the first through the loss of production time, and the second by interrupting the monotony of factory work and its disarticulation from their traditional structures of life and production. The question about whether the ghost is "real" remains one that is haunted by the context through which it operates. In Ong's words, "this is a story of cultural struggle in which the dialectic between spirits of resistance and new forms of discipline is the key refrain of rural Malays as they enter into the world of laboring by the clock."[18] The "spirits of resistance" play with industrial capitalism and rupture its logics.

An epistemology of justice must take hauntings seriously, hauntings of all kinds and in all their plurality. What about "bad ghosts"? Does situating hauntings as justice in fact situate us within a binary that leaves out many other situations of hauntings that may not be connected to justice? Thinking through this conundrum, if some ghosts create other ghosts, as seen in Marxist visions for justice, how do we open ourselves to a true plurality of hauntings, good or bad, good and bad? Throughout this book, I have studied ghosts—how the category of "animal" haunts postcolonial studies, the meaning-plays in translations as they move through maps, and Mithu Sen actively performing being possessed. While these ghosts may be seen as "bad" ghosts by some, as they inspire feminist and queer playful counteractions, I argue that there is no way to make an a priori distinction between "good" and "bad" ghosts. The very binary of good versus bad may silence and obfuscate perspectives even though specters of all kinds haunt the state and governance.

In *Contingency, Hegemony, Universality*, Slavoj Zizek draws our attention to how governance and the state are dependent on its "*obscene spectral underside.*" Zizek points out that the White supremacist movement leads a spectral existence: "So the problem is not simply the marginal who lead the spectral half-existence of those excluded by the hegemonic symbolic regime; the problem is that this regime itself, in order to survive, has to rely on a whole gamut of mechanisms whose status is spectral, disavowed, excluded from the public domain."[19] Thus it is not simply the unrecognized who are rendered spectral as White supremacist structures also depend on spectral mechanisms to maintain its power. Many may argue that White supremacy is not spectral and is not much more tangible than we choose to think; however, Zizek's point is useful in helping us to think through many kinds of spectral actors. Thinking about "bad ghosts," would one then position the "good" as the dominant, as that which creates the bad ghosts? I struggle to think which societal frame has positioned the "good" as the dominant power. Making distinctions between "good" and "bad" ghosts runs into the problem of disallowing their working. Rather, thinking with hauntings as a persistently stubborn epistemology of justice means learning to live with ghosts and constantly alert to exclusions that our frames of theory and action produce.

Conversing with Ghost Women

Toni Morrison's speech at the Nobel Foundation banquet in 1993 drew on her conversations with ghosts, as she received the award "pleasantly haunted" by those who had walked the halls before her.[20] She added, "I will leave this hall, however, with a new and much more delightful haunting than the one I felt upon entering: that is the company of Laureates yet to come."[21] Haunted by her predecessors and by the future, Morrison's reference to ghosts and haunting was not a mere coincidence or a manner of speech. In a conversation with Renee Montagne on National Public Radio (NPR) in 2004, Morrison gives us many more details about the ghosts that have haunted her novels and her life.[22] In this beautiful interview, Morrison talks about her books *Jazz* and *Beloved* and the ghosts that helped her write them. When Montagne asks her to explain how it is that she was "pleasantly haunted," Morrison relays that for her, ghosts and hauntings are about being "alert" and are something to "relish."[23] Morrison emphasizes that it was a "haunting alertness" that colors her novels. She talks about opening her mother's trunk as a child of four years of age, and the trunk lid smashing down as she gazed at the glittering clothes. This incident created a secret tie between Morrison and her dead mother, and Morrison endeavored to recollect these memories as she wrote *Jazz*. We hear of another incident when Morrison sees a woman walk out of the water in front of her country home. This would go on to shape her narrative in *Beloved* about two slave women who loved each other.

Morrison's ghosts and their hauntings weave complex stories of memory, loss, slavery, brutality, and joy—of ancestors looking toward the future.[24] The present remains torn under the many gazes from the past and into the future, and Morrison's hauntings inspire a political and social imagination that would relish living with ghosts as attentiveness to history and a vision beyond the present. Ghosts and hauntings, whether the specters of Marx or Morrison, disturb a present status quo, break its comfortable linearity, and extol thinking and feeling anew. Many ghost women haunt the pages of this book, imploring an epistemology of unknowingness while shunning the arrogance that allows anyone to believe they can completely capture a person or situation. Moving through categories of living and dead, here and now, past and future, ghosts generate hauntological disarray. Much like Anzaldúa's emphasis on the consciousness of borderlands, hauntings move through contradictions, lightness and darkness, transforming both, effecting "a constant changing of forms."[25]

I am inspired here to keep thinking with ghost women, moving with them, to discover feminist worlds that remain clothed within categories or seen as old and dated. I often teach Gloria Anzaldúa's *Borderlands/La Frontera: The New Mestiza* alongside her children's books, including *Prietita and the Ghost Woman*. Children's books have a great deal to teach us all. In this story, illustrated by Maya Christina Gonzalez, Anzaldúa asks us to be "friends" with ghosts. The story begins with Prietita working in the garden of the local healer, *la curandera*. Prietita's little sister comes running to ask her to ask la curandera to help their mother, who is feeling sick. Prietita asks la curandera for help, but she is unable to do much because she does not have the healing plant she needs. She draws a picture of the plant for Prietita so that she can find it at King Ranch, a dangerous area not suitable for a little girl. Prietita ventures into it anyway.

Initially, Prietita stays close to the barbed wire that encloses the area, but as she searches for the plant, she moves deeper and farther into the woods. Soon the fence is nowhere in sight. She asks help from a dove, a salamander, bugs, and a deer, but she still can't find the plant. Prietita soon comes to an open area with a lagoon and sees "a dark woman dressed in white emerge from the trees and float above the water." Prietita beseeches the ghost woman to help her. The ghost woman helps Prietita find the plant that will cure her mother and guides her safely back home through the woods and disappears. La curandera takes the branches of the healing plant from Prietita and tells her, "I am very proud of you. You have grown up this night."[26]

This simple story, illustrated with bright imagery, is wonderfully provocative in asking us to move through our fears of darkness, of strangers, and to venture forth to seek new friends. Anzaldúa tells us about her own childhood growing up in south Texas near the King Ranch and her grandmother's scary stories about *la Llorona*, the ghost woman. These stories were widely prevalent in Mexico and the Southwest, where most everyone was terrified of this ghost woman. Anzaldúa, however, was determined to undo the stereotypical representations. Delving into her Chicana/Mexicana cultural history, she soon discovered that indeed there was a positive source of energy and healing. Consequently, she wrote this story to inspire children to discover many truths and move beyond the simple surface of issues and things.[27]

What does it mean for feminisms to converse with ghosts, as Anzaldúa implores us to do? How do our methods of knowing, our epistemologies, and ontological assumptions shift through ghostly encounters? While ghost women beckon us to be alert and note the slippages in our political registers, as Morrison shows us, they also point to continuities and disjunctions among our past, present, and future. We see that ghost women, though in the shadows, perform many tasks. They also move with us through the woods, and like a friend, they work with us, helping us in our tasks. Though they appear uninvited and glide on surfaces, they also undo our assumptions about others and the unknown. Moreover, moving beyond utilitarian functionality, ghosts lead us to question who "we" are, the limits of our communities, who can enter them, who we are prepared to play with, and if we are prepared to be played with.

As Sen's *It's Good to Be Queen* shows, ghost women haunt feminist friendships and urge us to build solidarity with women from different walks of life. The exhibit offers a critique of the promises of transnational friendships that oftentimes simply engage with the other on one's own terms. Subverting the protocols of being a guest and a friend, Sen's aesthetic politics thus draws out modes of relating through differences. Absences and shadows guide this aesthetic politics, whether seen in the absence of the artist or artwork on the day of the exhibit. The hair that hangs from the shower head or a greasy fish on a pillowcase are also spectral apparitions, unexpected intrusions, and visitations conjured by the message asking Sen to be tidy and use a specific pillowcase. These spectral hauntings of hypocrisies in the name of hospitality urge us to consider what it would mean to be truly hospitable, and to open our doors to friends in all shapes and forms.

If Anzaldúa's ghost woman models what it means to be a true friend by being a catalyst for growth and discovery, we move beyond a model of friend-making that simply reiterates the status quo or maintains the norm. Sen's aesthetics also haunt our modalities of relating across differences by exaggerating presences and absences. Through an incessant questioning of what and who can be present or seen as legitimately present, Sen's art exhibits draw out the absences with playfulness and buoyancy. Her use of hair that is out of place, alongside other artifacts and performances, situates multiple layers in meaning of being in place and its concomitant exclusions. Haunted by presences and absences, Sen's art inspires a playful epistemology of working with ghosts. Invoking the words of Banu Subramaniam, "How do you learn to see ghosts? And what do you see once you learn to see them?"[28]

Queer Ghosts

In *Ghost Stories for Darwin: The Science of Variation and the Politics of Diversity*, Subramaniam invites us to learn and see with ghosts as a way to unravel connections and lineages from the past to the present and between "naturecultural" continuities. In many ways, working with ghosts is discerning histories and their violent renderings and those who live fugitive lives. Writing about the recurring presence of ghosts and their roles in Bollywood and other Indian movies, Subramaniam argues, "The ghosts by their constant and insisting presence coax and shepherd the slow uncovering of the past, the uncomfortable but undeniable truth. In the end, the guilty are apprehended and the innocent consigned to eternal heterosexual bliss. The injustice corrected, the ghosts disappear into oblivion with peaceful and satisfied souls."[29] In these narratives, the ghosts serve a purpose, a heterosexual agenda. Often, in many Bollywood movies, someone becomes a ghost because of unrequited or failed heterosexual romance; for example, a lover is killed because he or she belonged to a different caste or religious community. The ensuing storyline moves to a grand finale where the ghost can ultimately rest, and heterosexual couples live happily ever after. These ghosts serve as social agents for "heterosexual bliss," as Subramaniam points out. Moreover, the ghosts disappear in the grand finale with the restitution of a heterosexual utopia, which, in many Bollywood movies, is antithetical to hauntings. The appearance of ghosts signals the absence of "heterosexual bliss" but a yearning toward it, all the while queering social imagination toward heterosexual bliss's unfulfilled promise. Although ghosts in Bollywood movies queer by disrupting normalcy, José Esteban Muñoz takes us a step further, to ghosts as queer agents.

In *Cruising Utopia: The Then and There of Queer Futurity*, Muñoz writes about the importance of ghosts in fathoming a queer political imagination. He emphasizes that queerness is an ideal that we will never reach because at its heart it is always about generating other possibilities and other ones again. Working with Ernst Bloch's thoughts on hope and utopia, Muñoz argues, "If queerness is to have any value whatsoever, it must be viewed as being visible only in the horizon." Situating how ghosts have been used to emphasize the absences in heterosexual societies, Muñoz converses with ghosts to imagine futures and utopias: "The double ontology of ghosts and ghostliness, the manner in which ghosts exist inside and out and traverse categorical distinctions, seems especially useful for a queer criticism that attempts to understand communal mourning, group psychologies, and the need for a politics that 'carries' our dead with us into battles for the present and future."[30] Queer memory, to Muñoz, enthuses a different politics, one that infuses it with longing for other possibilities and haunts its present parameters. Looking at queerness as utopic politics, Muñoz's book also situates hauntings as central to queer utopias. Working against a given and a here and now, queer politics spills far beyond programs of policy and action.

Questions related to time and history have been central to queer theory, as has its reckoning with multiple temporalities and ghosts, and this book has continued the endeavor to unscript normative temporalities with particular attention to play and hauntings. The drawing of maps and nations is an attempt to homogenize space and time. Queer transnationalism and its meaning-plays draw attention to asynchronous temporalities and a politics of becoming and un-becoming that haunt any one theory of time and space, history and geography. Queer transnationalism's endeavor to unravel maps within maps, movements back and forth, haunts any static category or premise. Feminist and queer politics also contain active exclusions; they cannot be sacrosanct about their ability to see ghosts. Susan Stryker's critique of queer theory, for instance, highlights problems with queer studies: "The field of transgender studies has taken shape over the past decade in the shadow of queer theory." Transgender study's critical work, as with disability studies and intersex studies, reveals queer theories' inability to move outside a frame for sexual identity.[31] Queer theory, in its critique of heteronormativity, ironically settles into a familiar normative logic that prevents it from seeing ghosts. Queer ghosts, in a way, haunt themselves to remain queer, as Muñoz reminds us.

Ghost women, queer ghosts, communist ghosts, and many other ghosts propel us toward complex histories and ways of knowing. As Derrida reminds us, it is important to think of ghosts in the plural and as more and less than one. The cacophonous plurality pulls forth erasures and silences, absences and traces. It is not simply that ghosts do the work for us but that they make us work toward feminist and queer visions by haunting our frames of analysis. In eerie replication, our binary models of viewing the world are projected onto ghosts that we see, that is, male or female, straight or queer; working with a feminist and queer politics of haunting we must note this mirroring to create more livable worlds. My attention to translations in this book has a similar epistemological inspiration. In order to be alive to its ethics, we must listen to shadows and erasures when translating. Translations in queer transnationalism signal to an impossibility and to an epistemology of listening and responding to differences. The transnational and the translational within their circuitous routes show how the queer subject is always in excess or outside the frames of representation. Chapter 2 emphasizes the need to queer translations and to posit translations at the heart of transnational inquiry. Arguing against singular understandings of identity or of "coming out," I remain haunted by multiple maps that spiral over and under ground, contouring transnationalism and translations as a playful plurality. This persistent haunting signaled through "always translating" helps us think of a political imagination that is willing to travel through different orbits.

Like Muñoz's queer ghosts that work against a here and now by haunting the status quo, Namjoshi's plaited animal-human becomings featured in chapter 1 signal a sexual politics that refuses to be contained within categories. Through her exaggerated and subtle work with animals and animality, Namjoshi's work helps discern entanglements among race, gender, sexuality, nationality, and their insidious uncoupling. By separating issues or identities we create ghosts that flit between the ostensibly rigid identity walls. Writing against this epistemological containment, "becoming animal and becoming transnational" work toward a playful subversion through a spirited conversation with a cow. The utopic longing that traverses through this project is, to use the words of Jasbir Puar, an "effort to reintroduce politics into the political."[32]

Ghosts, Play, and Postcolonial Hauntings

Hauntings and play weave their way through this book. The playful politics that I emphasize, whether through Sen's aesthetic politics or Namjoshi's engagements with animals and animality, operate against and through hauntings. When Sen gifts her audience fragments of the Taj Mahal or stands possessed in front of an international audience, her politics haunts by bringing to the forefront the political economy of tokenization and exoticization of women. Playfully irreverent, Sen's gestures and undoing of language formulations urge us to listen and listen carefully. Alongside, Namjoshi's matter-of-fact dialogues with animals through zoomorphic and anthropomorphic frames makes her texts pulsate with different voices— the visible and invisible voices that shadow categorizations of animals and animality. Conversing with colonialisms and their hauntings, these playful modalities provoke thought and activism to face the "duress" of violent histories. Activism that works with hauntings would insistently question the outcomes of its actions and the inevitable shadows of those outcomes.

We live now in an age of continual crisis, facing disasters, extinctions, and turmoil at both local and global scales. In such an epoch, attending to hauntings and play gathers increasing urgency. The global ascendancy of the extreme right, neoliberal economics, shattering of public spaces and citizen forums, tightening of borders and control, widening social stratifications through a pandemic, and displacements—these all necessitate working with ghosts. As Avery Gordon points out, ghosts serve as "social figures" that draw forgotten histories, refugees, shadows, and memories into political imaginations.[33] We cannot grapple with climate change, for instance, without reckoning with hauntings. With rising sea levels, changing ecological habitats, and disappearing of species, death, memories, and haunted landscapes stand as testimonies to the arrogance of the Anthropocene. In *Arts of Living on a Damaged Planet*, editors Anna Tsing, Heather Swanson, Elaine Gan, and Nils Bubandt comment, "Ghosts remind us that we live in an impossible present—a time of rupture, a world haunted with the threat of extinction. Deep histories tumble in unruly graves that are bulldozed into gardens of Progress."[34]

Our haunted landscape riddles the hubris of modernity and progress. The global pandemic has centered the failure of public infrastructure and further accentuated divides between the rich and the poor, while the poor are also being made "essential." The public and private, home and abroad, and essential and nonessential are meaning-plays haunted by histories of contestation and exclusion. As we rescript understanding of containment, safety, and categories under COVID-19 capitalism, working with meaning-plays helps us, more than ever, to understand structures—social, political, and epistemological—and their workings.

As we live through haunted landscapes, politics, and economics, seeing and speaking with ghosts can center political alertness and restlessness in creating visions for the future. The ghosts enter and exit, flit in and out, visit at will, haunt persistently, and play with categories and conceptions of control and containment. Interconnectedness, complicity, and entanglements play with singularity and separation. Place and time dance back and forth in cyclical contamination. Spivak, in *Ghostwriting*, says that much of her understanding of spectral politics comes from reading James Mooney's work published in 1896, *The Ghost-Dance Religion and the Sioux Outbreak of 1890*.[35] Following cues from the subalternists to "follow the ghost," Spivak elaborates on the ghost dance as a practice of being haunted by the past and by ancestors, of, indeed, calling upon such hauntings.[36] In this way she contrasts the ghost dance with rituals that worship the past as a static object. The ethical and analytic power of the ghost dance lies precisely in its attention to the presence and future of ghosts and ancestors, of hauntings. The ghost dance has a long history among Indigenous American groups who, through the dance, call on the many ghosts created by the American genocide to assist in reviving Indigenous autonomy. The details of the dance vary among groups that practice it, but in all cases it incorporates social activism and social healing.[37] For Spivak, the ghost dance emphasizes "relations" between past and future, and it cannot be reduced to a singular proposition, such as, "The ghost dance is an attempt to establish the ethical relation with history as such, ancestors real or imagined." Spivak explains that the "'end' of the ghost dance," different from most social-justice frames, is "to make the past a future." In continuing the past into the future, the ghost is both a "*revenant*" ("a returner") and an "*arrivant*" ("a person who arrives").[38] In this entry and exit, return and arrival, we discern relations and traces and endeavor to reach an ethical engagement with our histories and future trajectories. As we frame visions for justice, I urge us to incorporate hauntings and play as braided, entangled ethics that can keep postcolonial and transnational feminisms alive to the exclusions and violence in the world around us.

Postcolonial Hauntings centers play and hauntings as indispensable for transnational postcolonial feminisms. By complicating play and hauntings through considerations of their heterogeneity, this book moves us beyond thinking of them as having one rationale or personae. Coupling heterogeneity with an emphasis on layers of spectral politics, when ghosts can also be haunted by other ghosts that remain excluded, I situate play and hauntings as the inspiration for change. Being attentive to the world around us means to know play and hauntings as coconspirators that constantly illuminate facets of our world and those outside it. This restless ethic animates the book and provides hope for justice that can constantly haunt itself.

Un-Summary

Play and hauntings have infiltrated *Postcolonial Hauntings* to disturb trajectories in thought and activism that simply perpetuate the status quo of the world. Among the questions addressed are these: How might postcolonial subjects use animality and animalization to sabotage their pejorative usage? How do we move beyond imperial modes of hospitality and friend-making? If translations are a necessity in feminist and queer transnational movements, how do we understand the translator's play with meaning? Whether deciphering frames of animality and animalization, questioning transnational friendships and hospitality, situating the counterpolitics in feminist art, or understanding queer transnationalism with its emphasis on translations, the questions that have animated *Postcolonial Hauntings* emphasize the inextricable connection between play and hauntings and bring to the forefront selected key conversations in feminist and queer theory, teasing and undoing their stakes. The search for playful creative possibilities has fueled this book and has been aided by conversations with diverse theorists who also work to open fields of action and theory that have remained largely invisible in our neatly categorized world. I use these useful cross-combustions to draw in and draw out and ultimately to draw through the lines of theory to visualize a playful feminist political imagination that can work with postcolonial hauntings and speak to a transnational world.

I see the core contributions of this book to be several. First, the book establishes an ethical method for postcolonial transnational feminisms through reckonings of play with hauntings. Play or mischievous resistance remains an important trope for survival through borders—geographical, political, and social—and numerous studies have noted its incidence and recurrence; in discerning play's entanglement with hauntings we reveal an understanding about why, precisely, play remains important through continuations of violence in myriad forms. For example, if a guest plays with a host's protocols for decorum, we need to question the power equation that lays the host's protocol as sacrosanct, and what histories of violence, as in postcolonial seething conditions, inspire the guest to play with rules. Thinking about play as a sole reaction to an immediate cause fails to acknowledge play's spirited history, as history compels play's repeated occurrence.

Second and flowing from the argument above on the persistent nature of play, I stress the heterogeneous politics of play and hauntings. Play and hauntings are repeated through time, and they also work with politics of different hues. In other words, play and hauntings cannot be relegated only to "good" resistance and activism. Capitalism plays with consumers to make more profit, as do fascism and political dictatorships, through an economy of violence and deceit that jostles anew our parameters of comprehension. Hauntings work this way, too. While hauntings certainly shadow the present moment and instill responsibility and responsiveness to regimes of racism, sexism, and colonialism, let us not forget the spectral underground in ongoing White supremacy and hate movements. Thus, while working with play and hauntings as indispensable moments in postcolonial struggles, I remain alert toward the entangled work of play and hauntings in politics across the spectrum and in play and hauntings' repeated occurrences and urge for its serious consideration in theories and activisms. The critique of hegemonic structures also forefronts the heterogeneity of ghosts: ghost women, queer ghosts, communist ghosts, among others. A universal theory of haunting fails miserably to acknowledge other shadows.

Third, this book frames the critical role of language in border crossings and reframings in meaning-plays. Meaning-plays are ostensibly slippages through language systems as we move from one language to another, as seen in translations that are pivotal to a global world. In addition, meaning-plays tell us about subject negotiations and yearnings to maintain and complicate the nuances to identities and events. Meaning-plays, for example, as this book demonstrates, help queer subjects in India move through competing worlds of tradition and modernity and of national and transnational that haunt an unequivocal embrace of being queer. The movement of subjects through shifting cartographies and temporal and spatial discontinuities makes the work of meaning-plays central to transnational postcolonial feminisms. The central concomitant anchoring of play and hauntings engages with heterogeneous politics and shifting spatial positions within global power structures. I argue through the book that attentiveness to meaning-plays discerns the past and present, here and there, and moves us toward responsive ethics in our theories and activisms.

It is easy to discern play and hauntings in the world around us. We are living in a ghostly world. Major economies, societal structures, and political equations were unsettled with the onslaught of COVID-19, alongside reeling unemployment, the precarity of essential workers, death, destitution, and vulnerability. While social stratifications have been further attenuated and inequalities starkly apparent, we notice an accentuation of societal divisions based on class, race, gender, ability, and nationality under capitalism's infrastructure, where "essential" means disposable and killable. We have created new ghosts since 2020, alongside ghosts from the 1918 influenza pandemic and fascism that have repeatedly entered our social worlds. Media's prolific reportage of COVID-19 has used archives from 1919 to report on eerie similarities between "then" and "now." "Spanish flu" and "Wuhan virus" are joined in myriad ways through geopolitics, media framing, and medical archives that prevent an easy bracketing off from one time to the next. Meanwhile, the politics of fascism, border control, and neoliberal economic trajectories haunt a global populace, fracturing the hubris of solidarity and the "we" of suffering.

A macabre play renders temporality and spatial calculations as pressing concerns and as uncontrollable. Tropes of mastery beat a hastening retreat or reemerge in full battle cry to control media framings and articulations of the deadly virus. A play exhibited through false news and political chicanery moves in tandem with a play against arrogance, certitude, and definition as the virus mutates and changes shape. Even while COVID-19 rages through the world in different stages of mutation, there is an urgent push toward normalcy and a pre-2020 world, notwithstanding the political economy of the pre-2020 world that led to the catastrophe of COVID-19 in 2020. Rather than noting the infiltration between places and times, we operate with place and time as blocks that can easily be rearranged, choosing to ignore the always-already-changing present and the intricate web of events that fold on each other. A refusal to engage with hauntings persists alongside the concomitant play with reality. As this book has argued, the braiding of haunting and play demands attention because it highlights the cohering threads of power structures, temporality, and spatial meanings.

Here at the end, I invoke once more the visitation by Satyajit Ray's ghost king in the film, *Goopy Gyne Bagha Byne*. Like Spivak, who "follows the ghost" of the ghost dance as an ethical work of revival and autonomy, Ray, too, draws our attention to the buoyant play of ghosts who haunt our world with possibilities for change. Ray's ghost king, like Sen's transnational queen, subverts social and ethical orders in his dance and challenges us to remake the world by granting three boons. In the film, the musicians Goopy and Bagha chose to be well cared for, to travel among the people, and to spread joy through their art. If we were given three boons by a ghost king, what would we ask for? And why? Will we, too, choose to move buoyantly, in friendship, toward a politics of hope in more livable worlds?

Notes

Introduction

1. See for example, Gordon, *Ghostly Matters*; Chen, *Animacies*; Bennett, *Toni Morrison*; Ong, *Spirits of Resistance and Capitalist Discipline*; Saleh-Hanna, "Black Feminist Hauntology"; Muñoz, *Cruising Utopia*.

2. Karl Marx writes in *The Eighteenth Brumaire of Louis Bonaparte*, "Hegel remarks somewhere that all facts and personages of great importance in world history occur, as it were, twice. He forgot to add: the first time as tragedy, the second as farce." He critiques "new" revolutions and ideas by emphasizing, "The tradition of all the dead generations weighs like a nightmare on the brain of the living." See Marx in Simon, *Selected Writings*, 188.

3. See, for example, Trawick, *Enemy Lines*; Hutcheon, *Irony's Edge*; Lugones, "Playfulness"; Kaviraj, *Unhappy Consciousness*; Sicart, *Play Matters*; Chess, *Play like a Feminist*.

4. Satyajit Ray was the director, writer, costume designer, and lyrics and music composer for this film that was based on a story written by his grandfather Upendrakishore Ray Chowdhury. The protagonists of the film, Goopy Gyne and Bagha Byne, are characters from *Sandesh*, a Bengali children's magazine started by Chowdhury in 1913. The film exhibits a visual panorama of special effects that was unknown to Bengali cinema in the 1960s to showcase ghost dances and the blessings of a ghost king. See Ganguly, *Cinema, Emergence, and the Films of Satyajit Ray*; Robinson, *Satyajit Ray*.

5. Marx, *Communist Manifesto*, in *Selected Writings*, 158.
6. Derrida, *Specters of Marx*, 4.
7. Spivak, "Ghostwriting."
8. Spivak, "Ghostwriting," 67.
9. Hartman, *Lose Your Mother*, 133.
10. A. Roy, "Graveyard Talks Back."
11. A. Roy, "Graveyard Talks Back."

12. A. Roy, "Graveyard Talks Back."

13. Achille Mbembe's *Necropolitics*, for instance, draws out the inadequacy of Michel Foucault's theory of biopower and, instead, uses the concept of "necropolitics" to describe the creation of "death-worlds" or "new and unique forms of social existence in which vast populations are subjected to living conditions that confer upon them the status of the *living dead*." Mbembe, *Necropolitics*, 92, original emphasis. Scholars conversing with the creation of "death-worlds," for instance, in Shatema Threadcraft's work on necropolitics and gender, look at framings of dead bodies within specific geopolitical moments. Threadcraft urges us to see the difference between homicide and femicide in North America and to see the need to work closely with intersectionality when perceiving the politics of death. See Threadcraft, "North American Necropolitics and Gender."

14. Holland, *Raising the Dead*, 9.

15. Mbembe, *Necropolitics*, 66.

16. Robert JC Young in his essay "Postcolonial Remains" draws our attention to a PMLA roundtable in 2007, "The End of Postcolonial Theory?" where it was announced as being over. Young asks, "Why does it continue to unsettle people so much?" Young, "Postcolonial Remains," 125.

17. Kwame Anthony Appiah, for instance, in his oft-cited essay "Is the Post- in Postmodernism the Post- in Postcolonial" writes about postcoloniality as comprising "*comprador* intelligentsia": "a relatively small, Western-style, Western-trained group of writers and thinkers, who mediate the trade in cultural commodities of world capitalism at the periphery." Appiah, "Is the Post," 348.

In their special issue Decolonial and Postcolonial Approaches for *Feminist Studies* in 2017, the editors, Priti Ramamurthy and Ashwini Tambe, comment, "The goal of this special issue is to offer a venue for a dialogue between postcolonial and decolonial feminisms precisely because they appeared to speak past each other." Preface, 510.

Walter Mignolo, for instance, differentiates between the postcolonial and the decolonial and emphasizes that "both walk in the same direction, following different paths." He points out the origin of the decolonial can be seen during the cold war, in the third world, and in the labor of African and Afro-Caribbean theory and activism. For him, the postcolonial originates in the experience of British India and to Edward Said's book *Orientalism* published in 1978. See Mignolo, *Darker Side of Western Modernity*, 55.

18. Asher, "Spivak and Rivera Cusicanqui," 524.

19. Bill Ashcroft, Gareth Griffiths, and Helen Tiffin in *The Empire Writes Back* point out how Edward Said and Gayatri Spivak, for varied reasons, have rejected the term "postcolonial": "Said from an aversion to any systematic theory (all of which he regards as 'theological') and Spivak in favor of what she regards as the more inclusive term 'subaltern.'" Ashcroft, Griffiths, and Tiffin, *Empire Writes Back*, 198.

Stephen D. Moore in "Situating Spivak" notes about the politics of representation surrounding the publication of *The Post-Colonial Critic* in 1990, "Spivak is not so subtly transformed into *the* prototypical and quintessential postcolonial critic." Alongside he notes how Robert Young in his 1995 book *Colonial Desires* calls Edward Said, Homi Bhabha, and Gayatri Spivak the "Holy Trinity" of postcolonial work. Spivak throughout has sharply criticized the field with little affinity toward being a part of the Holy Trinity. Moore, "Situating Spivak," 23–24.

20. Spivak, *Critique of Postcolonial Reason*, 361.
21. Spivak, *Critique of Postcolonial Reason*, ix.
22. Spivak, *Critique of Postcolonial Reason*, x–xi.
23. Ahmed, *Strange Encounters*, 11.
24. Ahmed, *Strange Encounters*, 10.
25. Muñoz, *Disidentifications*, 11.
26. Spivak, *Critique of Postcolonial Reason*, xii.
27. Mbembe, *On the Postcolony*, 15, original emphasis.
28. In a roundtable discussion on queer temporalities, Carolyn Dinshaw comments, "Postcolonial historians have been most influential in this process, and the turn toward temporality has been thrilling: it opens the way for other modes of consciousness to be considered seriously—those of ghosts, for example, and mystics." Dinshaw et al., "Theorizing Queer Temporalities," 178.
29. See Edelman, *No Future*; Halberstam, *In a Queer Time and Place*; Kara Keeling, *Queer Times, Black Futures*.
30. Gandhi, *Postcolonial Theory*, viii, ix.
31. Loomba, *Colonialism/Postcolonialism*, 12.
32. Loomba, *Colonialism/Postcolonialism*, 13.
33. McClintock, "Angel of Progress," 87.
34. Sikh traditions and religion grew in the Punjab area of South Asia, and Sikhism has grown as a countertradition to Hinduism. Sikhism as a religious practice anchors service to the community as one of its guiding principles.
35. Lugones, "Playfulness," 4, 10; 16; 15; 16; original emphasis.
36. Kaviraj, *Unhappy Consciousness*, 28–29.
37. Hartman, *Scenes of Subjection*, 13–14.
38. Chowdhury, *Transnationalism Reversed*, 9.
39. Grewal and Kaplan, *Scattered Hegemonies*, 17.
40. Mohanty, *Feminism without Borders*, 2.
41. Leela Gandhi refers to the "very volatile and tenuous partnership" between feminism and postcolonial studies and draws our attention to issues that fracture this companionship. Gandhi, *Postcolonial Theory*, 83.
42. Alexander, *Pedagogies of Crossing*, 183.
43. Spivak, *Aesthetic Education*, 3; 4; 4; 4 5; 4; 10–11.
44. Spivak, *Aesthetic Education*, 104.
45. See Spivak, *Aesthetic Education in the Era of Globalization*, ix. Spivak states, "A double bind is rather more than the suggestion that having found it, you can play it."
46. Misri, *Beyond Partition*, 4.
47. Misri, *Beyond Partition*, 4.
48. Butler, *Frames of War*, 100.

Chapter 1. Becoming Animal, Becoming Transnational

1. Fanon, *Wretched of the Earth*, 8.
2. Biswas, "Why the Humble Cow."
3. It remains important to recognize, as Radhika Govindrajan emphasizes in *Animal Intimacies*, that "not *all* cows" enjoy the same status in India. Govindrajan showcases how *pahari* cows and Jersey cows are differentiated in Uttarkhand. Through nuanced ethnography, she argues that the difference between the cows emerges through specific materialities that need recognition: "Bovine materiality thus came to play an important part in shaping the nature and outcome of Hindu nationalist projects of cow protection in contemporary India." Govindrajan, *Animal Intricacies*, 66.
4. See Suri, "Ban on Beef."
5. Spivak, *Readings*, 56, 58, 56.
6. The concepts of "biopower" and "biopolitics" have taken on a life of their own. They are used to connote "administration of life," "biological politics," "technology of life," and the "entanglements of life and power." See Chatterjee, Roy, and Subramaniam, "Spectres."
7. Agamben, *Homo Sacer*, 7, 7, 8.
8. See Fox, "India's Sacred Cow"; Singh, "1 Lakh Cattle."
9. Barber, *Strong Democracy*, 20–21.
10. Gatens, "Corporeal Representation," 83.
11. Gatens, "Corporeal Representation," 83.
12. See Doniger, "Hinduism."
13. Biswas, "Why the Humble Cow"; Mangaldas, "India's Got Beef with Beef."
14. Dave, "Something," 42.
15. The Eurocentric basis of Anderson's scholarship has been critiqued in conversations on nation building in the postcolonial world. See, for example, Partha Chatterjee, "Whose Imagined Community?"
16. Ong, *Flexible Citizenship*, 4.
17. Haraway, *When Species Meet*, 274.
18. Woods, "Nature and the Refrigerating Machine," 99.
19. Povinelli, *Geontologies*, 19.
20. Povinelli, *Geontologies*, 19.
21. Irish, "Coronavirus."
22. Srinivas, *Cow in the Elevator*. Writing about the city of Bangalore in India and its accelerated modernization, Srinivas notes the ironies of globalizing forces where cows also ride elevators: "In January 2009 I found myself trying to help lure a reluctant cow named Kamadhenu into a mirrored elevator" (34). This specific example refers to a house-blessing ceremony in a new apartment complex in Bangalore that required the sacred presence of a cow. As the apartment was on the eight floor, the cow's mode of transportation was the glitzy elevator. Srinivas provides an excellent account of the puzzles of modernity where we meet many

improbable situations in mundane contexts. India's sacred cows thus also ride elevators as India travels through a modernized global economy.

23. B. Jackson, "Words Create Worlds," 173.
24. Mann, "Suniti Namjoshi," 111.
25. Mann, "Suniti Namjoshi," 111, original emphasis.
26. Meighoo, *End of the West*, xii.
27. Namjoshi, *Goja*, 78–79, added emphasis.
28. "Raja" and "rani" refer to "king" and "queen" in many Indian languages, including Bengali and Hindi. The addition of "saheb" to the title adds a salutation of respect.
29. Namjoshi, *Goja*, 10.
30. Namjoshi, *Goja*, 11.
31. Namjoshi, *Goja*, 67.
32. Namjoshi, *Goja*, 66.
33. Namjoshi, *Goja*, 87, original emphasis.
34. "Feminism."
35. Dasgupta, "'Do I Remove My Skin?" 101.
36. Dasgupta, "Do I Remove My Skin?" 101.
37. Namjoshi, *Because of India*, 28.
38. Namjoshi, *Fabulous Feminist*, 24.
39. Namjoshi, *Fabulous Feminist*, 24.
40. Namjoshi, *Because of India*, 29.
41. See Doniger, "Zoomorphism in Ancient India." Wendy Doniger suggests that the Panchatantra was put together around 500 CE and drew on older Buddhist traditions: "The Panchatantra is a textbook of political science, probably intended for the education of princes, but its cast of characters was widely diffused into all levels of Indian literature, from folktales in the vernaculars to court poetry in Sanskrit" (18).
42. Namjoshi, *Fabulous Feminist*, 20.
43. Namjoshi, *Fabulous Feminist*, 20.
44. Namjoshi, *Fabulous Feminist*, 20.
45. Swayamvara refers to a public ceremony in ancient India where a woman chose her husband from amongst many suitors.
46. Namjoshi and Hanscombe, *Flesh and Paper*, 63.
47. Namjoshi and Hanscombe, *Flesh and Paper*, 62.
48. Namjoshi, *Conversations of Cow*, 13; 14; 23; 24; 24–25.
49. Namjoshi, *Fabulous Feminist*, 53–54.
50. Namjoshi, *Fabulous Feminist*, 53–54.
51. Namjoshi, *Conversations of Cow*, 13. Brahmins are one of the *varnas* (classes) that constitute the Hindu social structure. They constitute the priestly class and occupy a revered position in the caste structure. A Brahman, originally imported from India, is a hybrid breed of cattle raised in the United States and known for their adaptation skills and ability to withstand extreme heat and parasites. Namjoshi plays with multiple connotations, including being a

Brahmin and Brahman cattle. In this meaning-play it is important to reiterate the casteism that is projected and fueled by the current beef bans. Brahmins and their identity are aligned with cows, and lower-caste people face violence as beef eaters. See Doniger, "Hinduism."

52. Namjoshi, *Conversations of Cow*, 20–23.
53. Brown, *States of Injury*, 167.
54. Namjoshi, *Conversations of Cow*, 32, 53.
55. Namjoshi, *Conversations of Cow*, 72.
56. Cary Wolfe in *What Is Posthumanism?* explains that posthumanism "comes both before and after humanism: before in the sense that it names the embodiment and embeddedness of the human being in not just its biological but also its technological world. . . . But it comes after in the sense that posthumanism names a historical moment in which the decentering of the human by its imbrication in technical, medical, informatics, and economic networks is increasingly impossible to ignore" (xv). Alongside different renditions of posthumanism are various ways of approaching ecofeminism. See, for example, Mies and Shiva, *Ecofeminism*, and Adams and Gruen, *Ecofeminism*. Works centering queer politics and ecologies include Mortimer-Sandilands and Erickson, *Queer Ecologies*, and Seymour, *Bad Environmentalism*. We also have scholarship that riddles the categories of animal, animate, and inanimate. See Chen, *Animacies*. Scholars drawing attention to transnational animal studies include Ahuja, *Bioinsecurities*; Dave, "Something." Chen's *Animacies*, Z. I. Jackson's *Becoming Human*, and Boisseron's *Afro-Dog* are striking analysis about racialization and animalization. This list is far from exhaustive and simply brings together a few examples to highlight the tremendous scholarship fueling animal studies.
57. Derrida, *Animal That Therefore I Am*, 23.
58. Braidotti, *Posthuman*, 68, original emphasis.
59. Wynter, "Unsettling the Coloniality," 262.
60. Deleuze and Guattari, *Thousand Plateaus*, 238, 239, 272, 277.
61. For instance, Rosi Braidotti asks, "Can feminists, at this point in their history of collective struggles aimed at redefining female subjectivity, actually afford to let go of their sex-specific forms of political agency? Is the bypassing of gender in favor of a dispersed polysexuality not a very masculine move?" In Grosz, *Volatile Bodies*, 162–63. Alongside Braidotti's critical engagement with Deleuzian thought, we can recall Alice Jardine's forceful criticism of the masculine frame motivating this theory from her oft-cited essay "Women in Limbo." Jardine asks, "Is it not possible that the process of 'becoming woman' is but a new variation of an old allegory for the process of women becoming obsolete?" (54). Feminists have articulated their strong concerns about a theory coached very much through the bodies of Man with a capital *M*. Meanwhile, other feminists such as Elizabeth Grosz have provided us with a different possibility inherent in becomings. She notes that it would not be entirely correct to presume that Deleuze and Guattari are unaware of power divisions and asymmetries on a global level: "Instead, as I read them, they seem to be rendering more complex the nature and forms that these oppressions take." *Volatile Bodies*, 173.

62. Bignall and Patton, *Deleuze and the Postcolonial*, 1. "Nomadology" refers to Deleuze and Guattari's emphasis on subjects outside the state who can puncture the state's war machine. See Deleuze and Guattari's *Nomadology*. The rush toward creativity and abstractions, an exoticization of the other, and a failure to grapple with real histories are just some of the critiques Bignall and Patton mention. Bignall and Patton, *Deleuze and the Postcolonial*, 2.

63. Bignall and Patton, *Deleuze and the Postcolonial*, 2, 3, 12.

64. Deleuze and Guattari, *Kafka*, 42, 46–47, 13, 35, 36, 13, original emphasis.

65. *A Thousand Plateaus* is meant to be read as separate plateaus and not teleological chapters. Brian Massumi points out that the word "plateau" originates from an essay written by Gregory Bateson describing Balinese culture that was seen to operate separate from an economic frame. Deleuze and Guattari, *Thousand Plateaus*, xiv. Seen as an exercise in nomadic thought or thought unrestricted by normalized state-bound structures, Deleuze and Guattari offer a fresh impetus to move beyond asserting truth or false claims. As Brian Massumi contends, "The question is not, is it true? But, does it work? What new thoughts does it make possible to think? What new emotions does it make it possible to feel? What new sensations and perceptions does it open in the body?" In Deleuze and Guattari, *Thousand Plateaus*, xv.

66. Deleuze and Guattari, *Thousand Plateaus*, 239.

67. Deleuze and Guattari, *Thousand Plateaus*, 240, original emphasis.

68. Recall here Donna Haraway's oft-cited critique of becoming animal: "The old, female, small, dog-and cat-loving: these are who and what must be vomited out by those who will become-animal. . . . I am not sure I can find in philosophy a clearer display of misogyny, fear of aging, incuriosity about animals, and horror at the ordinariness of flesh, here covered by the alibi of an anti-Oedipal and anticapitalist project." Haraway, *When Species Meet*, 30.

69. Deleuze and Guattari, *Thousand Plateaus*, 241.

70. Deleuze and Guattari, *Thousand Plateaus*, 240–43.

71. Many other mock categorizations of animals critique the extreme anthropocentrism coloring our picturing of animals. Note, for example, Louis Borges's three-fold categorization of animals into "those we watch television with, those we eat and those we are scared of." Quoted in Braidotti, *Posthumanism*, 68.

72. John Gray tells us, "Unless they are kept indoors, the behavior of house cats is not much different from that of wild cats." Gray, "House Cats and Wild Cats."

73. See Harrison, "Holy Cow!"

74. Govindrajan, *Animal Intimacies*, 68.

75. See Bedi, "How Protecting Cows."

76. Puar, *Right to Maim*, 36, 58, 56.

77. Wendy Doniger, about the status of the cow in Indian society and its evolving role through time, points out: "As I see it, the arguments against eating cows are a combination of a symbolic argument about female purity and docility (symbolized by the cow who generously gives her milk to her calf), a religious

argument about Brahmin sanctity (as Brahmins came increasingly to be identified with cows and to be paid by donations of cows) and a way for castes to rise in social ranking." "Hinduism."

78. Namjoshi, *Fabulous Feminist*, 54.
79. Namjoshi, *Conversations of Cow*, 80, 85, 91, 125.
80. Namjoshi, *Goja*, 78–79.

Chapter 2. Translations and Overlapping Belongings

1. Spivak, *Aesthetic Education*, 270.
2. See, for instance, de Lima Costa and Alvarez, "Dislocating the Sign"; Arondekar and Patel, "Area Impossible."
3. Spivak, *Aesthetic Education*, 258, 259.
4. Spivak, "Can the Subaltern Speak?" 27, 24, original emphasis.
5. Macharia, "On Being Area-Studied," 185.
6. Mikdashi and Puar, "Queer Theory and Permanent War," 216.
7. Anjali Arondekar's work on queer transnationalism engages with spatial politics and configurations of the local and global through an examination of multiple circuits of power and subjectivity. She criticizes Dennis Altman's claims about the power of American queer theory and politics that indulge holistically in "global queering." "Border/Line Sex," 554. Arondekar argues against queer Westernization seen as a blanket conversion of indigenous gay identities into Western queer configurations. Arondekar points to important lacunae in Altman's study where he fails to note varied complications and entanglements between the local and global "Border/Line Sex," 555.
8. Dave. *Queer Activism*, 17.
9. Dave, *Queer Activism*, 21.
10. Povinelli and Chauncey, "Thinking Sexuality," 440.
11. See Shah, *Stranger Intimacy*; Eng, *Feeling of Kinship*; Rodriguez, *Queer Latinidad*; Puar, *Terrorist Assemblages*.
12. Povinelli and Chauncey, "Thinking Sexuality," 439.
13. Povinelli and Chauncey, "Thinking Sexuality," 446.
14. Cruz-Malave and Manalansan, *Queer Globalizations*, 2.
15. Gopinath, *Unruly Visions*, 5.
16. Arondekar and Patel, "Area Impossible," 154.
17. Arondekar and Patel, "Area Impossible," 153. Ragini Tharoor Srinivasan in her essay "Possible Impossibles between Area and Queer" writes about *GLQ*'s volume on area impossible and some interstices between "area" and "queer." She draws our attention to Kashmir: "Like the fields of area studies and queer studies. Kashmir is always already home to many, even if, finally, it belongs to no one" (129).
18. de Lima Costa and Alvarez, "Dislocating the Sign," 557–58.
19. de Lima Costa and Alvarez, "Dislocating the Sign," 562.
20. de Lima Costa and Alvarez, "Dislocating the Sign," 557.

21. See also Richa Nagar's illuminating *Hungry Translations*. Nagar emphasizes translations as "agitation": "This agitation narrates people, stories, events, and dreams through collectively owned journeys not in a hope to reach perfection, but in a hope to disorder the dominant languages and paradigms through which we often encounter knowledges and knowledge makers" (9).

22. Tsing, *Mushroom*, 62.

23. Tsing, *Mushroom*, 62, original emphasis.

24. Shiho Satsuka in *Nature in Translation* writes about meanings of nature and its constant translations by Japanese tour guides in Canada's Banff National Park. Satsuka argues that the "translation of nature is inseparable from the cultural politics of what it means to be human and what it is like to be a 'free' and 'liberated' subject living in the continuously globalizing world" (219–20).

25. See Cruz-Malave and Manalansan, *Queer Globalizations*.

26. Benjamin, *Illuminations*, 69, 79.

27. Spivak, *Aesthetic Education*, 252.

28. Spivak, "Translating," 37.

29. Spivak, "Translating," 37.

30. Spivak, "Translating," 37.

31. Spivak, "Translating," 38.

32. Spivak, "Translating," 37.

33. Mitchell, *Iconology*, 44. Many thanks to Kimberly K. Lamm for directing me toward Mitchell's works.

34. Mitchell also writes, "The history of culture is in part the story of a protracted struggle for dominance between pictorial and linguistic signs, each claiming for itself certain proprietary rights on a 'nature' to which only it has access." *Iconology*, 43.

35. Hillary L. Chute discusses the legitimacy accorded to writing as against drawing and tells about an incident with Art Spiegelman's *Maus II* that portrayed Jews as mice and Nazis as cats. The book was listed in the *New York Times Book Review* list for "fiction." Spiegelman requested that the book be added to a "nonfiction/mice" category in their list. An editor from the *Times* said, "Hey, let's go down to Soho and ring Spiegelman's doorbell. If a giant mouse answers, we'll put it in nonfiction." Subsequently, the *Times* did move the book to its nonfiction list. Chute, *Disaster Drawn*, 1–2.

36. Chute, *Why Comics*, 23, original emphasis.

37. Jakaitis and Wurtz, "Introduction," 2, 21.

38. Anderson, *Imagined Communities*, 44–46.

39. McClintock, *Imperial Leather*, 374.

40. McClintock, *Imperial Leather*, 374–75.

41. Justin Hall, in *No Straight Lines*, reminds us of important comic artists as early as the 1940s, for example, Touko Laaksonen.

42. J. Hall, *No Straight Lines*, editor's note.

43. J. Hall, *No Straight Lines*, editor's note. Hall writes, "The future is bright, queer, and full of comics" (editor's note).

44. Chute, *Why Comics*, 349–50.
45. Chute, *Why Comics*, 349.
46. Starred reviews from the *Austin-American-Statesman* and *Booklist* in Bechdel, *Fun Home*, n.p. For more on Bechdel's works, see Utell's excellent 2020 edited volume, *Comics of Alison Bechdel*.
47. Bechdel, *Fun Home*, 36.
48. Bechdel, *Fun Home*, 17.
49. N. Mukherjee, "*Kari* by Amruta Patil."
50. N. Mukherjee, "*Kari* by Amruta Patil."
51. See N. Mukherjee, "*Kari* by Amruta Patil," and Gravett, "Amruta Patil."
52. Gravett, "Amruta Patil."
53. Patil, *Kari*, 58.
54. Nationalism's gendered imaginary has been noted by many scholars. Cynthia Enloe eloquently emphasizes that nationalism has "typically sprung from masculinized memory, masculinized humiliation and masculinized hope." McClintock, *Imperial Leather*, 353. Going back to Anderson's original formulation of a nation as a fraternal community, the masculine projections on the body of the nation cannot be dismissed. A nation's gendered imagery has many articulations, whether seen in terms of "mother-land" or "mother-tongue." Femininity is often appropriated as symbol, as "trope of the other" subject to selective inclusions and exclusions exemplified in wars fought to "liberate" women, women as tokens in masculine politics, or as reproductive bodies that draw the borders of nation group. About the "reproductive heterosexuality" and role of women that frames nationalism, Spivak in *Nationalism and the Imagination* notes, "Nationalism negotiates with the most private in the interest of controlling the public sphere" (57). Questions of death and birth are tied to matters of origin and belonging, issues that allow for coding based on national belonging. Women as wombs birthing the future of the nation instill reproductive heteronormativity at the core of national imaginings (43). Throughout *Nationalism and the Imagination*, Spivak repeats over and over again that nationalism understood as "the product of a collective imagination constructed through rememoration" is firmly tied to "reproductive heteronormativity" (40, 42).
55. Phelan, *Getting Specific*, 52.
56. Phelan, *Getting Specific*, 52.
57. Martin, *Situating Sexualities*.
58. Dave, *Queer Activism in India*, 24.
59. Bechdel, *Fun Home*, 70, 220–21.
60. Patil, *Kari*, 79, 80.
61. King, "There Are No Lesbians Here," 43.
62. Dave, *Queer Activism in India*, 20.
63. Patil, *Kari*, 31.
64. Patil, *Kari*, 36.
65. Mukherji, "Graphic Ecriture," 164.
66. Bechdel, *Fun Home*, 9, 30, 104, 76.
67. Chute, *Why Comics*, 146, 47, 370.

68. Patil, *Kari,* 43.
69. Patil, *Kari,* 6–7, 8, 115.
70. Bechdel, *Fun Home,* 119, 120.
71. Bhabha, *Location of Culture,* 247.
72. Ritchie, "How Do You Say," 557–58, 560–61, 563.
73. Liu, "Why Does Queer Theory Need China," 314.
74. Sedgwick, *Tendencies,* 146, original emphasis.
75. Benedict Anderson states unequivocally in the introduction to *Imagined Communities,* "Indeed, nation-ness is the most universally legitimate value in the political life of our time" (3). He does acknowledge that defining "nationalism" or "nation" is "notoriously difficult" (3). Ultimately, Anderson defines nation as "an imagined political community—and imagined as both inherently limited and sovereign" (6). As an imagined community, members of a nation may not see each other, "yet in the minds of each lives the image of their communion" (6). A nation is a limited entity, as Anderson maintains, because it doesn't include everyone and has boundaries that distinguish it from others, even "if elastic" (7). It is sovereign because of its origin in a post-enlightenment era that destroyed dynastic regimes and sought to establish freedom (7). And, the nation is imagined as a community, a "fraternity," as Anderson points out (7).
76. Sedgwick, *Tendencies,* 146.
77. Sedgwick, *Tendencies,* 147.
78. Sedgwick, *Tendencies,* 147.
79. Sedgwick, *Tendencies,* 147.
80. Sedgwick, *Tendencies,* 148.
81. Sedgwick, *Tendencies,* 150.
82. Sedgwick, *Tendencies,* 150.
83. Anderson, *Imagined Communities,* 1.
84. P. Chatterjee, "Whose Imagined Community?" 216.
85. P. Chatterjee, "Whose Imagined Community?" 216.
86. Butler and Spivak, *Who Sings the Nation-State?* 59, 60, 67.

Chapter 3. Un-Mithu's Politics

1. Fanon, *Black Skin, White Masks,* 2.
2. Chow, *Not Like a Native Speaker,* 9.
3. Chow, *Not Like a Native Speaker,* 14.
4. Chow, *Not Like a Native Speaker,* 14–15.
5. Mithu Sen is embroiled in the politics of her artworks. She translates her name (i.e., Mithu) from its Bengali meaning as "black candy," which was also the title of her exhibit in 2010. Sen has also played with her name in multiple artworks as "Myth(u)." She has un-framed her own name through different kinds of aesthetic politics. I hope to signal at these interventions, alongside the deeply personal nature of her works.
6. Sinha, "Act of Persistence."
7. This chapter in Aristarkhova, *UNMYTH,* forthcoming.

8. Mithu Sen, personal conversation with author, New Delhi, India, July 2012. Sen has always been very conscious about her dark-toned skin color and its deviation from norms of beauty in Bengali society. In fact, she was advised not to wear the color pink as it would not suit her skin tone. Sen has expressed her rebellion to this societal prejudice in many exhibits, including a 2003 exhibit *I Hate Pink*.

9. Mithu Sen, personal conversation with author, New Delhi, India, July 2012.

10. Lugones, "Playfulness," 15, 16–17, original emphases.

11. See Siegel, *Laughing Matters*. Siegel writes about the trickster figure in ancient Indian texts and points out, "He exists in order to remind us of the game, that the game is all" (292). For instance, Siegel describes how Visnu uses magic to trick the demons.

12. Adajania, "Weight of Nightmares," 101.

13. Thomas, "Mithu Sen."

14. See S. Chatterjee, "What Does It Mean."

15. Trinh, *Elsewhere, Within Here*, 13.

16. Brown, *Walled States, Waning Sovereignty*, 19, 24.

17. Spivak, *Readings*, 135.

18. Butler, *Frames of War*, 11.

19. D'Mello, "Mithu Sen."

20. For more information, see Anderson, *Imagined Communities*, and P. Chatterjee, "Whose Imagined Community?"

21. Ashcroft, Griffiths, and Tiffin, *Empire Writes Back*, 221.

22. Sen, "Field Meeting."

23. Sen, "Field Meeting."

24. Derrida, *Monolingualism*, 1.

25. Derrida, *Monolingualism*, 5.

26. Trinh, *Elsewhere, within Here*, 47–48.

27. See Phan, "Amazon Echo."

28. See Fowler, "Alexa Has Been Eavesdropping."

29. Trinh, *Framer Framed*.

30. D'Mello, "Artist Mithu Sen."

31. Quoted in D'Mello, "Artist Mithu Sen."

32. Butler, *Undoing Gender*, 1.

33. Derrida, *Specters of Marx*, 22, 28.

34. See Seymour, *Bad Environmentalism*, 154–55.

35. Lugones, "Playfulness, 'World'-Travelling," 17.

Chapter 4. Feminist Transnationalism and the Political Dimension of Friendships

1. Aristarkhova, "Being Queen," 17, 15.

2. Aristarkhova, "Being Queen," 18.

3. Aristarkhova, "Being Queen," 19.
4. Aristarkhova, "Being Queen," 20.
5. Sen, "Guest-Host-Hospitality-Tolerance," 81.
6. Sen, "Unhome."
7. Yank and Mathur, "UNHomed."
8. Yank and Mathur, "UNHomed."
9. Derrida, *Politics of Friendship*, 306.
10. Chowdhury and Philipose, *Dissident Friendships*, 3.
11. Derrida, *Politics of Friendship*, 306.
12. Derrida, *Rogues*, 27, original emphasis.

13. Derrida, *Rogues*, 73. Derrida writes, "[I]in a strictly Platonic sense, that there is no absolute paradigm, whether constitutive or constitutional, no absolutely intelligible idea, no *eidos*, no *idea* of democracy. Therefore, in the final analysis, no democratic ideal. For even if there were one, and wherever there would be one, this 'there is' would remain aporetic, under a double or autoimmune constraint. This is not the first or the last word of some democracy to come, even if it is a necessary or obligatory word or passage, an obligation for the democracy to come." *Rogues*, 37.

14. Derrida, *Rogues*, 38.

15. See for example, Trinh's emphasis on "democratizing democracy" as a key project for civil society in *Elsewhere, Within Here*, 124.

16. Derrida, *Politics of Friendship*, viii–ix, ix, original emphasis.

17. Derrida, *Politics of Friendship*. Derrida traces the politics of friendship through Aristotle, Cicero, Montaigne, Nietzsche, and others.

18. Derrida discusses how Aristotle differentiates between three forms of governments or constitutions and three forms of friendships, "each of them proportional to relations of justice (VIII, 10, 1160a 31 and 13; 1161a 10), in such a way that if man is a 'political' being made to live in society (IX, 9, 1169b 28), and if, then, he is in need of friends, properly political friendship is nevertheless only a species of friendship, a derived one, the useful friendship demanded for concord, accord, consensus." *Politics of Friendship*, 230.

19. Derrida, *Politics of Friendship*, 8, 20, 19, 23, 22, original emphasis. Derrida quotes from Aristotle where Aristotle emphasizes that primary friendship is not for everyone for it involves a process of selection. According to Aristotle, one cannot "choose a friend like a garment." and a friend cannot be had "*without trial*" and nor in a single time span. *Politics of Friendship*, 20.

20. Borradori, *Philosophy*, 99, 127, 128–29. Tolerance speaks in the following way: "I am leaving you a place in my home, but do not forget that this is my home." *Philosophy*, 127.

21. Gandhi, *Affective Communities*, 9, 10, 26, 26. See chap. 5 of *Affective Communities*.

22. Gandhi, *Affective Communities*, 3, 5–6. Gandhi brilliantly writes about a number of South Asian and European friendships that flourished within colonialism and moved much beyond its rubric. She writes about Edward Carpenter,

M. K. Gandhi, Sri Aurobindo and others where interpersonal relations and networks formed a dynamic anti-imperial counter power. See Gandhi, *Affective Communities*.

23. Aristarkhova, "Being Queen," 15, 17.
24. Aristarkhova, "Being Queen," 17.
25. Borradori, *Philosophy*, 129.
26. Aristarkhova, "Being Queen," 18–19; Mithu Sen, personal conversation with author, New Delhi, India, July 2012.
27. Jones, "Hair Trade," 131.
28. Jones, "Hair Trade," 131.
29. Jones, "Hair Trade," 121–22.
30. Mercer, "Black Hair/Style Politics," 251.
31. See Cabanas, "Ana Mendieta"; Enright and Walsh, "Beautiful Trap."
32. Mithu Sen has previously embarked on a project where she exchanged her artwork for a letter written to her with love. As a critique of a market-driven art world, Sen's project sought to foster actual relationships and unique aesthetic experiences.
33. See S. Chatterjee, "What Does It Mean."
34. Aristarkhova, "Being Queen," 19.
35. Aristarkhova, "Being Queen," 19.
36. Mithu Sen, personal conversation with author, New Delhi, India, July 2012.
37. Sen, "Guest-Host-Hospitality-Tolerance," 81.
38. Aristarkhova, "Being Queen," 22–24. This is an excerpt from the email. See Aristarkhova, "Being Queen," for the entire email.
39. Ross, "Queen Mithu," 47.
40. Derrida quoted in Borradori, *Philosophy*, 128.
41. Derrida quoted in Borradori, *Philosophy*, 129.
42. Gandhi, *Affective Communities*, 32.
43. Gandhi, *Affective Communities*, 32, original emphasis.
44. Lugones and Spelman, "Have We Got a Theory," 383.
45. Lugones and Spelman, "Have We Got a Theory," 385–89.
46. Lugones and Spelman, "Have We Got a Theory," 389.
47. Mohanty, *Feminism without Borders*, 242.
48. See also J. Dean, *Solidarity of Strangers*. Dean's "solidarity of strangers" provokes a movement toward a process-oriented formation of the "we" in feminist communities (3).
49. Chowdhury and Philipose, *Dissident Friendships*, 7.
50. Tong, *Feminist Thought*, 235.
51. Lugones and Spelman, "Have We Got a Theory for You," 379.
52. Lugones and Spelman, "Have We Got a Theory for You," 387.
53. Lugones and Spelman, "Have We Got a Theory for You," 389.
54. Lugones and Spelman, "Have We Got a Theory for You," 389–90.
55. hooks, "Sisterhood," 392.

56. hooks, "Sisterhood," 404.
57. Lorde, "Master's Tools," 333.
58. Derrida, *Politics of Friendship*, 23.
59. Oguibe, "Queen in Her Chamber," 37.
60. Hancock, *Politics of Disgust*, 25, 26, 119. Hancock points out that there was a "limited embrace" of immigrants and a politics that sought to "Americanize" them, for instance, Irish and Italian immigrants. See Hancock, *Politics of Disgust*, 30.
61. See Collins, *Fighting Words*.
62. Hancock, *Politics of Disgust*, 122.
63. Oguibe, "Queen in Her Chamber," 37.
64. Butler, "Imitation and Gender Insubordination," 22–23, original emphasis.
65. Elizabeth Chin's work is useful to think about the queering with hair, which we could also interpret as part of Sen's curious politics. Chin writes about how poor black children in New Haven, Connecticut, braid the hair of their white dolls like their own hair. Unable to consume "ethnically correct dolls," girls braid their dolls' hair and make the dolls racially queer. Chin writes, "Seeing these dolls as racially queered is appropriate not only because naturalized categories of race are being bent, but also because it is a notion which, unlike hybridity, is fundamentally playful." "Ethnically Correct Dolls," 308. Following Erica Rand's analysis about "queering," where making Barbie queer is not solely premised on sexuality but also on subverting the respectable status quo, Chin's analysis brings to the forefront how by playing with Barbie's hair, the children have made a "play on whiteness" (308).
66. Beth Citron in Sen, *It's Good to Be Queen*, 84.
67. Gandhi, *Affective Communities*, 188.
68. Lorde, "Master's Tools," 333.

Chapter 5. Spectral Politics

1. See Saha, "Feeding the Spirits."
2. Stoler, *Duress*, 5.
3. Stoler, *Duress*, 5, 7.
4. Horkheimer and Adorno, *Dialectic of Enlightenment*, 215, 6, 8.
5. Borradori, *Philosophy*, 28.
6. Borradori, *Philosophy*, 28.
7. Spiegelman, *In the Shadow*, 1, unpaginated.
8. Spiegelman, *In the Shadow*, 2, front matter, 8, unpaginated in section "Comic Supplement."
9. Borradori, *Philosophy*, 109, original emphasis.
10. Borradori, *Philosophy*, 89, 92.
11. Marx, *Selected Writings*, 158, 157, 162, 169, 163.
12. Derrida, *Specters of Marx*, ix.

13. Derrida, *Specters of Marx*, xviii, xix, original emphases.
14. Derrida, *Specters of Marx*, 6, xx, 3, 6, 7, original emphasis.
15. Derrida, *Specters of Marx*, 107.
16. Spivak, "Ghostwriting," 65, 66.
17. Spivak, "Ghostwriting," 80, 78–79, 79, 81, 82. Spivak says, "*Specters of Marx* lets me read *Far from Medina* as a ghost dance, a prayer to be haunted, a learning to live at the seam of the past and the present." "Ghostwriting," 78.
18. Ong, *Spirits*, 204, 205, 207, 10.
19. Butler, Laclau, and Zizek, *Contingency, Hegemony, Universality*, 313–14, original emphasis.
20. Morrison, "Banquet Speech."
21. Morrison, "Banquet Speech."
22. Montagne, "Toni Morrison's 'Good' Ghosts."
23. Montagne, "Toni Morrison's 'Good' Ghosts."
24. See Bennett, *Toni Morrison*. Bennett studies Morrison's ghosts as queer and draws our attention to entanglements of race, gender, and sexuality in Morrison's works through their spectral politics.
25. Anzaldúa, *Borderlands/La Frontera*, 113.
26. Anzaldúa, *Prietita and the Ghost Woman*, [23, 31].
27. Anzaldúa, *Prietita and the Ghost Woman*, [34].
28. Subramaniam, *Ghost Stories for Darwin*, 21.
29. Subramaniam, *Ghost Stories for Darwin*, 7, 1–2.
30. Muñoz, *Cruising Utopia*, 11, 46.
31. Stryker, "Transgender Studies," 214.
32. Puar, "'I would rather," 63.
33. Gordon, *Ghostly Matters*, 8.
34. Tsing, Swanson, Gan, and Bubandt, *Arts of Living*, G6.
35. Spivak, "Ghostwriting," 70.
36. Spivak, "Ghostwriting," 70.
37. See S. Hall, "James Mooney Recordings."
38. Spivak, "Ghostwriting," 70, 71, original emphasis.

Bibliography

Adajania, Nancy. "The Weight of Nightmares: A Meditation on Mithu Sen's Self-Portraits." In Mithu Sen, *Half Full*, 99–103. Exhibition book. New Delhi: Nature Morte and Bose Pacia, 2007.
Adams, Carol J., and Lori Gruen, eds. *Ecofeminism: Feminist Intersections with Other Animals and the Earth*. New York: Bloomsbury, 2014.
Agamben, Giorgio. *Homo Sacer: Sovereign Power and Bare Life*. Translated by Daniel Heller-Roazen. Stanford, CA: Stanford University Press, 1998.
Ahmed, Sara. *Strange Encounters: Embodied Others in Post-Coloniality*. London: Routledge, 2000.
Ahuja, Neel. *Bioinsecurities: Disease Interventions, Empire, and the Government of Species*. Durham, NC: Duke University Press, 2016.
Alexander, M. Jacqui. *Pedagogies of Crossing: Meditations on Feminism, Sexual Politics, Memory, and the Sacred*. Durham, NC: Duke University Press, 2005.
Anderson, Benedict. *Imagined Communities*. London: Verso, 1991.
Anzaldúa, Gloria. *Borderlands/La Frontera: The New Mestiza*. San Francisco: Aunt Lute, 2007.
Anzaldúa, Gloria. *Prietita and the Ghost Woman*. Pictures by Maya Christina Gonzalez. New York: Children's Book, 1995.
Appiah, Kwame Anthony. "Is the Post—in Postmodernism the Post—in Postcolonial." *Critical Inquiry* 17 (1991): 336–57.
Aristarkhova, Irina. "Being Queen." In Mithu Sen, *It's Good to Be Queen*, 15–32.
Aristarkhova, Irina, ed. *UNMYTH: Works and Worlds of Mithu Sen*. Mumbai, India: Mapin. Forthcoming.
Arondekar, Anjali. "Border/Line Sex: Queer Postcolonialities or How Race Matters outside the U.S." In *The Routledge Queer Studies Reader*, edited by Donald E. Hall and Annamarie Jagose, with Andrea Bebell and Susan Potter, 547–57. London: Routledge, 2013.

Arondekar, Anjali, and Geeta Patel. "Area Impossible: Notes toward an Introduction." *GLQ: A Journal of Lesbian and Gay Studies* 22, no. 2 (2016): 151–71.

Ashcroft, Bill, Gareth Griffiths, and Helen Tiffin. *The Empire Writes Back: Theory and Practice in Post-Colonial Literatures.* New York: Routledge, 2002.

Asher, Kiran. "Spivak and Rivera Cusicanqui on the Dilemmas of Representation in Postcolonial and Decolonial Feminisms." *Feminist Studies* 43 (2017): 512–24.

Barber, Benjamin R. *Strong Democracy: Participatory Politics for a New Age.* Berkeley: University of California Press, 1984.

Bechdel, Alison. *Fun Home: A Family Tragicomic.* Boston: Mariner, 2006.

Bedi, Rahul. "How Protecting Cows Became Political in Modi's India." *Irish Times*, December 1, 2019. https://www.irishtimes.com/.

Benjamin, Walter. *Illuminations: Essays and Reflections.* New York: Schocken, 1968.

Bennett, Juda. *Toni Morrison and the Queer Pleasure of Ghosts.* Albany: State University of New York, 2014.

Bhabha, Homi. *The Location of Culture.* London: Routledge, 2004.

Bignall, Simone, and Paul Patton, eds. *Deleuze and the Postcolonial.* Edinburgh: Edinburgh University Press, 2010.

Biswas, Soutik. "Why the Humble Cow Is India's Most Polarizing Animal." *BBC News*, October 15, 2015. https://www.bbc.com/news/world-asia-india-34513185.

Boisseron, Benedicte. *Afro-Dog: Blackness and the Animal Question.* New York: Columbia University Press, 2018.

Borradori, Giovanna. *Philosophy in a Time of Terror: Dialogues with Jürgen Habermas and Jacques Derrida.* Chicago: University of Chicago Press, 2003.

Braidotti, Rosi. *The Posthuman.* Cambridge: Polity, 2013.

Brown, Wendy. *States of Injury: Power and Freedom in Late Modernity.* Princeton, NJ: Princeton University Press, 1995.

Brown, Wendy. *Walled States, Waning Sovereignty.* New York: Zone, 2010.

Butler, Judith. *Frames of War: When Is Life Grievable?* London: Verso, 2009.

Butler, Judith. "Imitation and Gender Insubordination." In *Inside/Out: Lesbian Theories, Gay Theories*, edited by Diana Fuss, 13–31. New York: Routledge, 1991.

Butler, Judith. *Undoing Gender.* New York: Routledge, 2004.

Butler, Judith, and Gayatri Chakravorty Spivak. *Who Sings the Nation-State?* Calcutta: Seagull, 2007.

Cabanas, Kaira M. "Ana Mendieta: 'Pain of Cuba: Body I Am.'" *Woman's Art Journal* 20, no. 1 (1999): 12–17.

Chatterjee, Partha. "Whose Imagined Community?" In *Mapping the Nation*, edited by Gopal Balakrishnan, 214–25. London: Verso, 2012.

Chatterjee, Sushmita. "What Does It Mean to Be a Postcolonial Feminist? The Artwork of Mithu Sen." *Hypatia: A Journal of Feminist Philosophy* 31, no. 1 (2016): 22–40.

Chatterjee, Sushmita, Deboleena Roy, and Banu Subramaniam. "Spectres of Biological Politics: Conversations within and across South Asia." In *Birth Controlled: Selective Reproduction and Neoliberal Eugenics in South Africa and India*, edited by Amrita Pande, 36–59. Manchester, UK: Manchester University Press, 2022.

Chen, Mel Y. *Animacies: Biopolitics, Racial Mattering, and Queer Affect*. Durham, NC: Duke University Press, 2012.

Chess, Shira. *Play like a Feminist*. Cambridge, MA: MIT Press, 2020.

Chin, Elizabeth. "Ethnically Correct Dolls: Toying with the Race Industry." *American Anthropologist* 101, no. 2 (1999): 305–21.

Chow, Rey. *Not like a Native Speaker: On Language as a Postcolonial Experience*. New York: Columbia University Press, 2014.

Chowdhury, Elora Halim. *Transnationalism Reversed: Women Organizing against Gendered Violence in Bangladesh*. Albany: State University of New York Press, 2011.

Chowdhury, Elora Halim, and Liz Philipose, eds. *Dissident Friendships: Feminism, Imperialism, and Transnational Solidarity*. Urbana: University of Illinois Press, 2016.

Chute, Hillary L. *Disaster Drawn: Visual Witness, Comics, and Documentary Form*. Cambridge, MA: Harvard University Press, 2016.

Chute, Hillary L. *Why Comics? From Underground to Everywhere*. New York: Harper Collins, 2017.

Collins, Patricia Hill. *Fighting Words: Black Women and the Search for Justice*. Minneapolis: University of Minnesota Press, 1998.

Cruz-Malave, Arnaldo, and Martin F. Manalansan IV, eds. *Queer Globalizations: Citizenship and the Afterlife of Colonialism*. New York: New York University Press, 2002.

Dasgupta, Anannya. "'Do I Remove My Skin?' Interrogating Identity in Suniti Namjoshi's Fables." In *Queering India: Same-Sex Love and Eroticism in Indian Culture and Society*, edited by Ruth Vanita, 100–110. New York: Routledge, 2002.

Dave, Naisargi N. *Queer Activism in India: A Story in the Anthropology of Ethics*. Durham, NC: Duke University Press, 2012.

Dave, Naisargi N. "Something, Everything, Nothing; or, Cows, Dogs, and Maggots." *Social Text* 35, no. 1 (2017): 35–57.

Dean, Jodi. *Solidarity of Strangers: Feminism after Identity Politics*. Berkeley: University of California Press, 1996.

Deleuze, Gilles, and Felix Guattari. *Kafka: Toward a Minor Literature*. Translated by Dana Polan. Minneapolis: University of Minnesota Press, 1986.

Deleuze, Gilles, and Felix Guattari. *Nomadology: The War Machine*. Translated by Brian Massumi. Cambridge, MA: MIT Press, 1986.

Deleuze, Gilles, and Felix Guattari. *A Thousand Plateaus: Capitalism and Schizophrenia*. Translated by Brian Massumi. Minneapolis: University of Minnesota Press, 1987.

de Lima Costa, Claudia, and Sonia E. Alvarez. "Dislocating the Sign: Toward a Translocal Feminist Politics of Translation." *Signs: Journal of Women in Culture and Society* 39 (2014): 557–63.

Derrida, Jacques. *The Animal That Therefore I Am*. Translated by David Wills. New York: Fordham University Press, 2008.

Derrida, Jacques. *Monolingualism of the Other or the Prosthesis of Origin*. Translated by Patrick Mensah. Stanford, CA: Stanford University Press, 1998.

Derrida, Jacques. *The Politics of Friendship*. Translated by George Collins. London: Verso, 2005.

Derrida, Jacques. *Rogues: Two Essays on Reason*. Translated by Pascale-Anne Brault and Michael Naas. Stanford, CA: Stanford University Press, 2005.

Derrida, Jacques. *Specters of Marx: The State of the Debt, the Work of Mourning, and the New International*. Translated by Peggy Kamuf. New York: Routledge, 1994.

Dinshaw, Carolyn, Lee Edelman, Roderick A. Ferguson, Carla Freccero, Elizabeth Freeman, Judith Halberstam, Annamarie Jagose, Christopher Nealon, and Nguyen Tan Hoang. "Theorizing Queer Temporalities: A Roundtable Discussion." *GLQ: A Journal of Lesbian and Gay Studies* 13, no. 2 (2007): 177–95.

D'Mello, Rosalyn. "Artist Mithu Sen on (Un)Mansplaining, Her Satirical Performance Piece from the 2019 Venice Biennale." *Firstpost*, June 4, 2019. https://www.firstpost.com/living/artist-mithu-sen-on-unmansplaining-her-satirical-performance-piece-from-the-2019-venice-biennale-6727331.html.

D'Mello, Rosalyn. "Mithu Sen." *Platform*, 2019. http://www.platform-mag.com/art/mithu-sen.html.

Doniger, Wendy. "Hinduism and Its Complicated History with Cows (and People Who Eat Them)." *Conversations*, July 16, 2017. http://theconversation.com/.

Doniger, Wendy. "Zoomorphism in Ancient India: Humans More Bestial than Beasts." In *Thinking with Animals*, edited by Lorraine Daston and Gregg Mitman, 17–36. New York: Columbia University Press, 2006.

Edelman, Lee. *No Future: Queer Theory and the Death Drive*. Durham, NC: Duke University Press, 2004.

Eng, David L. *The Feeling of Kinship: Queer Liberalism and the Racialization of Intimacy*. Durham, NC: Duke University Press, 2010.

Enright, Robert, and Meeka Walsh. "The Beautiful Trap: Janine Antoni's Body Art." *Border Crossings* (2010): 38–54. Academic OneFile, EBSCOhost.

Fanon, Frantz. *Black Skin, White Masks*. Translated by Richard Philcox. New York: Grove, 2008.

Fanon, Frantz. *The Wretched of the Earth*. Translated by Richard Philcox. New York: Grove, 2004.

"Feminism, One of Her Voices." *Hindu*, February 20, 2000. https://www.uni-saarland.de/fileadmin/upload/lehrstuhl/ghosh-schellhorn/Tas_Datenbank/South_Asia___Diasporas/Namjoshi_The_Hindu___Feminism.pdf.

Fowler, Geoffrey A. "Alexa Has Been Eavesdropping on You This Whole Time." *Washington Post*, May 6, 2019. https://www.washingtonpost.com/.

Fox, Michael W. "India's Sacred Cow: Her Plight and Future." *Animal Issues* 3, no. 2 (1999): 1–35.
Gandhi, Leela. *Affective Communities: Anticolonial Thought, Fin-de-Siècle Radicalism, and the Politics of Friendship*. Durham, NC: Duke University Press, 2006.
Gandhi, Leela. *Postcolonial Theory: A Critical Introduction*. New York: Columbia University Press, 1998.
Ganguly, Keya. *Cinema, Emergence, and the Films of Satyajit Ray*. Berkeley: University of California Press, 2010.
Gatens, Moira. "Corporeal Representation in/and the Body Politic," In *Cartographies: Poststructuralism and the Mapping of Bodies and Spaces*, edited by Rosalyn Diprose and Robyn Ferrell, 79–87. Sydney: Allen and Unwin, 1991.
Gopinath, Gayatri. *Impossible Desires: Queer Diasporas and South Asian Public Cultures*. Durham, NC: Duke University Press, 2005.
Gopinath, Gayatri. *Unruly Visions: The Aesthetic Practices of Queer Diaspora*. Durham, NC: Duke University Press, 2018.
Gordon, Avery. *Ghostly Matters: Haunting and the Sociological Imagination*. Minneapolis: University of Minnesota Press, 1997.
Govindrajan, Radhika. *Animal Intimacies: Interspecies Relatedness in India's Central Himalayas*. Chicago: Chicago University Press, 2018.
Gravett, Paul. "Amruta Patil: India's First Female Graphic Novelist." *Paul Gravett*, 2012. http://www.paulgravett.com/articles/article/amruta_patil.
Gray, John, "House Cats and Wild Cats Aren't Actually That Different." *Literary Hub*, December 1, 2020. https://lithub.com/house-cats-and-wild-cats-arent-actually-that-different/.
Grewal, Inderpal, and Caren Kaplan, eds. *Scattered Hegemonies: Postmodernity and Transnational Feminist Practices*. Minneapolis: University of Minnesota Press, 1994.
Grosz, Elizabeth. *Volatile Bodies: Toward a Corporeal Feminism*. Bloomington: Indiana University Press, 1994.
Halberstam, Jack. *In a Queer Time and Place: Transgender Bodies, Subcultural Lives*. New York: New York University, 2005.
Hall, Justin, ed. *No Straight Lines: Four Decades of Queer Comics*. Seattle, WA: Fantagraphics, 2012.
Hall, Stephanie. "James Mooney Recordings of American Indian Ghost Dance Songs, 1894." *Library of Congress*. https://blogs.loc.gov/folklife/2017/11/james-mooney-recordings-ghost-dance-songs/.
Hancock, Ange-Marie. *The Politics of Disgust: The Public Identity of the Welfare Queen*. New York: New York University Press, 2004.
Haraway, Donna J. *When Species Meet*. Minneapolis: University of Minnesota Press, 2008.
Harrison, Virginia. "Holy Cow! India Is the World's Largest Beef Exporter." *CNN*, August 5, 2015. https://money.cnn.com/2015/08/05/news/economy/india-beef-exports-buffalo/.
Hartman, Saidiya V. *Lose Your Mother: A Journey along the Atlantic Slave Route*. New York: Farrar, Straus, and Giroux, 2007.

Hartman, Saidiya V. *Scenes of Subjection: Terror, Slavery, and Self-Making in Nineteenth-Century America.* New York: Oxford University Press, 1997.

Holland, Sharon. *Raising the Dead: Readings of Death and (Black) Subjectivity.* Durham, NC: Duke University Press, 2000.

hooks, bell. "Sisterhood: Political Solidarity between Women," In *Feminist Philosophies*, edited by Janet A. Kourany, James P. Sterba, and Rosemarie Tong, 391–404. Englewood Cliffs, NJ: Prentice-Hall, 1992.

Horkheimer, Max, and Theodor W. Adorno. *Dialectic of Enlightenment.* New York: Continuum, 2002.

Hutcheon, Linda. *Irony's Edge: The Theory and Politics of Irony.* New York: Routledge, 1995.

Irish, John. "Coronavirus: Hindu Group Hosts 'Cow Urine Drinking Party' to Cure Illness Despite Lack of Evidence." *Independent*, March 14, 2020. https://www.independent.co.uk/.

Jackson, Bianca. "'Words Create Worlds': Rethinking Genre in the Animal Fables of Suniti Namjoshi and Vikram Seth." In *Comparatively Queer: Interrogating Identities across Time and Cultures*, edited by Jarrod Hayes, Margaret R. Higonnet, and William J. Spurlin, 171–92. New York: Palgrave Macmillan, 2010.

Jackson, Zakiyyah Iman. *Becoming Human: Matter and Meaning in an Antiblack World.* New York: New York University Press, 2020.

Jakaitis, Jake, and James F. Wurtz. "Introduction: Reading Crossover." In *Crossing Boundaries in Graphic Narrative: Essays on Forms, Series, and Games*, edited by Jake Jakaitis and James F. Wurtz, 1–22. Jefferson, NC: McFarland, 2012.

Jardine, Alice. "Woman in Limbo: Deleuze and His Br(Others)." *SubStance* 13, no. 3–4 (1984): 46–60. https://doi.org/10.2307/3684774.

Jones, Lisa. "The Hair Trade." In *Talking Visions: Multicultural Feminism in a Transnational Age*, edited by Ella Shohat, 119–36. Cambridge, MA: MIT Press, 1998.

Kaviraj, Sudipta. *The Unhappy Consciousness: Bankimchandra Chattopadhyay and the Formation of Nationalist Discourse in India.* Delhi: Oxford University Press, 1998.

Keeling, Kara. *Queer Times, Black Futures.* New York: New York University Press, 2019.

King, Katie. "'There Are No Lesbians Here': Lesbianisms, Feminisms, and Global Gay Formation." In Cruz-Malave and Manalansan, *Queer Globalizations*, 33–45.

Liu, Petrus. "Why Does Queer Theory Need China? The Advent of the Modern Queer Novel." *Positions* 18, no. 2 (2012): 291–320.

Loomba, Ania. *Colonialism/Postcolonialism.* New York: Routledge, 2005.

Lorde, Audre. "The Master's Tools Will Never Dismantle the Master's House." In *The Essential Feminist Reader*, edited by Estelle B. Freedman, 331–35. New York: Modern Library, 2007.

Lugones, Maria. "Playfulness, 'World'-Travelling, and Loving Perception." *Hypatia* 2, no. 2 (1987): 3–19.

Lugones, Maria, and Elizabeth Spelman. "Have We Got a Theory for You! Feminist Theory, Cultural Imperialism, and the Demand for 'the Woman's Voice.'" In *Feminist Philosophies*, edited by Janet A. Kourany, James P. Sterba, and Rosemarie Tong, 378–90. Englewood Cliffs, NJ: Prentice-Hall, 1992.

Macharia, Keguro. "On Being Area-Studied: A Litany of Complaint." *GLQ: A Journal of Lesbian and Gay Studies* 22 (2016): 183–89.

Mangaldas, Leeza. "India's Got Beef with Beef: What You Need to Know about the Country's Controversial 'Beef Ban.'" *Forbes*, June 5, 2017. https://www.forbes.com/.

Mann, Harveen S. "Suniti Namjoshi: Diasporic, Lesbian Feminism, and the Textual Politics of Transnationality." *Journal of the Midwest Modern Language Association* 30, no. 1–2 (1997): 97–113.

Martin, Fran. *Situating Sexualities*. Hong Kong: Hong Kong University Press, 2003.

Marx, Karl. *Selected Writings*. Edited by Lawrence H. Simon. Indianapolis: Hackett, 1994.

Mbembe, Achille. *Necropolitics*. Durham, NC: Duke University Press, 2019.

Mbembe, Achille. *On the Postcolony*. Berkeley: University of California Press, 2001.

McClintock, Anne. "The Angel of Progress: Pitfalls of the Term 'Postcolonialism.'" *Social Text* 31–32 (1992): 84–98.

McClintock, Anne. *Imperial Leather*. New York: Routledge, 1995.

Meighoo, Sean. *The End of the West and Other Cautionary Tales*. New York: Columbia University Press, 2016.

Mercer, Kobena. "Black Hair/Style Politics." In *Out There: Marginalization and Contemporary Cultures*, edited by Russell Ferguson, Martha Gever, Trinh T. Minh-ha, and Cornel West, 247–64. Cambridge, MA: MIT Press, 1991.

Mies, Maria, and Vandana Shiva. *Ecofeminism*. London: Zed, 1993.

Mignolo, Walter D. *The Darker Side of Western Modernity: Global Futures, Decolonial Options*. Durham, NC: Duke University Press, 2011.

Mikdashi, Maya, and Jasbir K. Puar. "Queer Theory and Permanent War." *GLQ: A Journal of Lesbian and Gay Studies* 22 (2016): 215–22.

Misri, Deepti. *Beyond Partition: Gender, Violence, and Representation in Postcolonial India*. Urbana: University of Illinois Press, 2014.

Mitchell, W. J. T. *Iconology: Image, Text, Ideology*. Chicago: University of Chicago Press, 1986.

Mohanty, Chandra Talpade. *Feminism without Borders: Decolonizing Theory, Practicing Solidarity*. Durham, NC: Duke University Press, 2006.

Montagne, Renee. "Toni Morrison's 'Good' Ghosts." *NPR*, September 20, 2004. https://www.npr.org/.

Moore, Stephen D. "Situating Spivak." In *Planetary Loves: Spivak, Postcoloniality, and Theology*, edited by Stephen D. Moore and Mayra Rivera, 15–30. New York: Fordham University Press, 2011.

Morrison, Toni. "Banquet Speech." December 10, 1993. *Nobel Foundation*, 2023. https://www.nobelprize.org/prizes/literature/1993/morrison/speech/.

Mortimer-Sandilands, Catriona, and Bruce Erickson, eds. *Queer Ecologies: Sex, Nature, Politics, Desire*. Bloomington: Indiana University Press, 2010.

Mukherjee, Neel. "*Kari* by Amruta Patil." 2008. http://www.neelmukherjee.com/2008/04/kari-by-amruta-patil/.

Mukherji, Pia. "Graphic Ecriture: Gender and Magic Iconography in Kari." *Postcolonial Comics: Texts, Events, Identities*, edited by Binita Mehta and Pia Mukherji, 157–67. New York: Routledge, 2015.

Muñoz, José Esteban. *Cruising Utopia: The Then and There of Queer Futurity*. New York: New York University Press, 2009.

Muñoz, José Esteban. *Disidentifications: Queers of Color and the Performance of Politics*. Minneapolis: University of Minnesota Press, 1999.

Nagar, Richa. *Hungry Translations: Relearning the World through Radical Vulnerability*. Urbana: University of Illinois Press, 2019.

Namjoshi, Suniti. *Because of India*. London: Onlywomen, 1989.

Namjoshi, Suniti. *The Conversations of Cow*. London: Women's Press, 1985.

Namjoshi, Suniti. *The Fabulous Feminist*. New Delhi: Zubaan, 2012.

Namjoshi, Suniti. *Goja: An Autobiographical Myth*. North Melbourne, Victoria, Australia: Spinifex, 2000.

Namjoshi, Suniti, and Gillian Hanscombe. *Flesh and Paper*. Charlottetown, Canada: Ragweed, 1986.

Oguibe, Olu. "The Queen in Her Chamber." In Sen, *It's Good to Be Queen*, 33–37.

Ong, Aihwa. *Flexible Citizenship: The Cultural Logic of Transnationality*. Durham, NC: Duke University Press, 1999.

Ong, Aihwa. *Spirits of Resistance and Capitalist Discipline: Factory Women in Malaysia*. Albany: State University of New York Press, 1987.

Patil, Amruta. *Kari*. New Delhi: Harper Collins, 2008.

Patton, Cindy. "Stealth Bombers of Desire: The Globalization of 'Alterity' in Emerging Democracies." In Cruz-Malave and Manalansan, *Queer Globalizations*, 105–218.

Phan, Thao N. "Amazon Echo and the Aesthetics of Whiteness." *Catalyst: Feminism, Theory, Technoscience* 5, no. 1 (2019): 1–39.

Phelan, Shane. *Getting Specific: Postmodern Lesbian Politics*. Minneapolis: University of Minnesota Press, 1994.

Povinelli, Elizabeth A. *Geontologies: A Requiem to Late Liberalism*. Durham, NC: Duke University Press, 2016.

Povinelli, Elizabeth A., and George Chauncey. "Thinking Sexuality Transnationally: An Introduction." *GLQ: A Journal of Lesbian and Gay Studies* 5, no. 4 (1999): 439–50.

Puar, Jasbir K. "'I would rather be a cyborg than a goddess': Becoming-Intersectional in Assemblage Theory." *Philosophia: A Journal of Feminist Philosophy* 2, no. 1 (2012): 49–66.

Puar, Jasbir K. *The Right to Maim: Debility, Capacity, Disability.* Durham, NC: Duke University Press, 2017.

Puar, Jasbir K. *Terrorist Assemblages: Homonationalism in Queer Times.* Durham, NC: Duke University Press, 2007.

Ramamurthy, Priti, and Ashwini Tambe. Preface to Decolonial and Postcolonial Approaches. Special issue. *Feminist Studies* 43, no. 3 (2017): 503–11.

Ray, Satyajit, dir. *Goopy Gyne Bagha Byne,* by Ray and Upendrakishore Ray Chowdhury. Purnima Pictures, India, 1969. Black and white, color, 2 hours, 12 minutes.

Ritchie, Jason. "How Do You Say 'Come Out of the Closet' in Arabic? Queer Activism and the Politics of Visibility in Israel-Palestine." *GLQ: A Journal of Lesbian and Gay Studies* 16, no. 4 (2010): 557–75.

Robinson, Andrew. *Satyajit Ray: The Inner Eye.* Berkeley: University of California Press, 1989.

Rodriguez, Juana Maria. *Queer Latinidad: Identity Practices, Discursive Spaces.* New York: New York University Press, 2003.

Ross, David A. "Queen Mithu." In Sen, *It's Good to Be Queen,* 47–54.

Roy, Arundhati. "The Graveyard Talks Back: Fiction in the Time of Fake News." *Caravan,* February 12, 2020. https://caravanmagazine.in/.

Roy, Parama. *Alimentary Tracts: Appetites, Aversions, and the Postcolonial.* Durham, NC: Duke University Press, 2010.

Saha, Amrapali. "Feeding the Spirits: Ghosts and Food in Bengali Literature." *Goya,* October 29, 2018. https://www.goya.in/blog/feeding-the-spirits-food-and-ghosts-in-bengali-literature.

Saleh-Hanna, Viviane. "Black Feminist Hauntology: Rememory the Ghosts of Abolition?" *Penal Field/Champ Pénal* 12 (2015). https://doi.org/10.4000/champpenal.9168.

Satrapi, Marjane. *Persepolis.* 1st American ed. New York: Pantheon, 2003.

Satsuka, Shiho. *Nature in Translation: Japanese Tourism Encounters the Canadian Rockies.* Durham, NC: Duke University Press, 2015.

Sedgwick, Eve Kosofsky. *Tendencies.* Durham, NC: Duke University Press, 1993.

Sen, Mithu. "Field Meeting, Take 4: Thinking Practice—Mithu Sen Discussion 2, Day 2 (ACAW 2016)." *Mitthu Sen.* https://mithusen.com/projects/aphasia-2016.

Sen, Mithu. "Guest-Host-Hospitality-Tolerance." In Sen, *It's Good to Be Queen,* 81.

Sen, Mithu. *It's Good to Be Queen.* Exhibition catalog. New York: Bose Pacia, 2008.

Sen, Mithu. "UNhome in City IF Angels: A Hollywood Production." *Mithu Sen.* https://mithusen.com/projects/unhome-2017/.

Seymour, Nicole. *Bad Environmentalism: Irony and Irreverence in the Ecological Age.* Minneapolis: University of Minnesota Press, 2018.

Shah, Nayan. *Stranger Intimacy: Contesting Race, Sexuality, and the Law in the American West.* Berkeley: University of California Press, 2012.

Sicart, Miguel. *Play Matters.* Cambridge, MA: MIT Press, 2014.

Siegel, Lee. *Laughing Matters: Comic Tradition in India.* Chicago: University of Chicago Press, 1987.

Simon, Lawrence H., ed. *Karl Marx: Selected Writings.* Indianapolis: Hackett, 1994.

Singh, Rajmeet. "1 Lakh Cattle on the Loose, Claim 100 Lives a Year in Punjab." (Chandigarh, India) *Tribune*, September 1, 2019. https://www.tribuneindia.com/news/archive/punjab/1-lakh-cattle-on-the-loose-claim-100-lives-a-year-in-punjab-826294.

Sinha, Chinki. "An Act of Persistence." *India Today*, June 6, 2019. https://www.indiatoday.in/mail-today/story/an-act-of-persistence-1543501-2019-06-06.

Spiegelman, Art. *In the Shadow of No Towers.* New York: Pantheon, 2004.

Spiegelman, Art. *Maus I: A Survivor's Tale: My Father Bleeds History.* New York: Pantheon, 1986.

Spiegelman, Art. *Maus II : A Survivor's Tale : And Here My Troubles Began.* New York: Pantheon, 1991.

Spivak, Gayatri Chakravorty. *An Aesthetic Education in the Era of Globalization.* Cambridge, MA: Harvard University Press, 2012.

Spivak, Gayatri Chakravorty. "Can the Subaltern Speak?" In *Can the Subaltern Speak: Reflections on the History of an Idea*, edited by Rosalind C. Morris, 21–78. New York: Columbia University Press, 2010.

Spivak, Gayatri Chakravorty. *A Critique of Postcolonial Reason: Toward a History of the Vanishing Present.* Cambridge, MA: Harvard University Press, 1999.

Spivak, Gayatri Chakravorty. "Ghostwriting." *Diacritics* (Summer 1995): 65–84.

Spivak, Gayatri Chakravorty. *Nationalism and the Imagination.* Calcutta: Seagull, 2010.

Spivak, Gayatri Chakravorty. *Readings.* London: Seagull, 2014.

Spivak, Gayatri Chakravorty. "Translating in a World of Languages." *Modern Language Association (MLA)* (2010): 35–43.

Srinivas, Tulasi. *The Cow in the Elevator: An Anthropology of Wonder.* Durham, NC: Duke University Press, 2018.

Srinivasan, Ragini Tharoor. "Possible Impossibles between Area and Queer." *GLQ: A Journal of Lesbian and Gay Studies* 25, no. 1 (2019): 125–30.

Stoler, Ann Laura. *Duress: Imperial Durabilities in Our Times.* Durham, NC: Duke University Press, 2016.

Stryker, Susan. "Transgender Studies: Queer Theory's Evil Twin." *GLQ: A Journal of Lesbian and Gay Studies* 10, no. 2 (2004): 212–15.

Subramaniam, Banu. *Ghost Stories for Darwin: The Science of Variation and the Politics of Diversity.* Urbana: University of Illinois Press, 2014.

Suri, Manil. "A Ban on Beef in India Is Not the Answer." *New York Times*, April 17, 2015. https://www.nytimes.com/.

Thomas, Skye Arundhati. "Mithu Sen, 'I constantly change my mediums so the market will not be able to trap me.'" *Studio International*, May 25, 2017. https://www.studiointernational.com/.

Threadcraft, Shatema. "North American Necropolitics and Gender: On #BlackLivesMatter and Black Femicide." *South Atlantic Quarterly* 116, no. 3 (2017): 553–79.

Tong, Rosemarie. *Feminist Thought: A More Comprehensive Introduction*. 3rd ed. Boulder, CO: Westview, 2009.

Trawick, Margaret. *Enemy Lines: Warfare, Childhood, and Play in Batticaloa*. Berkeley: University of California Press, 2007.

Trinh T. Minh-ha, *Elsewhere, Within Here: Immigration, Refugeeism, and the Boundary Event*. New York: Routledge, 2011.

Trinh T. Minh-ha, *Framer Framed*. New York: Routledge, 1992.

Trinh T. Minh-ha, *Woman, Native, Other*. Bloomington: Indiana University Press, 1989.

Tsing, Anna Lowenhaupt. *The Mushroom at the End of the World: On the Possibility of Life in Capitalist Ruins*. Princeton, NJ: Princeton University Press, 2015.

Tsing, Anna Lowenhaupt, Heather Swanson, Elaine Gan, and Nils Bubandt, eds. *Arts of Living on a Damaged Planet*. Minneapolis: University of Minnesota Press, 2017.

Utell, Janine, ed. *The Comics of Alison Bechdel: From the Outside In*. Jackson: University Press of Mississippi, 2020.

Wolfe, Cary. *What Is Posthumanism?* Minneapolis: University of Minnesota Press, 2010.

Woods, Rebecca. "Nature and the Refrigerating Machine: The Politics and Production of Cold in the Nineteenth Century." In *Cryopolitics: Frozen Life in a Melting World*, edited by Joanna Radin and Emma Kowal, 89–116. Cambridge, MA: MIT Press, 2017.

Wynter, Sylvia. "Unsettling the Coloniality of Being/Power/Truth/Freedom: Towards the Human, after Man, Its Overrepresentation—An Argument." *CR: The New Centennial Review* 3, no. 3 (2003): 257–37.

Yank, Sue Bell, and Vasundhara Mathur. "UNHomed: The Radical Hospitality of Mithu Sen." *18th Street Arts Center*, 2019. https://18thstreet.org/unhomed-the-radical-hospitality-of-mithu-sen/.

Young, Robert JC. "Postcolonial Remains." In *Postcolonial Studies: An Anthology*, edited by Pramod K. Nayar, 125–43. West Sussex, UK: Wiley Blackwell, 2016.

Yuval-Davis, Nira, and Floya Anthias, eds. *Women-Nation-State*. London: Macmillan, 1989.

Zizek, Slavoj. "Holding the Place." In *Contingency, Hegemony, Universality: Contemporary Dialogues on the Left*, by Judith Butler, Ernesto Laclau, and Slavoj Zizek, 308–29. London: Verso, 2000.

Index

Note: Page numbers in *italics* denote figures.

absurdity, 28, 40, 42, 108
activism, 10, 18, 59; and animals, 45; and art, 88, 109; and decolonial friendship, 118; and the ghost dance, 139; and hauntings, 1, 123, 138–39, 140–41; queer, 59, 65; and translation, 56, 61–62, 69; and transnational postcolonial feminism, 20
Adajania, Nancy, 83
Adams, Carol J., 148n56
Adorno, Theodor W., 124–25
aesthetic education, 20, 145n45
affirmative sabotage, 16, 44, 49, 50, 52, 123, 140; defined by Gayatri Spivak, 31; playfulness of, 31, 50, 53. *See also* counterpolitics
afterlife: of colonialism, 8, 60; and postcolonialism, 8, 125; of slavery, 7. *See also* hauntings
Agamben, Giorgio, 33, 104
Ahmed, Sara, 9
Ahuja, Neel, 148n56
Alexa. *See* artificial intelligence (AI)
Alexander, M. Jacqui, 19
Alfassa, Mirra, 104
Altman, Dennis, 150n7
Alvarez, Sonia E., 61
ancestors, 131, 133, 139

Anderson, Benedict: Eurocentrism of, 146n15; imagined community, 35, 77, 153n75; masculine projection in, 152n54; on nation and nationalism, 76–77, 153n75; on print capitalism, 65
animal. *See* becoming animal
animality and animalization, 3, 6, 29; and colonial bestiary of Franz Fanon, 28, 87; and colonial hauntings, 138; colonial imagination of, 28; cow in India and, 29–30, 34–35; and feminist and queer identity politics, 52–53, 137; and political communities, 30, 32, 34, 35; as postcolonial counterpolitics, 4, 31, 140; and race, 148n56; and transnational politics, 30, 32, 51; of women, 3, 34
animal studies, 30, 36–37, 45–49, 148n56
anthropocentrism, 1, 35, 40, 45, 48, 49, 52, 149n71
Antoni, Janine, 109
Anzaldúa, Gloria, 24, 133–35
Appiah, Kwame Anthony, 144n17
area studies, 58, 61, 150n17
Aristarkhova, Irina, 97–98, 100, 105–6, 108, 111
Aristotle, 32; *The Eudemian Ethics*, 102; on politics and friendship, 102–3, 114, 155n18, 155n19

Arondekar, Anjali, 61, 150n7
artificial intelligence (AI), 91, *91*, 93; Alexa, 90–93
Ashcroft, Bill, 87, 144n19
Asher, Kiran, 9
Aurobindo, Sri, 104, 155n22

Barber, Benjamin R., 34
Bateson, Gregory, 20, 149n65
Bechdel, Alison, 21, 23, 65, 66–68, 70–74; *Fun Home*, 66–68, 70–74
Becker, A. L., 80
becoming animal 27–54; and becoming transnational, 30, 37, 42, 52, 53; as counterpolitics, 23, 30, 31, 48 (*see also* affirmative sabotage); and deterritorialization, 46, 51, 53; and exclusion, 32–34; and haunting, 23, 28; of Kafka, 47; and the state, 30, 32–34, 53; and subjectivity, 4, 34, 47; and transnational feminist politics, 31, 36, 37; and traveling between worlds, 40; and undoing of identity, 46, 49; and undoing violence, 28, 30, 31, 37, 48, 49, 52, 53; of women, 34, 37, 40. *See also* animality and animalization; Deleuze, Gilles, and Guattari, Felix; Namjoshi, Sunati
beef, 29, 30, 44, 49, 148n51. *See also* cow
belonging, 3, 24, 37, 70, 80, 100–101; and binary imagination, 30; communities of belonging, 10, 14, 29, 71, 75–76, 87, 98–99, 104; and language, 89–90; and maps, 73–75; and nation, 10, 42, 53, 60, 85, 99, 152n54; and postcolonial hauntings, 5, 55; and queer transnationalism, 60; and sexual subjectivities, 56; unbelonging, 5, 73, 76, 87, 104
Benjamin, Walter, 62
Bennett, Juda, 143n1, 158n24
Bhabha, Homi, 73–75, 104, 145n19
Bignall, Simone, 46–47, 149n62
binaries, 4, 5, 8, 19, 33, 50; and binary thinking, 3, 4, 23, 30, 45–50, 104; and counterpolitics, 30, 32; framings, 23, 79; and friendship, 104; hauntings as undoing of, 5, 127, 131–32, 137; man/animal, 23, 30, 46, 47, 51, 53; play with, 17; subversion of, 30; and text-image, 63; undoing of, 5, 48, 51
Black women, 108, 114, 115
Boisseron, Benedicte, 148n56
border-crossing, 17, 19, 37, 62, 115; and hair, 109; and politics of hope, 12; and postcolonial subjects, 14; translation as, 55–56, 141; and transnational friendship, 99–100
borders, 10, 11, 115; and colonialism, 77, 104–5; and cross-cultural comparison, 66; and ghosts, 4, 25, 117, 127, 133; and maps 72, 77; and nation-state, 10, 18, 32–33, 35, 85, 138, 142; and play, 14, 17, 28–29, 84, 140; and sexuality, 22, 51, 59, 60; shifting, 21; and transnational postcolonial feminisms, 3, 19, 79, 104, 119; and transnational travel, 22, 35, 89; undoing of, 23, 53, 86; and violent genealogies, 18; and women, 24, 152n54. *See also* border-crossing
Borges, Louis, 149n71
Borradori, Giovanna, 155n20
Braidotti, Rosi, 45, 148n61, 149n71
Bresson, Cartier, 72
Brown, Wendy, 44, 85
Bubandt, Nils, 138
buoyancy, 12, 20, 39, 47, 127; in the art of Mithu Sen, 24, 81, 94, 135; in feminist transnational relations, 100; in friendship, 142; ghosts and, 142; in writing, 13, 39, 47
Butler, Judith, 22, 77–78, 86, 95, 117

Camus, Albert, 70, 74
capitalism, 6, 51, 61, 69, 81, 127, 128; COVID-19, 138, 141; and ghosts, 123, 128, 130, 131; as a haunting, 99, 140–41; surveillance, 93, 125; technology, 93; and translation 56, 57, 61–62
Cesaire, Aime, 62
Chatterjee, Partha, 77, 146n15
Chattopadhyay, Bankimchandra, 15

Chauncey, George, 60
Chin, Elizabeth, 157n65
Chow, Rey, 80
Chowdhury, Elora Halim, 18–19, 101, 113
Chute, Hillary, 64, 65, 72, 151n35
Citron, Beth, 118
colonialism, 10, 69; afterlives of, 7–8; as a ghost, 124; as a haunting, 29, 127, 138, 141; and meaning-plays, 16; and temporality, 10; traces of, 124; and translation, 55. *See also* postcolonialism
coming out, 71, 74–75, 77–78; of the closet, 67–70
commodity, 13, 62, 65, 109
communalism in India, 7, 22, 29, 34
counterpolitics, 23, 31, 140; art and, 24, 100, 119, 140; becoming animal and, 23, 30–32, 36, 48; transnational, 30, 100, 119
COVID-19, 2, 35, 138, 141, 142
cow, 48–9, 51; Brahman cattle, 147n51; caste and, 149n77; and Hindu nationalism, 29–35, 49–50; and identity thinking, 43–44; lesbian, 29–31, 42, 52; as mother, 34, 52, 53; as postcolonial haunting, 29, 50, 127; status of in India, 23, 28–29; transnational, 36, 37. *See also* Namjoshi, Suniti
creativity, 46, 76, 114, 119, 149n62
crises, 2, 129. *See also* COVID-19
Cruz-Malave, Arnaldo, 60

Dasgupta, Anannya, 39
Dave, Naisargi N., 34, 59–60, 68, 69, 148n56
Dean, Jodi, 156n48
decolonial feminism, 8–9, 11, 118, 144n17
Deleuze, Gilles, and Guattari, Felix, 23, 37, 45, 50–3, 57, 148n61; becoming animal, 30, 45–49; and nomadology, 46, 149n62; *A Thousand Plateaus*, 47, 149n65
de Lima Costa, Claudia, 61
democracy: Derrida on, 101–2, 155n13; double bind of, 20; and feminism, 31, 51; as framed by Liberalism, 33–34; and friendship, 24, 99, 100–105, 115; and gender, 102; radical, 51, 99, 101, 104, 114–15, 117, 155n15; translation and, 56, 61–62; transnationalism and, 56, 99; yet to come, 101, 102
Derrida, Jacque, 99–105, 112–13, 114; on animal, 45, 53; deconstruction, meaning of, 86; on ghosts and specters, 6, 96, 128–29, 137; hauntology, 2, 129; on haunting, 6, 96; on language, 90; on 9/11, 126–27; on Marx's love for Shakespeare, 129, 130; on Marx's work with ghosts, 128–29; on politics of friendship, 117; *Specters of Marx*, 6, 96, 128–31; on temporality, 95; on visitation, 107; and women, 6. *See also* democracy; friendship
Devi, Mahasweta, 56, 62
Dinshaw, Carolyn, 145n28
Djebar, Assia, 130–31
Doniger, Wendy, 147n41, 149n77
double bind, 20, 145n45
drag aesthetics, 117

ecofeminism, 45, 148n56
effervescence, 12, 16, 72
Engels, Friedrich, 128
Enloe, Cynthia, 152n54
entanglements, 41, 53, 60, 75, 81, 86, 124, 126, 137–38, 146n6, 150n7
epistemology: ethical, 122; and hauntings, 122–23, 131; of justice, 131; play and, 10, 18, 77, 123, 135; of the "postcolonial," 11; of resistance, 2; and translation, 137; of unknowingness, 133
Erickson, Bruce, 148n56
ethics, 140, 141, 142; importance of ghosts in, 24, 139; of justice, 23, 128; of play, 20; and politics of hope, 22–23; postcolonial, 10; postfoundationalist, 4; of tolerance, 116; of translation, 62–63, 137. *See also* Aristotle

fables, 37–39, 54. *See also* Namjoshi, Suniti
Fanon, Franz, 28, 80, 87

Fitzgerald, F. Scott, 72
Foucault, Michel, 33, 57, 144n13
fragmentation, 24, 85, 138
fratriarchy, 102, 118
Freud, Sigmund, 124
friendship, 4, 22, 24, 97, 123, 142; anti-imperial, 155n22; and art of Mithu Sen, 109–13, 118–20; Derrida on, 101–2; "equality of virtue" in, 103, 114; feminist discourse on, 113–14; feminist transnational, 99, 100, 103–4, 113, 115, 118, 134; fraternal, 99, 102–3, 117; inclusions and exclusions in, 100; politics of, 100–105, 117; and national belonging, 4, 99–105; non-fraternal, 100; and patriarchy, 102; postcolonial, 99; as postcolonial haunting, 24; and radical democracy, 101, 117; sisterhood and, 19, 28, 114, 118; solidarity model of, 113–14; subversion of, 102; queering, 117–18. *See also* Aristotle; hospitality; border-crossing
feminist theory, 18, 100, 113, 114, 118
Fukuyama, Francis, 129
futures, 7, 18, 25, 47, 128, 130, 132; and ghosts, 124, 127, 133–34, 138–39; and nation, 116; and radical democracy, 101; feminist, 115; and utopias, 10, 15, 136

Gadamer, Hans-Georg, 82–83
Gan, Elaine, 138
Ganguly, Keya, 143n4
Gatens, Moira, 34
gaze, 24, 89, 94, 95, 133; of the specter, 129; Western, 85, 87, 88, 93
ghost dance, 12, 139, 143n4, 158n17; *Goopy Gyne Bagha Byne*, 2–3, 5, 142, 143n4
ghosts, 1–2, 4–7, 137–38; communist, 24; and events, 125–27, 138, 141; as exclusions, 25, 132; "good" versus "bad," 132; Freud and, 124; and Hamlet, 96, 129–30; heterosexual agenda of, 135; and hospitality, 103; and Marxism, 123, 128–30; Toni Morrison and, 132–33, 158n24;
queer, 123, 135–37; and remembering, 5; as social actors, 127; and temporality, 123–24, 138, 145n28; and ways of knowing, 137; women, 130–31, 133–34. *See also* hauntings
ghost stories, 4–5, 121, 122, 135
Gonzalez, Maya Christina, 133
Gopinath, Gayatri, 60–61
Gordon, Avery, 138
Govindrajan, Radhika, 49–50, 146n3
graphic narratives, 21, 23, 64; as "crossovers," 64–65; frames in, 23, 56, 64–65, 68; *Fun Home*, 66–68, 70–74; gutter, 64; image-text in, 63, 64, 75; and identity work, 68, 75; *In the Shadow of No Towers*, 125–26; *Kari*, 23, 64–75, 125; *Maus*, 64; and maps and unmappings, 71, 73, 75, 77, 89; as metonyms of transnational identities, 65; *Persepolis*, 64; and queer transnationalism, 66, 73–78; translation and, 73–78
graveyards, 7
Gray, John, 149n72
Griffiths, Gareth, 87, 144n19
Grosz, Elizabeth, 148n61
Gruen, Lori, 148n56

Habermas, Jurgen, 125
hair, 24, 67, *108*; in the art of Mithu Sen, 88, 89, 93, 96, 107–10, 115, 135; and friendship, 118; and hospitality, 117–18; politics of Black hair-styles, 109, 157n65
Hall, Justin, 65, 151n41, 151n43
Hancock, Ange-Marie, 115, 157n60
Hanscombe, Gillian, 41
Haraway, Donna, 35, 149n68
Hartman, Saidiya, 6–8, 16
hauntings: braided with play, 2–3; as critical for postcolonial studies, 5–6, 7–12; defined, 4–5. *See also* ghosts
hauntology. *See* Derrida, Jacque
heteronormativity, 63, 136, 152n54
Hinduism, 39, 43, 147n51
Hindu nationalism, 29, 34, 49, 127. *See also* cow
historical materialism, 128, 130

Holland, Sharon, 8
hooks, bell, 100, 114–15, 118
hope, 15, 63, 102, 136, 139, 151n21; disappointed, 124; and masculinized nationalism, 152n54; politics of, 12, 22–23, 90, 142
Horkheimer, Max, 124–25
hospitality: Derrida on, 103–4; and guest-host relations, 107, 111; hair and, 117; and imperial inhospitality, 24, 101, 140; as opposed to tolerance, 113, 116; play with, 98, 100, 117; radical, 98, 119; unconditional, 103, 107, 112. *See also* friendship
hubris, 25, 56, 127, 138, 142
Huizinga, Johan, 15, 82–83
humor, in the art of Mithu Sen, 84, 88, 95, 96, 119; as an element of play, 12, 15; in lingual anarchy, 92. *See also* laughter
hybridity, 12, 37, 47, 104, 157n65; cattle breeds, 147n51; of English in the colonies, 87; in graphic narratives, 63

inclusions and exclusions, 6, 33, 44, 46, 123; and friendship, 100; frames of, 32, 45; and lingual anarchy, 93; and nation, 152n54
inclusive exclusion, 33, 53
identity: and animality/animalization, 35, 46; crossings, 49; deconstruction of, 84; feminist politics of, 52; and hair, 109; as hauntings, 24, 50, 137; lesbian, 41, 68–70; loss of, 38; marketing of, 84–85; and meaning-plays, 15–16, 29, 36, 42, 60, 66, 79–80; national, 65, 77–78, 86; postcolonial, 3–4, 18; queer politics of, 52, 57, 59; and queer theory, 136; sexual, 67–68, 70, 78, 136; shifting, 71; and translation, 56–57, 60, 73; undoing of, 46
identity work, 23, 67, 70, 71, 74–75
imagined community, 36, 42. *See also* Anderson, Benedict
India, 3, 21–22, 28, 34, 135, 147n51; colonial, 15; fables, 147n41; as a floating signifier, 21; ghosts in, 5; heteronormativity of, 67; idea of, 14, 21, 84–85; and lesbian identity, 36, 41–42, 59; markets in, 13, 16; Muslim graveyards in, 7; queer, 11, 36, 59, 67; as site of postcolonial meaning-plays, 21–22, 141; and transnationalism, 42, 98; women, 24, 36, 84, 84–85, 89, 109, 149n77. *See also* Hindu nationalism; cow
Indian movies, 2, 4, 135; Bollywood, 135; ghosts in, 2–3, 5, 135; *Goopy Gyne Bagha Byne*, 2–3, 5, 142
It's Good to be Queen. *See* Sen, Mithu

Jackson, Z. I., 148n56
Jakaitis, Jake, 64–65
Jones, Lisa, 108
Joyce, James, 72
justice: ethics of, 23, 128; and exclusions, 6; and feminist and queer, 11, 123; and friendship, 102, 155n18; and ghosts, 129–30, 135; and play and hauntings, 3, 131–32, 139; social, 95, 139; and temporality, 96; transnational visions of, 122

Kafka, Franz, 47
Kaviraj, Sudipta, 15–17
King, Katie, 69–70

Lamm, Kimberly K., 151n33
language, 3, 12, 17, 18, 32, 83, 86, 141; and belonging, 89–90; English, 38–39, 54, 55–56, 77, 87, 122; and exclusions, 24, 32; grammar, 80; as haunting, 17; and heteronormativity, 63; and identity, 42, 82; and nation, 77–78; and play, 18; politics of, 87; and postcolonial subjects, 3, 4, 15–16, 80, 90; as prosthesis, 80; and queer transnationalism, 58–59, 74–75; and spirit possession, 93–95; undoing of, 87, 95, 138; undoing social hierarchies, 90. *See also* translation; languaging; lingual anarchy
languaging and unlanguaging, 63, 80, 90
laughter, 12, 28, 47, 90, 122; of ghosts, 130

Index 175

liberalism, 33–34; 35–36, 76
lingual anarchy, 24, 80–81, 87–96; and communities of (un)belonging, 87; as political strategy, 92; and unlanguage, 81, 87–91. *See also* Sen, Mithu
Liu, Petrus, 75
livable worlds, 95, 137, 142
Loomba, Ania, 11–12
Lorde, Audre, 100, 114, 119
Lugones, Maria: on decolonial friendship and feminist theory, 113–14, 118–19; on play as "'world'-travelling" 15, 17, 82–84; on playfulness, 96; on translation, 61

Macharia, Keguro, 58
Manalansan IV, Martin F., 60
Mann, Harveen S., 37
mappings, 11, 16–17, 23, 72; queer, 56–70, 74; third world, 16; and unmappings, 30
maps, 70–73, 75; Cartesian, 23; colonial, 10, 58; and meaning-plays, 56; and nation, 65, 136; overlapping 21, 24, 125; and translation, 74, 75, 132; and transnationalism, 77, 100, 136. *See also* mappings
Martin, Fran, 68
Marxism, 5–6, 96, 122, 123, 127–28, 143n2; and ghosts, 128–31, 133
Massumi, Brian, 149n65
mastery, 80, 124, 127, 142
Mbembe, Achille, 10–11, 144n13
McClintock, Anne, 11–12, 65, 152n54
meaning-plays, 11; defined, 15; as politics, 17; and postcolonial transnational feminism, 23; as practices of translation, 17. *See also* affirmative sabotage; play
meat, 33, 34, 35, 49
Meighoo, Sean, 37
Mendieta, Ana, 109
Mercer, Kobena, 109
Mies, Maria, 148n56
Mignolo, Walter D., 144n17
Mikdashi, Maya, 58
Minh-ha, T. Trinh. *See* Trinh T. Minh-ha

Misri, Deepti, 21
Mitchell, W. J., 63, 151n34
modernity, 9, 15, 19, 77, 125, 138, 141, 146n22
Mohanty, Chandra Talpade, 19, 100, 113
Montagne, Renee, 132–33
Montaigne, Michel de, 103
Mooney, James, 139
Moore, Stephen D., 144n19
Morrison, Toni, 24, 132–34, 158n24
Mortimer-Sandilands, Catriona, 148n56
mother, 3, 13–14, 22, 27–28, 67, 86, 122, 133–34; cow as, 32–37, 49, 52–53; nation as mother-land, 152n54; and welfare, 116, 117
Mukherjee, Neel, 66–67
Mukherji, Pia, 70
Muñoz, José Esteban, 10, 24, 136–37

Nagar Richa, 151n21
Namjoshi, Suniti, 21, 23, 36–42, 50; and affirmative sabotage, 52; and becoming animal, 28, 36, 37, 40–42, 53–54, 137; *The Conversations of Cow*, 30, 42–46, 58; on East and West, 30, 36, 38–41; and fables, 39–41; on feminist and queer politics, 51–52; on identity, 42–44, 52; and sexuality, 36, 41, 52; on Western feminism, 40
narcissism, 118
nation: and animal, 32, 35; and citizenship, 74; and friendship, 100; and gender, 76–78; and homosexuality, 50, 76; and identity, 67; and mothers, 116; purity of, 50. *See also* Anderson, Benedict; maps
nation-building, 30, 65
nationalism, 7, 10, 19, 64, 76–78, 85, 104, 127, 152n54; 9/11, 103–4, 125–27. *See also* Hindu nationalism

Oguibe, Olu, 115
Ong, Aihwa, 35, 131

Patel, Geeta, 61
Patil, Amruta, 21, 23, 64, 66–67, 74; *Kari*, 23, 64–75, 125
patriarchy, 19, 29, 36, 39, 93, 102

Patton, Paul, 46–47, 149n62
Phelan, Shane, 68
Philipose, Liz, 101, 113
play, 2, 15–17, and double bind, 20; entangled with haunting, 2–4; as epistemology, 18; irreverence, 17, 18, 28, 52, 86, 137; mischief, 11–14, 17, 52, 53, 80, 123, 140; politics of, 18, 22; and postcolonial and transnational studies, 9, 11, 17; revelry, 13, 81, 84, 89; and temporality, 18
postcolonialism, 8–9, 11; as failed historicity 9; and disidentification, 10; and Deleuze, 47; and ghosts, 127
postcolonial theory, 10–12, 20, 46–47, 144n16, 145n41; feminist transnational, 114
posthumanism, 36, 45, 148n56
Povinelli, Elizabeth A., 36, 60
Proust, Marcel, 72, 73
Puar, Jasbir K., 51, 58, 137

queen, 96, 97–98, 101, 105, 109, 111–12, 119; drag aesthetics and, 117; transnational, 115, 142; "welfare," 116–17
queering, 63, 100, 117–18, 136, 150n7
queer translationalism, 11, 23, 69, 140, 150n7; and comparison, 66, 74–75; and meaning-plays, 67, 136; and translation, 56, 60–64, 74–78, 137

Ramamurthy, Priti, 144n17
Ray, Satyajit, 2–3, 4, 12, 142, 143n4. *See also* Indian film
resonance, 37, 39, 49, 65, 109; as an aspect of temporality, 73; and coming out, 68; and haunting, 55–56, 79; and translation, 43, 62, 73, 77
Ritchie, Jason, 74
Robinson, Andrew, 143n4
Ross, David A., 112
Roy, Arundhati, 7
Rushdie, Salman, 87

Said, Edward, 144n17
Satrapi, Marjane, 64, 66
Satsuka, Shigo, 151n24
Sedgwick, Eve Kosofsky, 76–77

Sen, Mithu, 24, 79–120, 132, 136, 138; name, 153n5; skin color, 154n8
sensorium, 5, 83, 96, 111, 122
Seymour, Nicole, 148n56
Shiva, Vandana, 148n56
Siegel, Lee, 154n11
spectral visitations, 4, 101, 103, 129, 142; in the art of Mithu Sen, 107, 116, 120, 135. *See also* Derrida, Jacques
Spelman, Elizabeth, 113–14, 118–19
Spiegelman, Art, 64, 66, 125–27, 151n35; *In the Shadow of No Towers*, 125–26; *Maus*, 64
Spivak, Gayatri, 6, 142; on deconstruction, 86; on ghost dance, 139, 158n17; on ghost women, 130–31; on the postcolonial, 9,10, 144n19; on spectral politics, 6, 130–31, 138–39; on translation, 56–59, 62–63; on women in nation, 152n54. *See also* aesthetic education; affirmative sabotage; double bind
Srinivas, Tulasi, 146n22
Srinivasan, Ragini Tharoor, 150n17
Stewart, Desiree, 117
Stoler, Ann Laura, 124, 126
Stryker, Susan, 136
subaltern, 57, 139, 144n19
Subramaniam, Banu, 135, 146n6
Swanson, Heather, 138

Tagore, Rabindranath, 14, 86
Tambe, Ashwini, 144n17
temporality, 10–11, 68, 72–73, 142; "ana-chronique," 96; anarchy, 10; asynchronous, 11, 136; braiding, 18; and ghosts, 4, 5, 122, 123, 138, 140; heterosexual, 123; homogeneous, 129, 131, 136, 142; hybrid, 12; linear, 11, 72, 75; postcolonial, 10; queer, 10, 123, 136, 145n28; and subjectivity, 10
third world, 16, 85, 144n17
Threadcraft, Shatema, 144n13
Tiffin, Helen, 87, 144n19
tolerance, 98, 101, 113, 116–17, 155n20; limiting nature of, 105; and territorialization, 103; versus unconditional hospitality, 103, 112

translation, 23–24, 55–78, 123, 131; as agitation, 151n21; and epistemology 137; and love, 15; and meaning-plays, 17, 141; of nature, 151n24; and postcolonial subjects, 14; and transnational inquiry, 14, 137, 140

transnationalism: defined, 10, 35; feminist, 97–120; and graphic narratives, 66–77; as plaited, 40; queer, 60–64, 66–78, 136–37, 140, 150n7. *See also* travel

travel, 32, 37–38, 47, 50, 87, 142; and animal, 35–36, 46; and democratic feminist politics, 100, 123; and meaning-plays, 22; and play, 15, 17, 84; and translation, 55, 57–59, 61, 69–70, 137; transnational, 21–22, 29, 35, 50, 54, 99; "world"-travelling, 15, 17, 40, 61, 83

trickster, 83, 96, 154n11

Trinh T. Minh-ha, 19, 84, 92–93, 155n15

Tsing, Anna Lowenhaupt, 61, 138

"un-," 61, 86, 98, 136; uncanny, 37, 39, 117; undoing, 18, 22, 32, 61, 81, 83, 87, 95, 123, 140; undoing sovereignty, 85

untranslatability, 63, 103

Utell, Janine, 152n46

utopia, 10, 15, 136

violence, 39, 89, 123, 127; in becoming animal, 31, 45, 53; and hauntings, 1–2, 5, 7, 20, 25, 139–41; of categories, 12, 28; friendship in the context of; 24; and India, 21–22, 148n51; and resistance, 13, 39; toward Muslims, 7, 29

virus, 36. *See also* COVID-19

Walpole, Horace, 34

White and Black, 8, 37, 66, 80. *See also* binaries

Whiteness, 80, 109, 157n65; and normativity, 31, 114; White feminism, 113–14; White man, 43, 45; White privilege, 93; White supremacy, 114, 132, 141; White women 114, 116

Wolfe, Cary, 148n56

Wollstonecraft, Mary, 34

Women: animalization of, 34, 40; and becoming animal, 37, 45; of color, 15; exclusion of, 34, 42, 123, 130; exoticization of, 138; and feminist theory, 114, 148n61; as ghosts, 128, 130–34, 137, 141; and identity, 42, 59; invisibility of, 6, 24; and nation, 67, 102, 152n54; in shaping Islam, 130–31; third world, 3, 19; and transnational feminism, 19. *See also* Black women; Whiteness

Wurtz, James F., 64

Wynter, Sylvia, 45

yearning, 12, 18, 104, 129, 134; and meaning-plays, 141; to play, 82, 96; and time, 73; and translation, 63

Young, Iris, 114

Young, Robert JC, 144n16, 145n19

Zizek, Slavoj, 132

SUSHMITA CHATTERJEE is a professor in the Department of Ethnic Studies and Women's and Gender Studies at Colorado State University. She is the coeditor of *Meat! A Transnational Analysis*.

The University of Illinois Press
is a founding member of the
Association of University Presses.

University of Illinois Press
1325 South Oak Street
Champaign, IL 61820-6903
www.press.uillinois.edu